Is Biblical Morality Outdated?

A Physician's
Perspective

DR. DANIEL CARREL

To Myrtle Duty,
Thanks for your
interest in America's
future.

Dan Carrel DO

Prov 3:5,6

ACW Press
Nashville, TN 37222

Is Biblical Morality Outdated? A Physician's Perspective

Copyright ©2007 Daniel Carrel
All rights reserved

Cover Design by Alpha Advertising
Interior Design by Pine Hill Graphics

Packaged by ACW Press
PO Box 110390
Nashville, TN 37222
www.acwpress.com
The views expressed or implied in this work do not necessarily reflect those of ACW Press. Ultimate design, content, and editorial accuracy of this work is the responsibility of the author(s). The names of patients are fictitious and the case histories disguised with altered circumstances.

Publisher's Cataloging-in-Publication Data
(Provided by Cassidy Cataloguing Services, Inc.)

Carrel, Daniel.

    Is Biblical morality outdated? : a physician's perspective / Daniel Carrel. -- 1st ed. -- Nashville, TN : ACW Press, 2007.

        p. ; cm.

        ISBN-13: 978-1-932124-87-3
        ISBN-10: 1-932124-87-X
        Includes bibliographical references.

        1. Conduct of life. 2. Christian life. 3. Christian ethics. 4. Decision making--Moral and ethical aspects. I. Title.

BJ1251 .C37 2007
241--dc22   0704

Printed in the United States of America.

This book is dedicated to my parents, John and Geraldine Carrel, and my in-laws, Casey and Virginia Staal who have both recently celebrated their golden wedding anniversaries. I am grateful for their love and support. Our lives are enriched because of their obedience to God's principles.

ACKNOWLEDGMENTS

This book would not have been possible without a Holy God who loves the world and gave His Holy Word for our protection and our salvation.

Contents

Chapter One

A FATAL ERROR

M y computer monitor flickered.

"A fatal error has occurred. Your system will be shut down," glared at me from the computer screen. It was the first time I had ever seen that message.

"Did I destroy my computer?"

I pressed the OK button, and the message went away. The warning wasn't as disastrous as it sounded. Eventually, I became desensitized to that message. I visualized the computer's threat, but a serious consequence didn't follow.

In today's world we have become desensitized to sin and its destruction. Pastors and evangelical leaders warn us about alcohol, premarital sex, infidelity, drugs, and pornography, but the people on television, in the movies, and in song seem to do whatever they want and, most of the time, suffer no obvious adverse effect.

When spiritual leaders speak against these moral issues, they are labeled intolerant, narrow-minded bigots, fundamentalists, extremists, and other derogatory names. As a result, our culture has effectively glorified people who participate in evil, and demonized those who warn against sinful activities. There is a great deal of confusion in the minds of many people. We live in an age where "Good is called evil, and evil is called good" (Isaiah 5:20).

How can we teach our culture in an effective way about right and wrong?

Maybe, if we developed a new "Decision-Making" software program that played out the consequences of our decisions on a computer screen, it would help us make better decisions.

Let's imagine a teenage girl typing in the statement "I want to remain angry at my mom. I don't like her rules. I'm fifteen, and I should be able to do whatever I want."

The girl punches the "enter" key. A video displays the teenage girl in a disrespectful profane outburst at her mom, and then the camera focuses on the mom's tearful face. There is a long silence and tension. As the girl watches, she sees how she hurt her mom deeply. She chooses to continue the computer program to see how the scenes progress.

The next scene shows the teenage girl in a conversation with a young man. She is smiling as he compliments her about her report in class. As they walk to their next class, she is impressed with his kindness and compassion. After school, he stops by her locker, and they have a long talk. Eventually, they are seeing each other daily at school and talking on the phone in the evening. They talk about music, movies, and life dreams. Their relationship deepens. They seem so right for each other.

The next clip shows her reading a positive home pregnancy test. She sees herself crying. As her tears flow, her future plans blur. When she breaks the news to her man, he responds that he is not ready for responsibility and commitment. He's sorry, but it is her problem. The months that follow are sad and lonely. She is not interested in an abortion, because she wants the baby.

Another young man at school listens to her patiently. He spends more and more time with her. He isn't her ideal soul mate, but he helps fill the "love" void. She continues to progress in her pregnancy, but the irritations and anger in her heart drive the young man away. On the porch, she stands alone while he drives away.

The screen displays the next few scenes in black and white. She watches her tears flow and her lonely walks. There isn't much happiness in the close-up shots of her face. She seems to be lost in her thoughts.

She later births a baby girl and finds momentary happiness in a cuddly newborn. Her family and friends share the excitement with her. She gets a crib, some clothes and toys. The scene ends with her smiling again.

In the next scene, she sees herself fixing food and bottles for the baby. She appears irritated. Her work and responsibility seem to be a burden to her. The subsequent scenes show her getting up in the middle of the night to feed her baby and then collapsing back into her bed. The days become long because of her fatigue and her unending work.

In the next scene, she picks up her two-week-old baby and presses her cheek to the baby's forehead. The warmth alarms her. Then, the baby rolls her eyes back and has a seizure.

After the paramedics transport the girl and her baby to the hospital, her newborn undergoes numerous tests including a spinal tap. The nurses administer intravenous fluids, antibiotics, fever reducers, and seizure medication.

"Your baby has a herpes infection of the brain. We are treating the infection, but the chances of a normal recovery are very slim," the doctor explains to her.

She sits in the chair in the room and cries. A nurse comforts her.

As the weeks elapse, she spends her days at the hospital. She learns more about the disease from the nurses and doctors. She realizes she probably acquired the infection from her second boyfriend in the last few months of her pregnancy.

The next image portrays her five years later. She is at her apartment with her child. Her child is severely mentally retarded and bed-bound. The child is in diapers and can't speak. As she watches the end of the futuristic projection of her life, the 15-year-old girl is quiet.

Do you think the young lady at the computer would think differently about her attitudes and actions if she knew her future? Of course not every teenager's argument with a mom leads to a pregnancy and a mentally retarded baby. However, it does happen.

Maybe the software could explain reasonable rules for the home, or the software could provide some statistics, such as, a boyfriend–girlfriend relationship ends an average of three months after they first have sex. The software could explain that genital herpes affects one out of four pregnant women, and if the infection is transmitted during pregnancy and infects the baby, it can cause death or severe disability to the baby. Currently, it infects about 1000 newborn babies every year.[1]

Every day we make decisions. Those decisions define us. They determine our future. Do we need a computer software program to help predict the consequences of our actions, or is obeying the Bible enough? Can we have faith in a book that is old and, some say, outdated, or is its principles applicable to us today? Does God expect us to find fulfillment by following His ways, or should we look for our thrills in alcohol, drugs, illicit sex, pornography, gambling, adultery, homosexuality, and gluttony.

Recently, I asked a heroin addict at the jail, "What would you say to a Sunday School class of teenage boys about doing drugs?"

"I would tell them that if I knew then what I know now, I wouldn't have started."

"Why do you say that?"

"I spent thirty years looking for a heroin fix almost every day. On many days, by the time I put the needle in my arm, I was already perspiring and having stomach cramps from drug withdrawal. Occasionally, I would be vomiting or having diarrhea. My need to feed my heroin addiction was the driving force in my life. It caused me to neglect my wife, my kids, and my job. Over the years, I lost everything that was meaningful to me. The temporary pleasure of doing drugs wasn't worth what it cost me."

A female inmate at the jail was previously married, had three children, and worked as a paramedic. She didn't grow up in the inner city, but she developed an addiction to Vicodin that progressed to marijuana and cocaine which required her to develop an unfortunate familiarity with the inner city. Her marriage dissolved, and her drug addictions caused her to become involved with drug dealers.

Her habits led her to act more and more irresponsibly until she was arrested for involvement in an armed robbery. She wanted to get back to a normal life, but knew the process was going to be long and difficult.

These two people came from different backgrounds, yet their choices led to a common end-point. They lost self-control, and, eventually, they lost their money, jobs, families, and freedom.

They bought into a lifestyle that deceived them and cost them a great deal.

The answer to happiness and fulfillment is deeper than staying away from destructive habits. It involves having a relationship with God who can provide a life with meaning and purpose.

Is biblical morality outdated? In this book, you will see how God's laws were meant for our protection. His purpose is to work through our lives and give us an abundant life. Satan's purpose is to destroy our life (John 10:10).

Recently a preacher told the story of a boy on a school playground who saw three bigger bullies coming toward him to pick a fight with him. As the three stood in front of him, the boy drew a line in the sand and dared them to step over the line. The biggest bully stepped over the line, and the little boy responded, "I'm glad you decided to come over to my side. Now, it's you and me against those two."

I want people to see that they don't have to fight against God, Satan, and his demons. God is on our side. His ways are wise. I want to help you to get to know Him.

This book contains the stories of real people I've met in the emergency room, the doctor's office, or the jail. Some, I've seen in the morgue. Hopefully, through their life experiences you will see that there is a right and a wrong. There are immediate or delayed consequences to what we do in our lives.

Chapter Two

"CAN YOU GIVE ME TWENTY VICODINS?"

It was 4 AM, and the emergency room had been busy. As the patients started to file out, I was hoping to get a lunch break, but while I was finishing my paperwork, I saw the nurse escorting a limping man into a room and onto a stretcher.

He was wearing a blue plaid shirt and jeans and looked respectable. When the nurse finished her assessment, she came out of the room and handed me his chart.

"He jumped off a tractor, pulled a left groin muscle, and wants something for pain."

"I'll try to help him out."

"Give him a few minutes to change into a gown."

While I waited, I checked over the information on the chart. He lived just outside of town. He was 42 years old. His vital signs were normal.

As I walked into the room, I could see he was uncomfortable. He grimaced while he sat on the stretcher with his hurting leg extended.

"Good morning, Mr. Brock."

"Good morning, Doc."

"How did you hurt yourself?"

"I was on a tractor yesterday. When I jumped off into the muddy field, I got stuck. As I tried to pull my one foot free, my muscle ripped. I was able to work the rest of the day, but last night the pain was so bad I couldn't sleep. I figured I needed to come to the emergency room to get some pain meds."

"Why don't you lie back on the stretcher and let me examine where you are having your pain," I told him as I put on a pair of gloves.

When I palpated the muscles over the groin area and upper left thigh, he reacted in pain. I tried to be gentle, but he let me know I was hurting him. I didn't see any other problems.

"I'll have the nurse give you a shot and give you some ibuprofen to go home with."

"I'd rather skip the shot, and ibuprofen aggravates my ulcers."

"I'll give you a dozen Vicodins," I offered.

"Can you give me twenty so I can make it through the whole weekend?"

"Possibly. I'll be right back," I told him as I left the room. His last request wasn't consistent with the farmer image. Most farmers wouldn't have come in for a muscle pull. They would've taken some aspirin or acetaminophen and stayed home.

I had the secretary look up his past record. He had only been seen one previous time. He was given narcotics for pain. When he left, he stole a blank prescription, wrote out an order for narcotics, and forged the doctor's name. When he tried to fill the prescription, the pharmacist became suspicious and called our hospital. The nurse verified that the prescription was forged.

With that knowledge, I went back into his room.

"Mr. Brock, I can't give you any narcotics because you previously forged a narcotic prescription," I told him. Then I left the room and let him get dressed.

When he left, I noticed he walked out without a limp.

I encounter people frequently in my medical work who have lied to me. It is upsetting to me when I spend a significant amount of time and effort on people and then realize that their story is fictitious. They lie for various reasons, but usually they want drugs, disability, or time off work.

Rhonda, a 15-year-old, was brought to the emergency room because she was having seizures. Her mother was upset. After I asked the girl and her mother some questions and did a physical exam, I left the room to order some tests. Within a few minutes, Rhonda began to seize again, and the nurse called me back into the room. As I entered the room, I witnessed the girl shaking instead of having a grand mal seizure with tonic-clonic contractions and frothing at the mouth. The shaking lasted a few minutes and then stopped. She was faking the seizure. I didn't want to give her any medicine. The next time she started to seize I asked her mom to come outside of the room. When the mom made it outside of the room, I looked back into the room around the curtain. The patient was still shaking, and she was peeking out of her left eye to see if anybody was watching. I explained to the mom what was going on, and then I confronted the patient to see why she might be doing that. She denied that she was faking it. The mom didn't believe my explanation for the girl's seizure. I ran the blood tests which were normal, and then explained to the mom that she could take her daughter home and follow up with the family doctor to arrange for an electroencephalogram to further document that she wasn't having actual seizures. Why the young lady was doing that is still a mystery to me. Although I didn't have much time to do an extensive history, I did ask her about her home life, school, relationships and she denied any problems.

Occasionally the lies are somewhat harmless. On one Friday night, a husky football player came in with a forehead laceration. He told me he played linebacker and he had tackled an opponent with such force that he ripped open his skin. After I sewed up his skin, he confessed that he had head butted his friend before the game when they weren't wearing their helmets.

There are times that a lie can be fatal. Doug Herman, a national abstinence speaker, described how a man lied about his HIV status when he donated blood. Doug's wife received the man's blood after she had some bleeding during the delivery of their baby boy. She developed AIDS and died several years later.[1] Their son didn't get HIV, but their second child, a daughter, developed HIV infection through the birthing process and died of AIDS at 2 years of age.

In the world of finances, we are affected by lies. In the bankruptcy trial of WorldCom Inc., the federal prosecutor said Bernard Ebbers told "lie after lie" in order to keep the accounting books in line with what Wall Street expected and to keep their stock prices high. It resulted in an 11 billion dollar accounting shortfall which bankrupted the company. His lies cost thousands of people their jobs, and cost millions to stockholders.

THE STATISTICS

In America, lies are part of our culture. According to Bernice Kanner's book *Are You Normal* 91 percent of Americans regularly lie, 20 percent admitted that they couldn't go through the day without going along with a previous lie,[2] and more than 50 percent believe lying is not morally wrong. People lie about their age, their weight, and money as well as more serious matters. Other statistics include: 63 percent of Americans say they have called in sick to work when they weren't ill,[3] 17 percent say they have cheated on the their income tax,[4] 44 percent of employment seekers say they have lied on job applications,[5] and 82 percent of CEOs admitted they had cheated at golf.[6]

THE BIBLE

Satan, who is called the father of lies in John 8: 44, has lied for thousands of years. In Genesis 3:4-5, Satan lied to Eve about the consequences of eating the forbidden fruit, and the sin of Eve and her husband Adam has been passed on to the rest of mankind. In John 4:1-13, the devil tested and tempted Jesus with lies and deceit. Jesus didn't yield to the temptation, and He willingly sacrificed His body and blood on the cross to pay the penalty for sins.

Jacob lied to his father, Issac, to obtain the birthright in Genesis 27. Then, later in his life, he was deceived by his father-in-law when he wanted to marry Rachel. When Jacob lifted the veil of his wife during the marriage, he discovered Rachel's sister, Leah. His father-in-law deceived him again about wages. Then his sons lied to him. They told him his son Joseph was killed by a wild animal, when actually they sold him into slavery.

In Acts 5, Ananias and Sapphira lied about how much money they were giving to the church. Peter asked Ananias why he lied to God. Before he answered, Ananias fell down dead. Then his wife came to Peter unaware of what happened to her husband, and she lied also. She fell down dead. The story of this couple's death brought great fear among the people. It is just a reminder of how God feels about being lied to. He isn't happy when people lie to others either. Lying is listed as one of the things that God hates in Proverbs 6:17.

Evolution

One of Satan's biggest lies has been evolution. It has kept many people away from a belief in God, and it has eroded the faith of many Christians. If the human race evolved, then there is no need for God as a creator. If there is no God, then we are just animals with no purpose. We can do whatever we want.

When I was in medical school, I commuted twenty miles every day with a student who believed in evolution. We debated frequently, and exhausted our thoughts on the subject. In conclusion, we summarized our arguments into one statement "we both had faith in something we couldn't prove."

He believed in a theory that man thought up, and I believed in a statement in Genesis 1:1 "In the beginning God created the heaven and the earth." He believed in man, and I believed in God. If he was right, I didn't have much to lose. If I was right, he had a lot to lose. He would have an appointment with God after death and an eternity separated from God. We continued to ride together and share our philosophies, but neither one of us had convinced the other of our position. (Years later, after God had been working in his life, he did accept Jesus as his personal Savior.)

How Big Is the God I Serve?

While I was in college, I went to Florida and met two young Jewish men. After we talked about some spiritual issues, one of them asked me if I actually believed that Moses, literally, parted the Red Sea. Because I had just recently studied the complexity of the body's biological systems, I told them that if God created the kidney's ability to filter the body's toxins, the eye's ability to see, the brain's ability to think, and the heart's ability to pump blood for a lifetime, then God would have no problem parting the Red Sea.

We, as humans, have a hard time accepting God for who He is and worshipping Him. It takes a step of faith. Is your God big enough to create everything you see and everything you don't see? In Romans 1:20 the verse states that man should recognize God's power and creativity from the creation of the world. How can there be such a beautiful creation without a creator? We have no excuse for the rejection of God.

What do Americans Believe?

In a *National Geographic* magazine article "Was Darwin Wrong?" the authors discussed what we believe:

> According to a Gallup poll drawn from more than a thousand telephone interviews conducted in February 2001, no less than 45 percent of responding U.S. adults agreed that "God created human beings pretty much in their present form at one time within the last 10,000 years or so." Evolution, by their lights, played no role in shaping us.
>
> Only 37 percent of the polled Americans were satisfied with allowing room for both God and Darwin—that is, divine initiative to get things started, evolution as the creative means. (This view, according to more than one papal pronouncement, is compatible with Roman Catholic dogma.) Still fewer Americans, only 12 percent, believed that humans evolved from other life-forms without any involvement of a god.
>
> The most startling thing about these poll numbers is not that so many Americans reject evolution, but that the statistical breakdown hasn't changed much in two decades.[7]

"The Case for a Creator"

Lee Strobel, in his book *The Case for a Creator*[8] examined the evidence. Like many of us who were educated in public schools, Lee was taught about evolution as scientific fact. There was no need for a creator. Despite his Catholic upbringing, he became an atheist after his education in high school and college. After college in 1974, he worked as a journalist for the *Chicago Tribune* and was sent on an assignment to West Virginia to report on Christians who were upset about the "anti-God" textbooks that were being used in schools. He wondered why Christians were so upset when, as one skeptic put it, "modern science had already dissolved Christianity in a vat of nitric acid."[9]

He took his notebook to a town meeting, and a part-time truck driver and part-time preacher rallied a crowd.

"We're not evolved from slime. We're created in the image of God Almighty, and He's given us the best textbook in the world to tell us how to live!"

Lee wrote down what he heard, but he felt the people were ignorant of modern science and didn't stand a chance against the intellectuals of education. As he headed back to Chicago, he wrote out his article "Textbook Battle Rages in Bible Belt Country." In his mind, he remembered what William Provine of Cornell University spelled out. If Darwinism is true, then there are five inescapable conclusions:

> There's no evidence for God
> There's no life after death
> There's no absolute foundation for right and wrong
> There's no ultimate meaning for life
> People don't really have a free will[10]

Lee Strobel felt Christianity was taking its last gasps in the clutches of the ironclad evidence of evolution. However, because of his training in journalism and law, he didn't abandon his search for answers. He agreed with two-time Nobel Prize winner Linus Pauling, who stated "Science is the search for the truth."[11]

He watched a seven-part series on evolution which appeared on Public Broadcasting Systems network. The spokesperson asserted that "all known scientific evidence supports evolution and virtually every reputable scientist." In contrast to that statement, he saw a two-page advertisement that stated "one hundred biologists, chemists, zoologists, physicists, anthropologists, bioengineers, organic chemists, geologists, astrophysicists, and other scientists from institutions such as Yale, Massachusetts Institute of Technology, Tulane, Rice, Emory, George Mason, Lehigh, the University of California, Washington, Texas, Florida, North Carolina, Wisconsin, Ohio, Colorado, and elsewhere wanted the world to know that they are skeptical." Their statement read "We are skeptical of claims for the ability of random mutation and natural selection to account for the complexity of life. Careful examination of the evidence for Darwinian theory should be encouraged."[12]

In his search for answers, Lee Strobel interviewed Jonathan Wells, Ph.D. at the Discovery Institute in Seattle, Washington. Professor Wells wrote *Icons of Evolution: Why much of What We Teach about Evolution Is Wrong*[13] which explains the problems with the icons of evolution.

The first icon he tackled was the Stanley Miller Experiment in 1953 which produced amino acids when an electric spark was shot through an atmosphere similar to the original atmosphere. However, scientists now believe that the original atmosphere was not what Miller used in his experiment. If the experiment is conducted with what is felt to be similar to the earth's early environment (carbon dioxide, nitrogen, and water vapor), the result would be embalming fluid which doesn't get you to the first step in the origin of life. Then scientifically how did life begin? Nobody has a good explanation. Our textbooks still mislead our young people with the thought that it could have initiated out of nothing, but that is only because they do not want to concede to the non-scientific thought that there was intelligent design from a creator. Even biochemist and Nobel Prize winner Francis Crick who discovered the molecular structure of DNA concluded, "An honest man, armed with all the knowledge available to us now, could only state that in some sense, the origin of life appears at the moment to be almost a miracle."[14]

The next icon Wells wrote about was Darwin's "Tree of Life." Darwin's sketch represented the theory that all living creatures have a common ancestor. He believed that if a population was exposed to different conditions, then natural selection would modify the different populations. Eventually, two separate species would result. The theory suggested progressive change, which the fossil record never supported. Darwin believed future fossil records would prove his theory true, but it hasn't. Professor Wells stated Darwin's "Tree of Life" is not a good explanation, and he further emphasized, "If you consider all of the evidence, Darwin's tree is false, as a description of the history of life. I'll even go further than that: it's not even a good hypothesis at this point."

Another icon was that of the embryos of a fish, salamander, tortoise, chicken, hog, calf, rabbit, and human side-by-side at three stages of development. The similarity of the embryos supported Darwin's claim of a universal ancestor. In actuality, the embryos are not similar. The embryos were *drawn* to look similar. This misrepresentation was known in the 1860s, but the drawings still persist in textbooks today.

The last icon dealt with the progression from ape to man which supposedly occurred over 5 million years. The Java man was the missing link between ape and man. However, the Java man was an artist rendering of a skull cap, femur (thigh bone), and three teeth that were excavated by Dutch scientist, Eugene Dubois, on an Indonesian Island in 1891-1892. The truth is Java man was distinctly human and had a brain capacity well within the range of humans living today.[15] *Time Magazine* as recently as 1994 treated Java as a legitimate evolutionary ancestor.[16]

Professor Wells summarized his thoughts on Darwinian evolution by stating, "My conclusion is that the case for Darwinian evolution is bankrupt. The evidence for Darwinism is not only grossly inadequate, it's systematically distorted. I'm convinced that sometime in the not-too-distant future—I don't know, maybe twenty or thirty years from now—people will look back in amazement and say, 'How could anyone have believed this?' Darwinism is merely materialistic philosophy masquerading as science, and people are recognizing it for what it is."[17]

FALSE RELIGION

Another one of Satan's lies is that all religions are right. It doesn't matter which one you believe. However, if a person investigates religions it is clear that religions can't all be correct. It is possible to co-exist and tolerate each other, but somebody is right and somebody is wrong.

Wouldn't it be simple if there was only one religion? We could either believe in God or not. The chaos occurs because we have thousands of religions. Which one is right? Was there a time when there was only one religion? Is there only one true religion now? What is the truth? What are the lies? Let's examine the Bible and cults.

THE BIBLE

God's acts and His words were written down by men in the Holy Bible. It became the foundation for Christianity. It was meant to be a guide and a standard. God wanted mankind to read it, know it, and meditate on it. However, over the years, some have maligned, distorted, added to, taken away from, perverted, and mistrusted the Bible.

What does the Bible teach?

- The Bible is the final authority on all matters.
- There is one God who has a personal interest and involvement in our life.
- The Trinity is composed of the God the Father, Jesus Christ the son, and the Holy Spirit.
- Jesus Christ is God, not just a prophet.
- Jesus Christ resurrected.
- Jesus Christ is 100 percent God, and 100 percent man.
- Jesus Christ has authority to forgive sin.
- Jesus Christ has authority over nature, life, and death.
- He is omnipresent, omnipotent, omniscient, holy, and loving.
- He is to be worshipped as God.
- Salvation is by faith in Jesus Christ and not by our good works (Ephesians 2:8-9).
- Man is made in the image of God, but, because of sin, separated from God.
- The Holy Spirit indwells believers.
- There is an everlasting, conscious punishment of unbelievers and an everlasting, conscious blessedness of the righteous (Hebrews 9:27).

Satan's lie is that the Bible can't be trusted. It is not the Word of God. Jesus Christ was not God. As a result, 12,000 false religions have surfaced. All these religions stress the person's need to do something. Whereas in Christianity, the work of redemption has been done by Jesus Christ. Another distinguishing feature of Christianity is the resurrection of Jesus Christ from the grave. Christianity is the only religion with a resurrected Savior.

Cults or False Religions

The definition of a cult or a false religion is "a perversion or distortion of biblical Christianity."[18] The following are characteristics of cults:

- They claim to have a new truth.
- They have a new twisted interpretation of Scripture.
- They have their own scripture.
- They teach about a different Jesus.
- They reject orthodox Christianity.
- They have inconsistencies in their doctrine.
- They reject the Trinity.
- Dictator-type leadership, "Messenger of God."
- Salvation by works.
- Unfulfilled prophecy.
- Financial exploitation.
- Satanic influence.
- Secret practices.
- Aggressive proselytizing.

A Brief History of Religions

As we have gone through history, how did these other religions come into existence? In the beginning God created the world. He set up a sacrificial system to atone for sins which was a foreshadowing of the supreme sacrifice that Jesus Christ paid for sins on the cross. God chose the Jews as His people. The rest of humanity worshipped other gods or didn't worship any god. When Jesus Christ, a Jew, came and died for the sins of the world, the Christian church was formed. The Jews either accepted Christ and became Christians, or they rejected Christ and remained in the Jewish religion. The other major religions reject Jesus as God.

The Islamic faith says that Jesus is a prophet. Ergun Caner, who wrote *Unveiling Islam*[19] realized, after he heard about the saving grace of Jesus, that Islam was wrong about Jesus being a prophet. He said Jesus claimed to be God.

A person can't claim to be God and be a prophet. A prophet of Allah was supposed to lead people to God, not claim to be God. Claiming to be God is blasphemy, and blasphemy is a capital offense.

Caner questioned whether Jesus was insane, or whether He was and still is the God He claimed to be. He decided Jesus Christ was God and placed his faith in Him.

Satan is in this world to confuse people and to keep them from the truth. In 2 Corinthians 4:4 Paul wrote "the god of this age hath blinded the minds of them who believe not…" In 2 Corinthians 11:13 Paul penned "for such are false apostles, deceitful workers, transforming themselves into the apostles of Christ."

We know the truth by seeking the truth. Lee Strobel in his books *The Case for Christ* and *The Case for Faith* detailed his journey for the truth by investigating the evidences for Christ and Christianity. What he found caused him to abandon his atheism and embrace Jesus Christ.

Chapter Three

I DO, AND NOW I DON'T

W hat symptoms have you been having?" I asked Brenda, who was a thin blonde in her mid-thirties. She had been in the office previously with her husband, but I knew little about her.

"For the last month, I've had more nausea and diarrhea."

"Are the medicines helping you with the symptoms?"

"Yes, they are, but I take the medicines when I have problems. I just seem to be having problems more frequently."

"I do have a letter from your gastroenterologist. He states that the endoscopy of your stomach and colon last year were normal. He felt your symptoms were due to irritable bowel syndrome, which you are presently under treatment for."

"I am taking the pills, but I wondered if there was anything else that could help me get better."

Her eyes were tearful, and her prevailing sadness made me wonder what was going on in her life.

"What would you consider to be the major stress in your life right now?"

"I have been separated from my husband for the last 4 years," she quietly admitted while looking down. "I never expected this in my marriage. I took my vows seriously. I believe in being faithful."

"Have you been through counseling?"

"Yes, I have, but I still struggle."

"Why did you separate?"

"He was seeing someone else," she said while keeping her composure.

I waited. It was hard for her to say.

"How did you find that out?"

"His beeper went off a few times, and he didn't answer it. Eventually, I checked the number. It was a number I didn't recognize and I called it to see who it was. When a girl answered, I talked with her awhile. Later that evening, I asked my husband if the number that I called was his girlfriend. He confessed that it was. Then he moved out of our house and into her house. He talks with me frequently, yet he isn't willing to get back together."

I knew her physical symptoms were mostly related to her emotional turmoil. After I refilled her medicine prescription, I asked her to come back for a follow-up visit in a few weeks.

In my first week in an internal medicine office practice, I had already spoken to four patients about problems related to adultery. Another gray-haired female patient in her sixties with a long history of depression related to me that she was married to a philandering businessman, who spent too much time in bars. She was a little overweight and had short curly hair. She said he had been unfaithful to her for years. When he finally gave up the bar scene, he spent hours every day on the computer in chat rooms talking to women all over the country. When she complained, he told her that she should be happy that he wasn't running around anymore. She stayed married to him for the benefit of the family and the family business.

Another mom brought her 12-year-old girl into the office.

"She refuses to do any schoolwork, and I want her to be tested for Attention Deficit Disorder," the mother informed me.

"How long has she had this problem?"

"About one year. For the last semester, she didn't do any homework, and, now, she has to go to summer school."

"Is she doing any drugs?"

"She says she isn't, and I haven't had any reason to suspect anything."

"How is your family situation?"

"Her dad did move out five years ago to live with his girlfriend."

"How do you think that impacted your daughter?" I asked knowing that most kids will have problems years after their parents break up.

"She was hurt. She loves her dad. I thought she got over it."

"I will set her up for an evaluation for ADD and some counseling," I told the mom although I suspected most of the problems were related to the father's abandonment.

The last patient I saw that week with adultery-related problems was a pleasant gentleman in his 60s. After he told me how much he liked his previous doctor who just had a baby and was taking time off, he told me that he was thankful that I was available to take over his case.

As I looked over his chart, I noticed that he had a history of high blood pressure and depression. His blood pressure was under control, and I thought I would ask him how he was doing with his depression.

"Is your anti-depressant still helping you?"

"I feel better on it than I do off it. I've been on several different medicines, but none of them completely takes away my down feelings."

"Was there a specific event in your life that you felt led to your depression?" I asked him.

"Yes, there was. I don't like to talk about it," he said as he paused and looked out the window. "I still get angry and emotional. Thirty-three years ago, I was married. I would be out of town on business for a few days at a time. One day when I came home, my wife told me that she was pregnant and the baby wasn't mine. I suspected who the father was. A few times when I came home, the minister would be sitting in the kitchen smoking a cigarette. I asked her if he was the father. She admitted that he was."

As he told me that story, tears were flowing down his cheeks. He apologized and took some time to wipe away the tears and blow his nose.

"After that, we separated and then divorced. She had a baby boy. She raised him, but she never disciplined him. He became a problem child. I did what I could to help him. When he became an adult, he drank alcohol heavily. I stay involved in his life, but he has caused me a lot of emotional and financial stress."

My patient lived every day with heartache over his wife's betrayal. He could have moved on with his life, but he didn't. He had been through some counseling, but he never got over his pain. Within a few months, the emergency room notified my office that he had a major stroke and died.

In one week of an office practice, I felt immersed in the tragedy of American family life; lack of commitment, lies, deceit, unhappiness, hurt children, and unending conflict and bitterness.

About half of all divorces are due to sexual immorality. It affects all of us in one way or another. Our society glamorizes unfaithful housewives, sex in the workplace, and friendships with the opposite sex. Is there a need for guidelines? Does that fit with our self-centered "I want it all" culture? Is adultery acceptable if love is moving you in that direction?

One young nurse told me that another couple was fun and friendly to her and her husband. They spent time together going out to dinner and movies. One night, the other couple asked them to consider swapping mates for the evening. They explained that they had done that with several other couples, and it was an enriching experience for both marriages. This young nurse was skeptical, and she broke off the friendship.

PREVENTION

Is "Thou shalt not commit adultery" in Exodus 20:14 a prudish rule that omits adult fun and expression? Is it a commandment that doesn't allow us to liven up our lives? Or is it a commandment for our own protection and for the good of society?

In Christian circles, according to a *Christianity Today* survey, adultery is committed by 23 percent of non-pastors surveyed and by 12 percent of pastors.[1] In the same survey, the major factor contributing to extramarital relationships was physical and emotional attraction (78 percent) which was considerably more than marital dissatisfaction (41 percent). Most of the time, it is attraction more than dissatisfaction that gets people to cross the line. In non-Christian surveys, the percentage of unfaithfulness in males that had been married for more than two years is reported at 72 percent.[2]

In 2 Samuel 11, King David, who was a man after God's own heart, looked upon Bathsheba from his balcony as she bathed. Now, if he would have stopped right there and turned away, he could have avoided adultery, murder, and divisive family problems. Instead, he lost his self-control and gave in to what he was thinking. Lust is a battleground for most men.

In Matthew 5:27-29, Jesus said to take your eye out if it offends you. He didn't actually mean for people to pluck their eye out, but it was a warning of the severity of what we look at.

One preacher told the story of a young man and an elderly man in his eighties that were sitting on a park bench. A nicely dressed young woman walked by. The young man said he couldn't wait until he got older and lust wasn't such a problem. The older man replied, "Me too."

Lust is a struggle of the mind, and it needs to be controlled.

I once heard a speaker say that he was married and yet fell in love with another woman. He said his wife had also fallen in love with another man. Neither of them acted on their feelings. They honored their commitment. They remained faithful and married to each other. He made that point to emphasize that we can't trust our feelings. We need to live by principles and develop clear boundaries. At some time in our marriage, we may develop feelings for someone else. Those feelings will come and go much like they did in elementary school, middle school, and high school.

In Jerry Jenkins' book *Loving Your Marriage Enough to Protect It*, he was proactive in protection for his marriage. He said he first wrote a magazine article "Of Scandals and Hedges" about some of his prudish rules that he developed for his marriage. He shared six hedges (don't meet alone with another woman, be careful about touching, set guidelines for how you compliment other women, guard your tongue when you are tempted to flirt, remember your wedding vows, spend time with the family). He felt the hedges protected him, his wife, his family, his employer, his church, and the reputation of Christ. He wrote don't try to "conquer or stand and fight, or pray about or resolve, but to flee lust."[3] He thought the magazine article might be too personal. However, more people responded to that article than anything that he had ever written. People asked for more practical ideas on the topic, and he wrote a book for people to use to help protect their marriages.

While I was in medical school, one of the professors encouraged us to set boundaries in our relationships to patients. He said if a patient is flirting with you; don't get caught up in it. It is not because you are intelligent, good looking, successful, charismatic, or too good to be true. It is because "the patient is crazy." Remember that, he said, and it will keep you out of trouble. His wise words stuck in my mind. Only a crazy woman would pursue and tantalize a married man. As I think about my years in practice, the only patients that made a pass at me were either crazy, demented, drugged, or intoxicated.

Jerry Jenkins also tells a story about his experience in a top flight hotel. He and an elderly colleague were getting settled into their room when they smelled perfume and heard a spraying sound near the door. The colleague went and opened the door. A middle-aged lady in a mini-skirt was leaning seductively in the doorway.

"You lonely, hon?" she asked.

"I'll never be that lonely," he said, and shut the door.[4]

In order for us to be faithful in our marriages, we need to be concerned about meeting the needs of our spouses. Women need conversation, honesty, financial security, family commitment, and affection, while men need affection, recreational companionship, an attractive spouse, home front support, and admiration. Most importantly, men and women need to value their marriage. Even men with the best looking spouses are capable of lust. We need to focus our attention on what we have, rather than on what we don't have. Some men justify their affair by saying their wife is dumpy, unintelligent, boring, and lazy, but the truth is they knowingly broke God's commandment and are looking for an excuse.

THE CONSEQUENCES

I was talking to one of the other emergency room physicians about his religious beliefs. He explained his lack of interest in any religion. He said his parents were divorced, and they had attended church. He didn't see where religion was helpful to them. He told me that he respected my religious beliefs, but that he believed most Christians were the worst examples of how we are supposed to live. He cited one of his neighbors who criticized him because he and his wife were divorced from previous marriages. However, he recently learned that this Christian neighbor had given his own wife a venereal disease that he had picked up from a prostitute.

This Christian man not only picked up a venereal disease and transmitted it to his wife, but he tarnished Christianity. Unfortunately, it happened, and it happens way too often to Christian people.

Back to King David in 2 Samuel 11, what did his thoughts lead to?

When David saw beautiful Bathsheba with her dark tanned skin and long black hair, he wanted her. Although he was married and so was she, he took her for himself. His sin culminated in a pregnancy, the death of Bathsheba's husband, and the death of his child. Later, his family went through turmoil. David's son, Amnon committed incest with his sister, Tamar. Subsequently, David's other son, Absalom, told his men to kill Amnon to avenge the act against Tamar (2 Samuel 13:23-29). David's disobedience and sinful actions may have opened the door for his family to cross the line also.

Does that still happen today? We live in such a sexually free culture. Scott Peterson made national news when he declared his pregnant wife missing on December 24, 2002. Later, she was found dead in the San Francisco Bay. In his trial, the prosecuting attorney portrayed him as a lying philanderer who didn't act the part of a grieving husband after his pregnant wife disappeared.[5] When details of an affair with Amber Frey were presented to the jury as the motive for the murder, the evidence against Scott was mounting. The jury felt there was enough circumstantial evidence to convict him of murder.

In a case in Michigan, a Baptist pastor with 14 years of successful ministry had an affair with a married woman in his congregation. He eventually left his wife and five kids as well as his position as pastor, and moved back to his hometown several hours away. Soon after that, his mistress left her husband and two kids and followed him. The jilted husband figured out what was going on. He traveled to the town where the pastor had moved and knifed him to death.[6] After news of the tragedy reached the small town, the mood of his 180 member former congregation was sad. The interim pastor commented that "They are really feeling the loss of a beloved pastor who had a profound impact on their lives." One of the deacons commented that the people were trying to focus on the good that he did for the church and for the community. They didn't want to focus on the fact that the man left his wife and five children, and the woman left her husband and two children. A poor choice affected seven children, left one man dead, and sent another to prison for life.

A married lady in our city became emotionally involved with a smooth talking man who boarded horses at her stables. After the man found out about a million dollar life insurance policy on the lady's husband, he shot, stabbed, and slit the husband's throat. A long embarrassing trial brought out the details of the affair for the whole city. In the end, when the murderer was convicted, the wife said "I feel like the biggest fool on the face of the Earth." She knew that nothing could repair the damage she had caused.[7]

My pastor, Bo Moore, gave some statistics when he spoke on adultery which can lead to fatherless homes. He said 70 percent of the almost two million inmates in the United States grew up without a father in the home. Seventy-five percent of children who live in a fatherless home will experience poverty, as compared to 20 percent of children who grow up in a two-parent home. The number one fear among children is the loss of one or both parents. Adultery devastates children.

Adultery doesn't deliver the happiness as much as people think it will. In one survey, 80 percent of those who break up their marriage to marry another said they shouldn't have done it. The divorce statistics also bear out that second and third marriages have a higher divorce rate than first marriages. Many times the same struggles a person runs from in a divorce, they encounter in their next marriage. All marriages have struggles that need to be worked through. If the lure of eternal bliss with a new partner is tempting you, realize that married people who believe that sex outside of marriage is wrong are happiest.

Adultery undermines trust in a marriage. On our wedding day, my wife and I made a commitment to each other. We said that we would love each other and no other. Of course over our married life, my wife has met many good looking men who are more talented musically, more godly, more athletic, more charismatic, more charming, more eloquent at speech, more humorous, more intelligent, and more romantic than I am. Many men will say very nice things to her, and compliment her. However, she made a commitment that she will love me until death. She didn't say she would love me when she felt like it or when it was convenient.

I have met many good looking women, but I have vowed before God to give my attention and love to my wife. I am not free to pursue others. God expects me to take my vows seriously. I remind my wife that I do love her and am faithful to her.

We both are committed. We can break that commitment at any time. Either one of us can destroy the trust we have for each other. God doesn't want us to do that. He has provided for each of us a helper, a soul mate, a friend, and a lover. We are to cherish that relationship, nurture it, and let it be an example to our children. God help us in that endeavor. It is a huge responsibility. Many people are affected by it.

CAN PEOPLE MAKE IT THROUGH AFFAIRS?

In an article in *Physician* magazine, a doctor shared his heartache and warned others.

> I sometimes look to the nurses with whom I work for some normalcy, just as they look to me. We want to see a smiling face, hear a joke and experience something that pulls us temporarily out of the blood and the breathlessness, the drunkenness and the stupidity that often accompany our work. We depend on one another throughout the day until we can go home to the ones we love.

A potential stumbling block in this arrangement is that, like many physicians, I work with some lovely women. Bright and professional, some of them have a manner of speech, a favorite perfume, a lilt of laughter or a curve of body that makes them appealing.

Years ago, in a time when my faith was weak from neglect, when I suppressed emotions and ignored warning signs, sin was lurking. I was absorbed completely in my career, unhappy and unmotivated in my marriage, immature and self-centered. All of these factors converged so that I committed adultery with a young woman in my office.

I wanted this woman. I was determined to have this woman's attention and touch. Rather than accept her wisdom and try to salvage order in my life, rather than respect God's commandments and walk away from another's man's wife, I plunged us both into the chaos of an affair. In the process, I shut off the wisdom, faith, and Scriptures I had learned as a child and young adult. I made the choice to disobey. Of course, so did she, though I blame myself most of all.

She and I learned about adultery over many months. We learned that nothing is as discreet as we thought and how news of scandal travels fast. We learned that betrayal occurs in the heart before it ever involves the body. We learned that it was thrilling and tragically romantic, but exhausting on every level. It was physically exhausting as we tried to convey messages and arrange meetings beneath the veneer of normal life. It was emotionally exhausting as we rode the highs of our time together to the lows of jealousy and anger when we were apart.

Ultimately, it ended, though not before our spouses found notes and poems left in ridiculous places. Not before we became habitual liars. Not before I ignored my wife's birthday and left her swinging between rage and tears as I consistently disregarded her attempts to reach me.

I see now that marriage can survive adultery and even thrive afterward. Fortunately, by Christ's death and resurrection—and by my repentance—my sin was forgiven. Likewise, by my wife's mercy and my renewed commitment, our marriage moved on to levels of trust, romance, and intimacy that we had never known before. In some ways, the affair shocked us into a new life.

Still, even though it lies in the past, even though everyone survived, the memory haunts me at times. I wish I could go back to the day I began my trek into the wilderness of adultery and make the right decision. I wish I could go back to the first night of my betrayal, and take my wife to dinner instead and ask her about her dreams and needs. I wish I could take her home and make love to her, ignoring the confusing murmurs of temptation in favor of real love, of romance blessed and sanctioned by God.

If I could change it all, the young woman and I might be able to speak without the uncomfortable memory of the sin we wandered in far too long. And I wouldn't have felt ashamed the last time I shook her husband's hand.

As for me, I tread carefully now. I see some of the traps laid out by Satan. I know my vulnerabilities. I accept that I am a combination of soul and body—and that both have their weaknesses. I accept the reality, spoken in pulpits too seldom, that Christians are not free from sinful desires, but perhaps, at times, more assailed by them. I see that it is my response, not my temptation, that determines my walk with God. I pray about this, knowing how I enjoy the company of the women I work with, knowing how easy and dangerous even proximity can be. And, as I thank God for the gentle hand He showed me when I needed it most. I also thank Him for the woman who shares my life and my children; I ask Him to keep me from making the same mistake again. Because even as His mercies are infinite, so is the foolishness of man.[8]

In 1 Corinthians 7:1-5, Paul commented on the ways of proper sexuality "let every man have his own wife, and every woman have her own husband." God gave us one mate to focus our time and energy on. He wants us to lift our mate's ego, communicate with them, serve them, and look for ways to please them.

We are to do the same to God. When the Israelites were not faithful to God and turned to idols, it cost them. They spent many years in captivity. When people fall into the trap of adultery, they are in captivity also.

In John 8:3-11, Jesus dealt with a lady who committed adultery. The people were gathered around her ready to stone her, but Jesus pointed out that we are all guilty of sin. We shouldn't be condemning others, but we need to be aware that adultery leads to God's judgment. It is best not to head down that road to destruction.

Chapter Four

E M P T Y

"Did I lose my baby?" Annette, a 35-year-old brunette, asked me with tears trickling down her face. Her husband was at her side.

"Yes," I told her gently with my sincere sympathy. She buried her head in her husband's chest and sobbed heavily. He cried with her.

"I'll be back," I whispered to the husband when he glanced up.

I quietly left the obstetrics' room in order to let them grieve privately. Only 5 weeks before, they had celebrated a positive pregnancy test. This morning, she started bleeding and cramping and arrived in the emergency room having an obvious miscarriage. Their hearts were broken.

When I returned to their room some time later, they had composed themselves. Their tears had stopped flowing. However, their faces were engraved with sadness.

"I contacted your doctor, and he arranged to take you to surgery to stop the bleeding. The operating room staff will be down to transport you. In the meantime, I have a few other questions I need to ask you," I explained to her. "Have you had any other pregnancies?"

"Yes, I have. I had a normal pregnancy and delivery a few years ago. Then at 3 months of age my baby girl died," she replied and paused while she battled a surge of emotions. I waited.

"I'm sorry to hear that," I responded sympathetically.

"She was a beautiful healthy baby with no signs of problems," she continued. "Then one day she had trouble breathing and turned blue. I drove her to the hospital. As I ran through the emergency room entrance, a nurse stopped me, looked at my baby, took her from me, and rushed her into the emergency room treatment area. Another nurse came up to me, put her arm around my shoulder, and guided me into a private family waiting room. I was crying and trying to answer the nurse's questions, but I could only think about my baby. I would interrupt her questions with my frantic questions. 'What is going on? Is she going to live?' The nurse assured me that the doctors would do everything they could do."

"Eventually, the doctor came in and confirmed my worst fears. He told me he did everything he could, but my baby died of an abnormal heart," she explained and then began crying again.

My heart grieved also. Children are so precious. The thought of losing a child is a parent's worst nightmare. My own child was three months old when the woman related that story to me.

"Emotionally, my baby's death severely affected me for years. I missed her. My sleep wasn't restful, and I didn't feel like eating. A dark cloud continually overshadowed my life. I got counseling and took an antidepressant," she explained as she wiped away her tears with a Kleenex.

"I had another pregnancy several years before our little girl died. Because I was young and the timing wasn't right, I ended up getting an abortion," she added quietly and remorsefully.

My mouth was silenced. My mind tried to understand another aspect of her grief.

"I've gone over that decision many times," she volunteered as she stared blankly. "But I can't change the past, and I've dealt with it."

My heart went out to them. The pain they had endured in their young life was very apparent. I wish I had more time to spend with them, but we were interrupted by the surgery staff that came to take her away. I never saw them again, though I think about them often. They appeared successful, and most likely they were. In a few minutes, they opened up a part of their life that few people had been privilege to. They carried a burden. They wanted children, and they didn't have any. They were empty.

THE STATISTICS

Abortion was legalized in 1973, while I was in high school. Since that time, abortion has resulted in the deaths of 47 million babies or almost 1.5 million babies a year. Abortion is the number one cause of death in America although it is not listed on the charts because it is not considered a cause of death. The next most common cause of death would be heart disease at 700,142, then cancer at 553,768, then stroke at 163,538, and then emphysema and chronic bronchitis at 123,013. We abort almost 1.5 million babies a year compared to a total of 2.4 million people that died from all other causes of death combined.[1] Abortion is the most common surgery performed on women. The next most common is Cesarean sections (one million per year) as reported by the CDC.[2]

I have heard politicians proclaim "Abortion should be safe, legal, and rare," but abortion is common. Of the 3 million unintended pregnancies each year, half end in abortion.[3] It is also very lucrative business. In the March 2005 newsletter from Right to Life of Michigan, Barbara Listing stated that Planned Parenthood, the largest abortion provider on the planet, made $104 million in 2004 from abortions alone. She said there is one adoption referral for every 138 abortions. Planned Parenthood hands out condoms to prevent pregnancy and abortions. However, according to Consumer Reports who released a major study on the quality of condoms, the condoms that Planned Parenthood gave out ranked the worst of all 23 brands tested.[4]

When I entered the medical field, I met many women who had already had abortions. Some had a great deal of grief and regret, while others did not have any regrets. One woman told me that she did not feel bad after any of the ten abortions that she had.

I have discussed abortion openly a few times with other doctors and nurses.

"When does a fetus become a living being?" I have asked. With ultrasounds, the beating heart is visible at 18 days of gestation, and the brain waves are detected at 40 days. It is obvious the fetus is living early in the pregnancy. However, I realized that my views were hitting the ears of women who had already had abortions. I stirred up some emotions I wasn't prepared to deal with. I realized these women needed counseling and support. They needed to hear about a loving God that forgives. Years ago those resources were not available, but today counselors are waiting in Christian-based centers in many major cities and small towns to help deal with the physical, emotional, and spiritual pain.

One of my sons, when he was four years old, asked my wife "If a woman kills her first baby, does God give her another one?"

"Yes, He can because we serve a loving, forgiving God," she answered him.

However, many women that have had abortions have expressed those fears. There are consequences to the abortion act physically, spiritually, and emotionally. Abortions more than double the risk of future sterility because the womb may be scraped too deeply or an infection may develop. A woman's spiritual and emotional state also can have an effect on future fertility.

Post-Abortive Men

The emotions of men vary according to how the man was involved in the abortion. Did he insist or force the woman into an abortion, or did he allow her to make the decision? Did he try to stop the abortion, or was he unaware his child was aborted until after the fact?

There is help for men. Richard Beattie, who wrote *David's Harp*, a devotional for men, wrote out his testimony. He was sixteen when he got his girlfriend pregnant. He wanted to get a job and get married, but her mom arranged for an abortion.

He never told his parents or anyone else. He sobbed all by himself in the corner of an empty room. He was no longer a virgin. What he believed would help him be a man had taken something out of him.

When his girlfriend got pregnant again, he went to his parents. He thought they would agree with his marriage plans, but they wanted to meet with her parents. When all four parents counseled together, they chose abortion again. The parents kept the young couple apart until after graduation. Then they drifted apart.

Five years later, he met the wife of his dreams, and they got married. He never told her about the abortions. After he got involved in two affairs and his marriage was on the brink of divorce, he broke down and told her everything. He finally began to heal.[5] Now he is helping others work through their past struggles.

THE PRO-CHOICE VIEWPOINT

In a medical journal, I read about a pioneer in woman's health care. She wrote about how she used to counsel women about abortion, although it was never easy. Before Roe vs. Wade, women who decided to abort were flown to England for their procedures.

Later in the article she told how her daughter, who became a physician, practiced with her in the 1980s and 90s. They offered abortions, early in the first trimester of pregnancy, as part of their family practice services. Every day, people marched in front of their office with placards showing dismembered mature infants. Although the police kept the protestors at the required distance, it was still an uncomfortable situation. Due to threatening phone calls, they had to get unlisted phone numbers. She worried about the safety of her grandchildren, especially after the oldest came home from grade school asking if she really killed babies. A friend at school said his father told him that.

In the next paragraph, she stated, "Our fears were definitely not unfounded. Those who did not agree with the abortion laws were murdering women and the physicians who tried to help them. In 1993 the obstetrician and gynecologist, Dr. David Gunn, was killed just outside his office. At his death vigil I stated, 'Personal reflection and public debate, without fear of reprisal, is our only hope for reconciliation for finding common ground that will eliminate violence.'"[6]

THE POLITICAL DEBATE

Since I have been in high school, the debate over legal abortion has raged on. One side has argued for the rights of women to birth, love, and feed the number of children they desire. The pro-life side has argued that abortion is not a healthy choice for women physically, emotionally, or spiritually.

George W. Bush in a speech at the March for Life Walk in Washington D.C. on January 24, 2005 stated "I encourage you to take heart from our achievements, because a true culture of life cannot be sustained solely by changing laws. We need, most of all, to change hearts. And that is what we're doing, seeking common ground where possible, and persuading increasing numbers of our fellow citizens of the rightness of our cause."[7]

WHAT DOES THE BIBLE SAY?

Deuteronomy 5:17 commands "Thou shalt not kill." If you believe life begins at conception, then abortion is murder. Of course, it is not right to kill the abortionist either.

Exodus 21:22-23 explains that if two people are fighting and in the process hurt a pregnant woman resulting in the death of the baby, the offender must be executed.

In Colossians 3:5, Paul exhorts Christians to set our affections on things that matter to God and not on having sex outside of marriage. If we obey his command about limiting sex to marriage, we eliminate the problem of having unplanned children outside of marriage. Nearly 900,000 teens get pregnant every year in America. Once a teenager is pregnant, none of the resulting scenarios is without problems physically, emotionally, and spiritually. According to a 1995 survey, 51 percent of teens that became pregnant gave birth; 35 percent sought abortions; 14 percent miscarried. Less than 1 percent chose to place their children for adoption.[8]

When God commanded that we limit sex to marriage, it was for good purpose. It eliminates out of wedlock children and it decreases sexually transmitted diseases. The Centers for Disease Control in Atlanta, Georgia agrees. They recommend abstinence or a lifelong monogamous relationship as the only means of safe sex.

WHAT ARE THE CONSEQUENCES OF ABORTION?

The complications of abortion include infection, bleeding, death, sterility, tubal pregnancy, ongoing pelvic pain, and more. Women who abort are two times more likely to abuse alcohol, five times more likely to use drugs, three times more likely to commit suicide than the general population, and seven times more likely to commit suicide than women who have given birth in the previous year. The rate of breast cancer is increased 50 percent, because having babies and breastfeeding decrease the risk of breast cancer.[9]

Post-Abortion Syndrome symptoms include the following:[10]

Guilt—what an individual feels after going against one of nature's strongest instincts; a mother protecting her young.

Anxiety—tension in the form of inability to relax, irritability, dizziness, pounding heart, nausea, worry about the future, difficulty concentrating, and disturbed sleep. She may avoid anything to do with babies.

Psychological numbing—avoidance of emotions. It hampers their ability to form and maintain close relationships.

Depression—thoughts of suicide, uncontrollable crying, decreased self-concept, decreased motivation, lack of enthusiasm for activities and relationships. In a survey by the Elliot Institute of post-abortive women, 33 percent reached a level of depression so deep that they would rather die than go on.

Anniversary syndrome—54 percent of post-abortive women noted an increase in their symptoms around the anniversary of the abortion and/or the due date of the aborted child.

Re-experiencing the abortion—"flashbacks" of the abortion experience occurring during pelvic exams or at the sound of a vacuum cleaner. Nightmares involving themes of lost, dismembered, or crying babies.

Preoccupation with becoming pregnant again—a significant percentage of women who abort become pregnant again in one year.

Anxiety over fertility issues—fear that they will not be able to become pregnant again.

Interruption of the bonding process with present and/or future children—fearing another loss, the post-abortive mom may not bond well with her other children.

Survival guilt—abortion is a difficult decision for many women, and the decision boils down to "It's me or you, and I choose me."

Development of eating disorders—anorexia or bulimia as a form of self-punishment, or a means to become unattractive, or a means of control for the woman who feels that her life is totally out of control.

Alcohol and drug abuse—a way to cope with the pain.

Other self-punishing behaviors—abusive relationships, promiscuity, failure to take care of herself medically, emotionally, and/or physically.

Brief reactive psychosis—the individual's perception of reality is drastically distorted.

Do Christians Have Abortions?

It is especially discouraging to hear that many Christian young people are having abortions. One girl said, "I'm a good Christian girl. I had to have an abortion." A volunteer for Right to Life felt terrible that some of the young women walking into the abortion clinic were wearing "WWJD" bracelets, and Christian college sweatshirts. One day a girl walked into the clinic wearing a T-shirt with the spiritual concept "Seven days without prayer makes one weak." The young lady said she was a follower of Jesus. Another young lady was studying her Bible Study Fellowship notes while she waited to have an abortion.[11] About 18 percent of those who abort claim to be Christians.

IS THERE HOPE FOR THOSE WHO HAVE HAD ABORTIONS?

Ramah International is a non-profit ministry that assists those who have gone through abortion.[12] "A voice is heard in Ramah—mourning and great weeping. Rachel is weeping for her children and refusing to be comforted because her children are no more. This is what the Lord says, 'restrain your voice from weeping and your eyes from tears. For your work will be rewarded. Your children will return from the land of the enemy'" (Jeremiah 31:16). Ramah International hopes to heal these women by allowing them to grieve their children's death and eventually return to a normal life. "So there is hope for your future, declares the Lord" (Jeremiah 31:17).

For many, the hope for the future is to stop abortion from hurting other lives.

SPECIAL LETTER ON ABORTION

Hello Friend,

I want to invite you into one of the most private moments of my life. It was the moment my life was sliced in two, if you will. I say it was sliced into two because the person I was before this moment was drastically different from the person I quickly became for many years to come.

I was 19. I was the daughter of a pastor. I was attending a Christian college and dating the son of a pastor. I was having fun, enjoying both the newfound freedom of college and a really neat dating relationship with a Christian guy.

Sounds picture-perfect so far, right? Suddenly the unthinkable happened. I got pregnant. My boyfriend was less than supportive and seemed to threaten to turn my whole world upside down if I carried the pregnancy to term. He taunted me with stories of getting me kicked out of college. (The college expelled pregnant, unwed students.) He even relayed my own assessment—that my mother would probably have a mental breakdown. He convinced me that I didn't have much choice.

I aborted my baby. He would have graduated in 2000, and there isn't a day that goes by when I don't think about him.

I could have been engulfed in the most horrible grief imaginable, but I didn't have anyone to face it with me, and I wasn't willing to do it alone. I chose to numb myself. I drowned my feelings with drugs and promiscuity for many years. I just wanted to escape the overwhelming pain. And in many ways, I did. The only thing I believed during that time was that I made the right decision for that period of my life.

But one day, I found that there was no escaping it. I had to face it. While it was the most painful time in my life, grieving my child brought healing. Finding forgiveness from Christ furthered the journey that brought me to peace that passes all understanding. Then God gave me the inspiration that He could work even abortion to His good.

The world can debate abortion all it wants, but the fact remains there is pain.

I am so much happier now than I was when I was in denial and had convinced myself that I had only aborted a "blob of tissue." I am very loved by a wonderful husband, and I find tremendous fulfillment in a productive and successful career helping other women heal from abortion. The Lord has allowed me to rescue a few children who would have been aborted had their mothers not heard my testimony.

What do I tell these women? What do I see working as they seek to heal? First, I tell them that they are not alone. The Alan Guttmacher Institute (the research arm of Planned Parenthood, the world's largest abortion provider) recently stated that, "At the current rate, 43 percent of women will have at least one abortion by the time they are 45 years old."[13] And you might find this surprising, but women in the church are not immune. Imagine that 43 percent of all women are postabortive— they sit in your congregations, work in your schools, climb corporate ladders to success, and exist in every part of our society. Despite those statistics, abortion is rarely discussed by those who have chosen it.

Second, I would have to say that a good step toward healing can start with confession. Oh, I had confessed it before God, but confessing it to a loving, godly adult through sharing my testimony was a major step in my journey to healing. James 5:16 says, "Confess your sins to each other…so that you may be healed." God gave us each other to encourage and provide help in the process of healing. Telling this truth was one of the most frightening things I've ever done, but it was worth it. I tell people to just make sure this person is one that they can trust.

I hope that you can't really identify with my story. I hope that you aren't hiding from the pain of abortion. I hope you can't feel the overwhelming grief. But if you can, let me encourage you to tell an older, wiser, and very godly woman. If you don't feel you can talk to your mom about it right now, find a local crisis pregnancy center to talk to one of their counselors—they can be found in the "Abortion Alternative" section of your Yellow Pages. I know that sounds tough, but it will be very worth it.

Speaking as someone who knows what premarital sex cost me, I can say that the best way to avoid pain is to remain abstinent until marriage. Your heart is very precious and should be saved for the perfect man. One of my greatest regrets is that I couldn't share my innocence with my husband. Regardless of the fact that the "sky doesn't fall" when you go a little further with your boyfriend than you would have liked, there are major consequences to your future. The boy who truly loves you will wait for marriage.

My prayer for you, if you have experienced abortion, is that you would join me in my journey. Never encourage or support a friend in making the choice to abort—regardless of their circumstances. Abortion is never the solution. It only makes matters worse by bringing more pain and regret into their hearts. Lead them to a crisis pregnancy center where they can find the truth about abortion and to continue their pregnancy.[14]

In God's Great Healing Love,
Sydna

Sydna Masse is the former director of Focus on the Family's Crisis Pregnancy outreach. She is now president and founder of Ramah International, Inc., a post abortion ministry (www.ramahinternational.org). She is the author of *Her Choice to Heal: Finding Spiritual and Emotional Peace after Abortion* (Chariot Victor). Her book tells her story in-depth and provides the opportunity for the reader to reflect on her own abortion situation and to begin the process of finding emotional and spiritual healing.

IN MEMORY

On Memorial Day, we remember those who have died. Especially we honor those who have given their lives for our freedom. On one Sunday, my pastor read off the fatalities of each of America's war casualties. It read as follows:

- Revolutionary War—4,435
- War of 1812—2,260
- Mexican-American War—13,283
- Civil War—529,332
- Spanish-American War—2,446

E M P T Y

- WWI—116,316
- WWII—405,399
- Korean War—54,246
- Vietnam War—56,121
- Persian Gulf War—148
- Iraq War—Over 2500

All the wars combined have killed over 1 million Americans. We need to remember and honor every one of these heroes who sacrificed their lives for our freedom. We also need to remember the 47 million babies, who have been aborted.

God knows every child even before they are formed in the womb.

"For thou hast possessed my inward parts; thou hast covered me in my mother's womb. I will praise thee; for I am fearfully and wonderfully made. Marvelous are thy works, and that my soul knoweth right well. My substance was not hidden from thee, when I was made in secret, and intricately wrought in the lowest parts of the earth. Thine eyes did see my substance, yet being unformed; and in thy book all my members were written, which in continuance were fashioned, when as yet there was none of them" Psalm 139:13-16 (KJV).

Chapter Five

"OH MY,
HOW I LOVE TO EAT"

After church one night, the young people were selling desserts and pizza. They were earning money for camp and the annual bike trip. As I made my way to the kitchen, my stomach growled as I became engulfed with the aroma of pizza. When I saw all the desserts, I felt like I was in fat-man heaven. Despite my desire to start with the sweets, I chose a piece of pepperoni pizza and a Coke. Then I had to make a decision between strawberry pie, peanut butter pie, chocolate butterscotch pie, and more. Since strawberry is a fruit, I selected that piece of pie even though it had a fattening graham cracker crust. When I finished eating, I was satisfied. I enjoyed the conversation with the others at the table, and I didn't feel too bad about my choices.

As the night lingered on, I noticed the young people were visiting tables trying to sell the overabundance of food that was still available. Yes, I did have money left in my wallet. Yes, I knew I could eat more food, and yes, a young lady appeared at our table asking if we wanted to buy something else while displaying fresh pizzas. Finally, after a brief second of mental debate, I broke down and bought, at half price, a piece of ham and cheese pizza. Then when the young people brought around the leftover desserts on trays, I selected the peanut butter pie with chocolate dripped delicately across the top and a spoonful of whipped cream added to top it off. It tasted better than it looked. As I put the last few spoonfuls into my mouth, I wished I had taken two pieces. Then, as if condemned by fate itself, my wife couldn't make it through the second half of her bee sting cake which consisted of chocolate, walnut, and a thick butterscotch frosting.

"Why stop now?" I thought to myself. I already had been self-indulgent. Despite a visual of myself sinking in deep water with a heavy ball and chain wrapped around my ankles, I moved my spoon towards her plate, and I finished off the last few bites of her cake.

Oh my, how I love to eat. Sometimes, I find food so irresistible. It is truly pleasurable. Maybe if I had a calorie counter built into my mouth that would close my jaws at a certain calorie limit, I wouldn't overeat.

Recently, I visited Rock City, a tourist attraction on a mountain in Georgia. As I walked the trail, I came to a narrow cleft between two boulders called "Fat Man Squeeze". I did have some room to spare, but I will need to be disciplined to continue to make it through that pass. I also have a vivid recollection of a vacation my dad took us on to a pig farm in Wadena, Minnesota. I remember seeing a squealing hog stuck in the mud because he was so heavy he could not move. After the farmer shot the hog, he brought in a crane to lift the hog up and take him to the butcher. I've often thought about that. I don't want to get to the point that I am so big I cannot move.

SUPERSIZE PATIENTS

I've seen patients that have gotten to that point. It is sad. I had one patient I saw in the emergency room who weighed 450 pounds. Her legs were swollen and infected. They were painful for her to walk on. She told me she got up to go to the bathroom and fell between her bed and dresser. She was wedged in such a way that she couldn't maneuver herself to get up. Her husband couldn't get her up either.

He called 911, and it took 8 paramedics, rescue personnel, and police officers to get her onto a tarp and into the ambulance. She was a nice lady, but her weight severely restricted her.

I see patients every day that struggle with weight problems. One Monday morning in the office, I saw five patients that weighed over 300 pounds and two of the five patients weighed over 350 pounds.

I asked a 60-year-old woman who dropped from 450 pounds down to 300 pounds after gastric bypass surgery to tell me what she thought I should tell young people about being overweight. She said "Don't ever get overweight in the first place. I went through this stomach reduction surgery in order to play with my grandkids and take care of them."

My overweight patients are sincere, friendly, and honest. They remind me of my family. We ate well. On the charts, we were overweight. We still are, and we struggle to discipline ourselves.

How is our nation doing? In 1980, our population was estimated to be 31.6 percent overweight and 14.4 percent obese. In 2000, The Center for Disease Control estimated that 33 percent were overweight and 31 percent were obese.[1]

BIOLOGIC OR ENVIRONMENTAL?

We have a growing problem. Is it biologic or environmental? There are some genetic disorders such as Prader-Willi Syndrome, Laurence-Moon Bardet Syndrome, and Albright's hereditary osteodystrophy that can cause obesity. There was an article "Living with a Locked Fridge"[2] that explained what it was like to live with three children with Prader-Willi Syndrome.

"We're the food police," the mother described.

"We should wear security badges," her husband added. "We're always doing surveillance, following our kids around, checking up on them."

They have three children with the genetic disorder. Prader-Willi Sydrome affects one out of 12,000 children, and it causes excessive appetite, obesity, and temper tantrums. The syndrome doesn't recur in a family 98 percent of the time. The other symptoms include short stature, weak muscles, food foraging, sleep problems, incomplete sexual development, cognitive disabilities, attention deficit disorder, learning problems, depression, and rages.

The parents do not have the syndrome.

"We might look like we do, but we don't," the mom commented. "Our weight problems come from eating to relieve stress. I've survived by a combination of prayer and chocolate, chocolate and prayer."

At family picnics, the parents would have to watch for their kids stuffing food into their sweat pants, and prevent their children from taking walks alone because they would dig through trash cans. If a rotten smell surfaced in the home, the dog was brought in to find the source. One time an old chicken bone was recovered under a mattress.

Their vigilance has paid off. Amanda, 26-years-old, has dropped from 335 pounds down to 288. Andrew, 21-years-old, has shed 100 pounds down to 226 pounds. Adam, 19-years-old, went from 356 pounds down to 192 pounds.

The mother prayed that her kids would be able to be together, and be happy and healthy. Her prayer was answered when she was able to get them into a home for Prader-Willi Syndrome patients in Oconomowoc, Wisconsin.

"My biggest fear was that God would take us before we had our kids settled," the mother said. "Now I know that if something happens to us, they'll be all right."

"Maybe we can finally do things as a couple," her husband added.

Genetics does play a role at times in people that are overweight, but most of the time in our society our overweight problems come from the overabundance of food in our society, and the lack of physical activity.

Obesity is almost as bad as smoking when health consequences are considered. It is associated with diabetes, coronary artery disease, hypertension, strokes, arthritis, sleep apnea, gallbladder disease, and cancer (uterine, breast, prostate, and colon). It kills 400,000 Americans prematurely every year, and it affects many people emotionally by causing low self-esteem and depression.

PREVENTION

Maybe you are tired of all the warnings you see in the media, and frustrated by the failure to shed pounds and keep them off, but prevention in young people should be our priority. They should at least know what their choices are and possible outcomes. The slogans that we see "Have it your way," "No Rules," "Just do it," imply that we can do whatever we wish, but the consequences of our wishes may be undesirable.

For instance, diabetes is a disease that is related to eating too much and lack of exercise in over half of the people who have it. Only 10 percent of diabetics are juvenile-onset which is caused by a virus or other conditions beyond a person's control. The number of diabetics in our society has grown from 4 million to 18 million in the last 30 years. In 2002, the cost of diabetes was estimated to be $132 billion. One out of 10 of health care dollars spent in the United States is related to diabetes.[3] The problem with diabetes is that it leads to very undesirable consequences such as heart disease, stroke, kidney disease, blindness, and numbness in the hands and feet (peripheral neuropathy). Heart disease strikes a person with diabetes twice as often as a person without diabetes.[4] People with diabetes are two to four times more likely to suffer strokes. Diabetes results in blindness in 12,000-24,000 people a year, and in kidney disease which results in dialysis or transplantation in 129,000 people a year. Diabetic peripheral neuropathy (numbness) and poor circulation causes 82,000 amputations a year.

I am reminded of the severity of diabetes every day. I saw one lady in the emergency room that had an infected swollen foot. She had no feeling in her feet and I wondered if she had stepped on something. I ordered an x-ray. When I looked at it, I saw a needle from an insulin syringe that was broken off and imbedded in the bottom of her foot. She had been walking on it for a week and didn't even know it.

One night in the early morning hours, my beeper went off. There was a code blue called to resuscitate a man in the hospital. I ran up a few flights of stairs to get to his room. The man, Charlie, was well known to the hospital staff because of his frequent visits. He was in his 60s. He was hospitalized for heart disease, and he was a diabetic. While I was trying to revive him with the nurses and technicians, I noticed he had both legs amputated. He didn't survive.

The nurse mentioned to me that the roommate was outside the room. When I left the room, I saw a man walking down the hallway toward me with his I.V. pole beside him. He appeared to be in his forties and had a dark moustache and medium length dark hair.

"Your roommate didn't survive," I informed him.

"I was afraid Charlie wasn't going to make it," he responded. "I knew he was in trouble when he started gurgling in his sleep. I called the nurse right away."

"Thanks for doing that. Charlie had severe heart disease, diabetes, and arterial disease. We did everything we could for him, but we couldn't bring him back."

"I know."

The nurse showed him to another room until his room was put back in order. I went back to the doctor's area to finish the paperwork. As I was writing, the nurse came in to talk.

"Thanks for talking to Charlie's roommate," she began. "He was pretty upset at first. He had been his roommate for about 4 days. They got along pretty well and enjoyed each other's company."

"He seemed to be understanding about Charlie's condition and death, but I'm sure it was a shock to him."

"I am going to move him to a different room."

"That's a good idea. By the way, what was the roommate in the hospital for?" I asked her out of curiosity.

"A heart attack and diabetes," she replied.

I felt bad. He was in the hospital for the same thing that Charlie had been in the hospital for. I imagine it must have been depressing for him to see a diabetic with both legs amputated, and then see him die.

A difficult aspect of medical work is the death of our patients, but a memory of fun times with people help us through. While we were running the code to try to save Charlie, one of the respiratory technicians, Jim, was telling me how much fun he and Charlie had. They would poke fun of each other. Jim, who was a husky Vietnam War veteran with curly long black hair and tattoos all over his forearms, was the brunt of a lot of Charlie's jokes. However, when Charlie came into the hospital this time, he was riding in a wheelchair because he just had his remaining leg amputated.

"I didn't give him any sympathy," Jim told me. "I didn't want him feeling sorry for himself. I told him 'Good to see you Charlie.

You look good.' Then I paused as I noticed both his legs amputated, 'you're a little shorter though.'"

CONSEQUENCES AND COST

Many people can prevent future problems by having discipline in their eating and a regular exercise program. I see people in their twenties and thirties that are overweight with diabetes, high blood pressure, and high cholesterol. These problems lead to other problems and costs prematurely.

As an example of cost, I received a printout of an 80-year-old's prescriptions from an insurance company. Many older patients are on a host of drugs. The average number of drugs that a hospitalized medical patient is on is 15. In this insurance report, this 80 year-old lady, was prescribed 49 prescriptions in three months for a total cost of $1846. The drugs were for hypertension, antibiotics for infections, insulin and pills for diabetes, pain medicine, blood thinners for heart disease, muscle relaxers, hormone pills, an antidepressant, a thyroid medicine, inhalers, medicine for heartburn, medicines for osteoporosis, a pill to lower blood fat, and a steroid to help her breathing. My point is that there are pills for many things, and the longer a young person can stay off prescription drugs the better they will be. Young people don't need to head down the trail of obesity with all its costs and complications.

CASE STUDY

"I'm tired, and I can't do my job. I get plenty of sleep, but I don't feel rested. What's wrong with me, Doctor?" The case was in a medical journal. The patient was a 43 year-old schoolteacher. I've heard the complaint also from different people. What is causing the fatigue? Is it caffeine, alcohol, excessive weight, sleep apnea, lack of exercise, pain, the heart, the lungs, the blood, an infection, the thyroid gland, the liver, arthritis, depression, or drugs? In this case, his blood tests were normal, but the sleep study revealed snoring and pauses in his breathing. His obesity resulted in obstructive sleep apnea. He was instructed to avoid alcohol, lose 10 percent of his weight, and get a continuous pressure mask to keep him breathing at night.[5]

Obesity is the major risk factor for sleep apnea, but it's not the only reason people quit breathing in their sleep. Some people have problems because the part of the nervous system responsible for breathing is not working properly. In our society with the increase in obesity, we have also seen a sharp increase in those with sleep-related problems. It is estimated 40 million people have sleep related problems, but 90 percent are undiagnosed. In obese patients, the excess tissue, lack of muscle tone, and possibly anatomic abnormalities result in the obstruction of the upper airway. As the obstruction gets worse, so does the apnea which can result in excessive daytime sleepiness, snoring, loss of productivity, hypertension, arrhythmias, marital problems, and depression. It is thought to be responsible for 100,000 motor vehicle accidents every year. The annual direct cost of sleep-related problems is $16 billion, and an additional $50-100 billion in indirect costs (accidents, litigation, property destruction, hospitalization, and death).

"Super Size Me"

The popular documentary about a man who ate fast food three times a day for one month demonstrated what inappropriate eating can do to a body over a short period of time. His cholesterol, liver tests, and blood pressure went up dramatically. The physicians that were caring for him suggested he stop his experiment. When I watched the movie, one of my college-age sons thought the guy was going to die. I told him that I have patients who have worse levels than that guy, and they continue in their bad eating habits year after year.

I asked one man what kind of food he ate after his cholesterol came back very high. He said he ate fast food every day, because he wasn't married and he never cooked for himself. Another lady worked at a bank, and she went out with her co-workers three times a week to the buffet. I suggested that she could lower her cholesterol by eating at the sandwich shop or making her own lunch. In the emergency room, I was questioning a 330-pound mother and her 300 pound daughter about their dietary habits. They told me they deep fried every meal.

In contrast to the "Super Size Me" movie, a lady ate every meal at a fast-food restaurant for several months. Instead of gaining weight, she lost 30 pounds by limiting her calorie input to 1400 calories a day.

CAN OBESITY BE TREATED?

Good eating habits and exercise are important to prevent obesity and to lose weight, but when a patient gets overweight and they fail repeatedly to lose their pounds then more drastic measures are needed. Medicines are available, but on an average most people lose about ten pounds with appetite suppressant drugs. For the obese and severely obese, many people choose the various types of stomach surgeries which make the stomach the size of a walnut and limit the amount of food intake. The surgeries, which cost $30,000-40,000, help patients lose an average of 55-97 pounds after one to two years.[6] The surgery has a 0-1.5 percent chance of death, 20 percent chance of infection, and a 25 percent chance of re-operation. In the office practice I was in, we had about 20 patients that had the procedure done and one lady went through the procedure three times. In the United States 20,000 surgeries were performed in 1995, and in 2005 120,000 surgeries are expected to be done.[7] It is a last resort type of procedure. There is no easy fix. Even when the weight is off, patients have to work hard to maintain the weight loss. A bariatric specialist said that after five to six years, one-third of patients will suffer from post-gastrectomy syndrome, which includes vomiting, gallstones, folate-acid deficiency, nausea, and bloating. About half of all patients will regain their lost weight after six or seven years.[8] One patient I took care of paid $27,000 out of her pocket to have the procedure. She lost over 100 pounds. She continued to work out two to three hours a day to keep the weight off, and was proud that she finally weighed less than her husband.

There are various types of diets like the Atkins Diet and the South Beach Diet which seem to be effective for some people, but the real test is whether the weight loss is sustained over several years. According to studies, about 95 percent of people will regain their weight in one year. The 5 percent of people that maintained their weight loss over several years credited their success to one hour of walking seven days a week and maintaining a disciplined diet. I tell people to start slowly with exercise with a goal of eventually walking one hour a day.

PERSONALLY, WHAT DO I DO ABOUT IT?

I have enrolled in a few accountability weight-loss programs where I recorded what I ate and how much I exercised. I recently entered a ten-week contest which offered a $150 prize for first place. I didn't win, but I did lose ten pounds in ten weeks. I know I need to maintain a lifestyle change in order to maintain an appropriate weight.

Years ago I took a course in weight loss from a diabetic nurse educator. She taught our class about calories, fat grams, fiber grams and exercise. Every day we recorded our calorie intake. She wanted our diets to consist of 2500 calories a day (the daily caloric intake of an average American is 3900 calories). When she talked about fat grams, she wanted us to restrict ourselves to 20 grams a day. When I looked up the fat grams for a Whopper, fries, and shake, I found out my fast food meal used up my fat grams for the whole week! Then I started to add up the fiber grams in my diet because we were suppose to eat 20 grams of fiber a day. I fell short in that category. The foods we eat are processed and refined. For example, when I eat an apple I am getting fiber and calories, and the energy gets into my body slowly. If I take the skin off the apple, and mash the apple into sauce, then I lose some fiber. If I take the sauce and make it into juice, I lose more fiber. One third of a glass of apple juice is the same amount of calories as three apples. I could easily drink four glasses of juice in a day, but I have never eaten 36 apples in a day.[9] Apples or any food in its natural state is better for us because it delays the time it takes for the energy to get into our system. It also provides more fiber which is helpful in our digestive process.

During the class with the diabetic educator, I became more aware of what I was eating and the targets I needed to aim for. I also read several books about weight loss. One was *Fit or Fat* by Covert Bailey which encouraged exercise to build muscle and thereby increase the rate of metabolism or the rate at which our bodies use up energy. Another book *Love Hunger* by Dr. Frank Minerth, Dr. Paul Meier, Dr. Robert Hemfelt, and Dr. Sharon Sneed examined the emotional side of overeating. The last book was *How to Become Naturally Thin by Eating More* by Jean Antonello, R.N., B.S.N. which concentrated on the right foods to eat.

UNEXPLAINED WEIGHT LOSS

A young lady told me that she lost 30 pounds in a month when she wasn't even trying. I was happy that she had been able to drop her weight to 230 pounds, but I was concerned that she had a medical problem. I asked her about symptoms of thyroid disease, diabetes, tuberculosis and cancer. She denied any problems. She denied any dieting. I asked her about drinking pop. She said that she switched from 2 liters of regular pop a day to 2 liters of diet pop a day. By doing that, she dropped a few thousand calories a day. I commended her for the switch and losing weight, but I also advised her to switch the diet drink to water. The biggest problems I see with pop is stomach irritation, kidney stones, and weight gain.

EXERCISE

When it comes to exercise, I recommend at least 30 minutes of walking five days per week. According to experts, if we as Americans do that, we can prevent 50 percent of adult-onset diabetics in the future.[10]

It is interesting to note the amount of walking that Jesus did. In Luke 24:13, Jesus and the disciples walked over seven miles. It was common for them to walk this distance daily to their destination.

Of course, there are other types of exercise that work. The important thing is to do something that works for you. One self-proclaimed couch potato stated that every time he got the feeling to exercise, he would lie down until the feeling went away. He got a few laughs with that line, but he wasn't keeping his body maintained. Another comedian stated that he practiced "slumbercise." He would put on a few ankle weights at bedtime, and then if he rolled over in the night he will burn a few extra calories. I appreciate their humor, but I know beneficial exercise takes work.

One of my patients told me her son lost over 300 pounds from diet and exercise. He was almost 500 pounds and after watching a program on television he decided to buy the right foods and exercise. He lost the weight and now he is dealing with the extra skin.

Dr. Nick

One of the most impressive weight-loss testimonies I read appeared in a magazine article "My Big (Formerly) Fat Greek Doctor." Dr. Nick, who was in his thirties and weighed 470 pounds, used to tell his patients "do what I say, not what I do" with a wink of his eye. Unfortunately, he developed testicular cancer and went through surgery and radiation therapy. He survived it. He figured since he dodged the cancer bullet, he knew he needed to dodge the obesity bullet also. He decided to take time off from his clinical practice and lose the weight. He chose a protein drink of 800 calories a day for his nutrition. He took a trip around the United States with his dad to visit every major league ball park as a distraction. He ended up losing over 200 pounds. He continued his weight loss by a rigorous exercise program to drop his weight down to 197 pounds. Now he continues to exercise and eat nutritiously.[11]

Good versus Evil

God does give us good things to eat, and He does it for our benefit.

Fat Theology

And God populated the earth with broccoli and cauliflower and spinach, green and yellow vegetables of all kinds, so man and woman would live long and healthy lives.

And Satan created fast food which brought forth the 99-cent double cheeseburger.

And Satan said to man, "You want fries with that?"

And man said, "Super size them." And man gained pounds.

And God created yogurt, that woman might keep her figure that man found so fair.

And Satan brought forth chocolate. And woman gained pounds.

And God said, "Try my crispy, fresh salad."

And Satan brought forth ice cream. And woman gained pounds.

And God said, "I have sent you heart-healthy vegetables and olive oil with which to cook them."

And Satan brought forth chicken-fried steak so big it needed its own platter.

And man gained pounds and his bad cholesterol went through the roof.

And God brought forth running shoes and man resolved to lose those extra pounds.

And Satan brought cable TV with remote control so man would not have to toil to change channels between ESPN and ESPN2.

And man gained pounds.

And God said. "You're running up the score, Devil."

And God brought forth the potato, a vegetable naturally low in fat and brimming with nutrition.

And Satan peeled off the skin and sliced the starchy center into chips and deep-fat fried them. And he created sour cream dip also.

And man clutched his remote control and ate the potato chips swaddled in cholesterol.

And Satan saw and said, "It is good."

And man went into cardiac arrest.

And God sighed and created quadruple bypass surgery.

And Satan created HMOs.[12]

SATISFACTION

As I ate my chocolate-chip cookie dough ice cream cone the other day, I thought back to what I had read in John 4:7-30.[13] Jesus told the Samaritan woman that if she drank the water from the well, she would thirst again; but if she drank from the water that He offered, she would never thirst again. She decided that she wanted the water that Jesus had to offer. Jesus told her to go get her husband. She replied that she had no husband. Jesus told her that she had had five husbands, and the man she presently lived with was not her husband. Jesus pointed out that she wasn't happy in her relationships because she didn't have the water that satisfies in life, which is a personal relationship with God through Jesus Christ. She went back and told her friends, and they all came out to hear what Jesus had to say. Then she accepted what He had to say and believed on Him.

As I continued to savor the taste of that ice cream cone, I thought about how I wasn't satisfied after the first Mackinac Island Fudge cone. I wanted a second cone, even though I was no longer hungry. I was looking for satisfaction and pleasure in food, yet it didn't completely satisfy. I could have had five more cones just for the pleasure of eating. However, I realized that my satisfaction in life does not come from food, but from God. The fruit of His Spirit is self-control. If my affections are set upon what God wants, I won't desire more than what I need.

My brother, Tim, my pastor and his wife, and a group of men learned about needs and wants when they went on a mission trip to build a church in the jungle of Guyana. Where they stayed there was no electricity, no running water, and no housing. They stayed in tents. One of the Guyana men that worked with them ate one meal a day. He ate fish and rice every day with some fruits and vegetables. He said that is all He needed.

My brother was impressed. "Imagine that, eating the same thing every day, and only what you need," he said.

Chapter Six

A WISE OR UNWISE RISK (GAMBLING)

Jack Whittaker, a chubby-cheeked grandpa wearing wire-rimmed glasses and a black cowboy hat appeared in the press photo with a broad grin and twinkle in his eye. Who wouldn't be happy after winning $314.9 million in the Powerball jackpot on Christmas Day 2002? He appeared on NBC's *Today* show with his wife, Jewell. The couple from Scott Depot, West Virginia, had just won the biggest undivided jackpot in the nation.

However, troubles have plagued the millionaire since his win. He was twice arrested for drunk-driving and was ordered to give up his license and go into an alcohol rehabilitation program. He was also accused in two lawsuits of assaulting female racetrack employees. His vehicle, business, and home were broken into. Then he was served a wrongful death lawsuit when Jesse Joe Tribble, his granddaughter's friend, was found dead in his home. Mr. Whittaker was not home at the time that Jesse died from illegal drugs, and his granddaughter, Brandi Bragg, did not seek medical help. Three months later, Brandi died of an overdose at her boyfriend's house.[1]

Many times all we see are the over-sized checks that lottery winners are holding up, or the television casino advertisements that glamorize the games and the excitement. Just the thought of winning big money without effort is tempting. We don't always hear about the winners who lose all their money.

"8 Lottery Winners That Lost Their Millions"

My son sent me an article entitled "8 Lottery Winners that Lost Their Millions."[2] The following is a synopsis of the article.

Evelyn Adams won the lottery twice totaling $5.4 million but lost it all and lives in a trailer house now. She said, "I won the American dream but I lost it, too. It was a hard fall. It's called rock bottom. Everybody wanted my money. Everybody had their hand out."

William "Bud" Post won $16.2 million in the Pennsylvania lottery in 1988, but now he lives on social security. He describes his experience as a total nightmare. His former girlfriend sued him for a share of the earnings. A brother was arrested for hiring a hit man to kill him, hoping to inherit some of the money. Other siblings pestered him until he invested in a car business and restaurant, which brought him no money and strained his relationship with them. He even spent time in jail for firing a gun over the head of a bill collector. Within a year, he was $1 million in debt.

"I'm tired, I'm over 65 years old, and I just had a serious operation for a heart aneurysm. Lotteries don't mean (anything) to me," Post summarized.

Suzanne Mullins won $4.2 million in the 1993 Virginia lottery, but now she is deeply in debt. She blamed her debt on the failure to make loan payments and the lengthy illness of her uninsured son-in-law who needed $1 million for medical bills.

Ken Proxmire won $1 million in the Michigan lottery. He moved to California and went into the car business with his brothers. Within five years, he had filed for bankruptcy.

"He was just a poor boy who got lucky and wanted to take care of everybody," explained his son, Rick. "There's no more talk of owning a helicopter or riding in limos. Dad's now back to work as a machinist."

Willie Hurt of Lansing, Michigan won $3.1 million in 1989. Two years later he was broke and charged with murder. His lawyer said he spent his fortune on a divorce and crack cocaine.

Charles Riddle of Belleville, Michigan won $1 million in 1975. Afterward, he was divorced, faced several lawsuits, and was indicted for selling cocaine.

Missourian Janita Lee won $18 million in 1993 only to file bankruptcy eight years later after giving to a variety of causes.

One southeastern family won $4.2 million in the early 90s. They bought a huge house and succumbed to repeated family requests for help in paying off debts. The house, cars, and relatives ate the whole pot. Eleven years later, the couple is divorcing, the house is sold and they have to split what is left. The wife got a very small house. The husband has moved in with the kids. Even the life insurance they bought ended up being cashed in.

The experts say that these sad-but-true stories are not uncommon. Money can cause more problems than it solves for many people who aren't knowledgeable in how to handle their finances. People either keep the money and lose family and friends, or they lose the money and keep the family and friends, or some lose the money, family and friends according to Susan Bradley, a certified financial planner and founder of Sudden Money Institute, a resource center for new money recipients and their advisors.

I've encountered a few people who voluntarily share their gambling stories with me. I talked with a school administrator about difficulties with students in schools. Eventually the topic got around to gambling, and he told me that his niece suffered financially because of her gambling. She gradually became involved in embezzlement that resulted in a prison term for her.

"I lost all my money playing poker," another young man admitted. "My rent payment is due, and I can't pay it. I thought I could earn a living playing a game of cards."

Another patient told me that he won $2500 when he hit the three wild cherries on a slot machine three years ago. Since that time, he has spent $100 every other week and hasn't won anything. He told me that he needed to stay away from the slot machines.

A Few Win and Millions Lose

The big losers are the 5 to 15 million pathologic or problem gamblers.[3] The other losers include the 86 percent of Americans that gamble in one form or another.[4] The numbers of gamblers are growing. In 1961, 61 percent of our population gambled. By 1990, the numbered had increased to 80 percent, and now we are at 86 percent. In 1978, two states had legalized gambling, and now we only have two states that do not have legalized gambling.[5]

In Rex M. Rogers book *Seducing America: Is Gambling a Good Bet?* he said that, in the United States, gambling is a $700 billion per year enterprise. We gamble more per day than we spend on groceries. We gamble more per year than we spend on movies, CDs, major league sports, books, and entertainment parks combined.[6]

It's Entertainment

Maybe I am getting carried away. After all, it is entertainment. An elderly patient of mine told me that she enjoys a weekend in Las Vegas once a year. She and her girlfriends spend money that they set aside for the trip, and then they come home. She told me they have such a good time. My barber was overjoyed when he won $1700 on the nickel slot machine. I was happy for him, but I wasn't tempted to empty my piggybank and head to the casino. Am I nuts? Why would I pass up such a fun way to pick up some easy cash?

What Are the Costs?

The decision we all have to make is whether we start gambling or not. What are the costs? Do you picture your future in a nice home and car because you won the lottery, or, more realistically, do you see yourself sitting in one of the 1000 chapters of Gambler's Anonymous, which are located in all 50 states, telling your hard luck story? For many it is a road of addiction that leads to depression and for some a suicide attempt. Of the addicted gamblers (5 to 15 million), there are two out of ten that attempt suicide, and one out of ten of their spouses attempt suicide.[7] When the statistics are compared, those with a pathologic gambling disorder are at increased risk for serious problems in life. The rate of job loss within the last year for those afflicted with pathologic gambling disorder (13.8 percent) and in non-gamblers (5.5 percent). The rate of bankruptcy filing for pathologic gambling disorder (19.2 percent) and in non-gamblers (4.2 percent). The rate of divorce (53.5 percent) as opposed to (18.2 percent), and the rate of incarceration (21.4 percent) versus (0.4 percent). One-third of the annual cost of pathologic gambling disorder represents criminal justice expenses.[8]

ARE THERE GOOD REASONS NOT TO GAMBLE?

In the book *Tony Evans Speaks Out on Gambling and the Lottery*,[9] two observations are made in the beginning of the book. First, God is not against wealth. In Deuteronomy 8:18, God gave the Israelites the power to get wealth, and, in 1 Timothy 6:17, God is interested in how we acquire our wealth and how we handle it. The second observation is that God does encourage risk taking or investing. In Matthew 25:14-30, Jesus tells the story of a man who gave money to his servants. After a long time, the man returned unto his servants. He commended and rewarded two of the servants because they had used their money and doubled it. Yet, the Lord scolded and punished the servant that didn't add to the money that was given him. The take-home message is that God gives us time, talents, and treasure that He wants us to use for His purposes.

If God is not against wealth or risk taking, then how do I know whether I am making a legitimate or an illegitimate gamble? In his book, Tony Evans presents ten questions.

1. Is it Greed?

One Sunday, a man came to church looking sad and despondent. The pastor noticed him and asked, "Why are you so sad?"

"Well, two weeks ago, my uncle died and left me $75,000. Then a week ago, my aunt died and left me $50,000."

The pastor said, "Wait a minute. Two weeks ago, your uncle died and left you $75,000. Last week, your aunt died and left you $50,000. Why are you so sad?"

The man answered, "Because nobody died this week."

The greedy man wants more, and is not content with what he has. Do I gamble because I want to get rich quick? Consider Proverbs 21:5, "The plans of the diligent lead surely to advantage, but everyone who is hasty comes surely to poverty." There are many who have tried to strike it rich on some scheme only to lose all their money. The road to success for most people involves planning and hard work.

2. Do I trust God?

Is God my supplier, or do I play the lottery because I have little confidence in God?

Proverbs 10:22 says "It is the blessing of the Lord that makes rich, and He adds no sorrow to it." God can give us riches in His time, and we can experience joy because of that. The devil can also provide riches, but his riches may come with misery if it was attained in the wrong way.

3. Has your gambling replaced productivity?

Are you trying to luck your way into things that you should be working productively for? Paul writes in Ephesians 4:28:

"Let him who steals steal no longer: but rather let him labor, performing with his own hands what is good, in order that he may have something to share with him who has need." Honest work brings benefit to others as well as oneself.

4. Am I taking a wise or an unwise risk?

My chance of injury in an automobile crash is one in 6,000. My chance of injury in a plane crash is one in 500,000. My chance of winning the lottery is one in 16,000,000.

A person that spends $50 a month on the lottery would spend $12,000 in twenty years. If he invested the money at 10 percent interest the person would have gained $34,365.

How would you feel if your banker called you and said he was going to risk your savings on the lottery? Jesus wants us to count the cost before we commit to something. (See Luke 14:28.)

5. Mastered by God or gambling?

When people become addicted to gambling, they are dependent on it. They enjoy it while they are doing it and miserable without it. They have to gamble. Nothing else matters including wife, kids, or their job.

Paul says in 1 Corinthians 6:12 "All things are lawful for me, but not all things are profitable. All things are lawful for me, but I will not be mastered by anything."

6. Does my risk exploit someone else?

In gambling, in order for one person to win, many people have to lose. Many people who make $10,000 or less a year spend up to one-fifth of their income on the lottery. If a con man were bilking poor people out of one-fifth of their income, the community would have his head. But the government is doing the same thing, and we call it a game.

7. Does it help or hurt society?

Do the laws we pass as a society provide for a better society? Are the lottery and gambling benefiting our society?

8. Does it do spiritual harm to others?

If I gamble, will others follow and not be able to control their gambling?

9. Is it legitimate fun?

God is not against fun. However, our fun should not replace our love for God (2 Timothy 3:4).

10. Is gambling good stewardship?

Is it okay with God if I risk His money?

A PATHOLOGIC GAMBLER

I enjoyed reading *Gambling Addiction—The Problem, the Pain, and the Path to Recovery*, by John Eades.[10] John spent twenty years working as a drug and alcohol addiction counselor. One night, John was persuaded by his wife and some friends to go out gambling.

Normally, he stayed away from the casinos because of the alcohol. However, on this evening he broke down and gave it a try. Even though he didn't win, he really enjoyed the nickel slot machines. Soon he was gambling every weekend and eventually on the week nights. In two years, he had lost a lot of money, and he was beginning to have problems at home.

One night after he spent all his cash at the casino, he arrived home. He met his wife in the kitchen and they started arguing. His wife became so distressed that she reached into her purse and pulled out a bottle of sedatives. Her doctor had prescribed the medication because she had such anxiety over his gambling that she couldn't sleep. She took off the cap and swallowed every pill. She didn't say a word, but her sad eyes relayed the message that she no longer wanted to watch him destroy their lives. Even though he tried to convince her to go to the hospital, she refused. She just began to sob deeply until he called 911. An ambulance transported her to the hospital. They pumped her stomach. When he was able to visit her, she looked so pitiful with a tube in her nose. Her spirit was defeated.

He didn't know what to say. He knew it was his fault. As he took her home from the hospital, he could see she was still very depressed. However, the next day, he felt he could cheer her up by taking her gambling. He used every excuse to gamble—even his wife's suicide attempt.

Despite almost losing his wife, he still continued to gamble. At Christmas, he decided to spend some money on nice presents for the family. He took the last one thousand dollars out of the credit union. He wanted to get his two grown daughters something nice. As the day wore on, he thought he could double his money if he played the slot machines. He went to the casino that night and played for seven straight hours. He ignored his wife's calls, forgot to take his blood pressure medicine, and didn't eat or go to the bathroom. When he started to feel sick, he stood up and immediately fell to the floor. As a guard came to his aid, others looked at him curiously. When the paramedics took his blood pressure, his numbers were at stroke level. Despite his condition, he was worried because his slot machine still had a few credits. He noticed one man step over him and go right to his slot machine and start playing it. He was too sick to protest. The ambulance took him to the hospital in Biloxi, Mississippi which was close to the casino. When his wife came, she had no sympathy, just anger and hurt.

After three years of a gambling addiction, John grew sick of his lies to his wife and himself. He went outside of the casino after gambling away his money and stood under the flashing lights as he watched the rain fall. Eventually, he walked to his car and drove away. As he headed home, he didn't want to face his wife again. He wrote the following about his thoughts at that time:

> As I pulled out onto the interstate, guilt and fear were my passengers. Shame engulfed me. I couldn't escape my thoughts that were coming faster than the oncoming cars. Who has cleaned out his checking and savings accounts? Who maxed out seventeen credit cards? Who sold things he treasured in order to get money to gamble? Who is totally wiped out and facing bankruptcy? Whose car always went faster as it neared Biloxi? Who filled his tank with gas before going gambling because he knew he wouldn't have enough money left to buy gas to get home with? Who used to lock his credit cards in the trunk before entering the casino only to come back later to get them out so he could keep playing? Who was a hypocrite? Who had broken his wife's heart? Who had destroyed everything he had worked his whole life to obtain? Who was the liar with a soul sickness that could not be described? The answer to every last one of these barb-wired questions racing through my mind was me. I was no longer who I used to be. I was a stranger to myself.

Just ahead was one last rest stop before entering Alabama, and I had a plan. I pulled into the mostly deserted rest stop and drove around to the back parking area. I found a spot where there were no cars and I parked. It was still sprinkling rain as I slumped down in the seat and stared at the drops as they slid down the windshield. I imagined I was like one of those raindrops, only I had slid down the slope of gambling addiction instead of the windshield. Jerking the keys out of the ignition, I fumbled through them until I found the key to the glove compartment. The answer to my overwhelming problems from gambling lay right there in that compartment. I have never been a brave person, but I knew the .357 Magnum pistol I carried there could do one thing: put a final stop to my gambling.

As I held the key between my fingers, I thought of how many times I had told alcoholics that suicide was a permanent solution to a temporary problem, and that there was always hope—no matter how bad things were. But I was too cowardly to take my own advice. Life was too hard and there was no way back for me. I had no self-respect left, no hope, and our future contained nothing but poverty. Sticking a gun in my mouth and pulling the trigger would end my life and my pain. I pushed the key into the glove compartment lock, turned it, and the lid fell down. I reached inside to get the gun, but couldn't feel it. I leaned over and looked inside. No gun. My first thought was that Karen had taken it out, thinking I might try to harm myself. At first I was angry, but then fearful about how close I had come to committing suicide. I was so scared I began to shake. Suddenly, I couldn't see out of the windshield, as tears poured down my face while I cried like a lost child. I may have been lost, but I knew where home was. Suddenly, I had an overwhelming urge to get home to Karen to thank her for saving my life. I drove straight to our house.

Karen was waiting up for me when I arrived home. I rushed over to her and hugged her as hard as I could.

She seemed confused about my sudden show of affection. I told her what I had almost done and said, "You must have known I was going to try something like that, and you took the gun out as a precaution." Karen hugged me and kissed me on the cheek. She looked up into my eyes and with sadness said, "Oh, Johnny, I took the gun out because I had to sell it. I needed the money to pay the power bill so they wouldn't turn our lights off." That night we stayed up and talked from the depth of our souls about what we could do to save our marriage—and maybe our lives.

Even though John promised he would never gamble again, he would still hide away money to spend at the casino. One day, when he planned to get away, his adult daughter, who was living with them, was missing with all of her anti-depressant pills. He feared she had overdosed. He postponed his gambling trip, and, after an extensive search, the rescuers found his daughter unconscious. She was alive. She was hospitalized for several days and survived. During her hospitalization, John surrendered his stored-up gambling money to pay for the hospital bill.

John did some serious soul searching. When he thought back about the counseling he did, he realized that most of his alcohol and drug addicts who did well were committed to Jesus Christ. He had seen them give testimony that God had loved them and had an alcohol- and drug-free plan for them. John also began a journey that led to a full understanding of Christ. He realized that his addiction had slammed him to his back, and he could only look up to God for help. He stated that unless an addict looks to God for help he will likely drop one addiction only to pick up another.

A GAMBLING SELF-EVALUATION

Is gambling a part of your life? Is it an addiction? I have included a self-evaluation test to see how much gambling may be affecting you.

Gamblers Anonymous 20 Question Survey

1. Did you ever lose time from work due to gambling?
2. Has gambling ever made your home life unhappy?
3. Did gambling ever affect your reputation?
4. Have you ever felt remorse after gambling?
5. Did you ever gamble to get money with which to pay debts or otherwise solve financial difficulties?
6. Did gambling cause a decrease in your ambition or efficiency?
7. After losing, did you feel you must return as soon as possible and win back your losses?
8. After a win, did you have a strong urge to return and win more?
9. Did you often gamble until your last dollar was gone?
10. Did you ever borrow to finance your gambling?
11. Have you ever sold anything to finance your gambling?
12. Were you reluctant to use gambling money for normal expenditures?
13. Did gambling make you careless of yourself or your family?
14. Have you ever gambled longer than you had planned?
15. Have you ever gambled to escape worry and trouble?
16. Have you ever committed or considered committing an illegal act to finance gambling?
17. Has gambling caused you to have difficulty in sleeping?
18. Have arguments, disappointment, or frustrations caused you to gamble?
19. Have you had an urge to celebrate any good fortune with a few hours of gambling?
20. Have you ever considered self-destruction as a result of your gambling?

Seven or more positive responses suggest pathologic gambling.

John went from addiction to recovery. He hopes churches will become involved in helping people overcome their addictions. His recovery included church worship, Bible study, fellowship, group recovery, changes in thoughts, feelings, behavior, and spirit. He was involved in prayer and meditation on Scripture. He continues to help other suffering addicts.

Other resources

Gamblers Anonymous
PO Box 17173
Los Angeles, CA 90017
800-266-1908
www.gamblersanonymous.org

Gam-Anon
PO Box 157
Whitestone, NY 11357
718-352-1671
www.gam-anon.org

Chapter Seven

"L ET'S G ET H IGH"

Robert, an African-American male in his late thirties, stood on the witness stand, lifted his shirt, and turned to show the jury his back. He had four healed bullet wounds over his left rib area.

"You can see the scars of the bullets," the attorney pointed out to the jury. "You can sit down, Robert."

After Robert settled back into the witness chair, the attorney continued his questioning.

"Are the men that shot you in this courtroom?"

"Yes, they are," he stated.

"Can you point them out?"

"They are the two men seated at the defendant's table," he said as he pointed to the two African-American men in orange jail attire.

"Please describe what happened on June 4, 1971."

"I was driving my friends, Fish and Star, to buy some drugs to deal. When I drove into the parking lot, the two defendants approached our vehicle. I gave them the money as I took the drugs, but they quickly took the drugs back. They pulled out their guns and started shooting into our car. I ducked and took some bullets to my back. I slumped forward and kept still even though I was in a lot of pain and I could feel the warmth of my blood running down my back. Eventually, they quit shooting. They started to run away. I was having some difficulty breathing, but I was able to start the car and take off. Star was unconscious and slumped forward beside me. She had blood in her hair and on her shirt where the bullets ripped through. Fish was by the door which he had opened to try to get out. He was half out the door. I reached over Star and grabbed him by the shirt to pull him into the car. His foot was still out the door when I took off."

"Did they pursue you?"

"Yes, they did."

"Did they fire more shots?"

"They were shooting as I was driving away."

"Then what happened?"

"As I was driving, I tried to attract some attention by driving recklessly through the city streets. After I turned through several intersections, I finally spotted a police officer. He must have noticed my car speeding with the passenger door cracked open and Fish's boot dragging along the street. He immediately turned on his lights and sirens and followed me. I didn't hear any more shots after that," he paused. "I finally felt safe enough to stop. Fish and Star were not moving. Neither of them had a pulse. They were both dead."

As a 15-year-old high school student, I listened to that testimony and viewed the impressionable courtroom drama as part of a school project. The ugly side of the drug world was openly displayed. In my mind, as a result of drugs and greed, two defendants were convicted of murder and were sent away to prison for the rest of their lives, two people were dead, and one person survived with four bullet wounds.

Drugs of Abuse Roll Call

Illegal drugs became popular in the 1960s and have continued to be a major part of our culture for the last 40 years. According to the Substance Abuse and Mental Health Services Administration, marijuana abuse is reported by over four million Americans, while cocaine abuse is reported by over 1.5 million, pain reliever abuse (Vicodin-type narcotics) is reported by over 1.4 million, tranquilizers at 435,000, stimulants at 378,000, hallucinogens at 321,000, heroin at 189,000, inhalants at 169,000, and sedatives at 158,000.[1] Twenty-four percent of teenage students say they use illegal drugs.[2]

What Does the Bible Say about Illegal Drugs?

In Romans 13, Paul wrote that we are to be obedient to the laws of the land. Government is supposed to protect its citizens from evil. At this point in time, illicit drug use has been ruled a detriment to our society.

Marijuana

"What is the problem with marijuana?" a college student asked.

"It is against the law," I advised him.

"It is no worse than alcohol."

"That is against the law also until you are 21, and I agree alcohol has its problems too."

Some people have smoked marijuana for the last 30 years without much apparent consequence, but there are consequences to smoking marijuana.

"Marijuana has put my life on hold for the last 20 years," a 36-year-old male inmate confessed to me. "It has kept me from maturing into a responsible adult."

"It has slowed my mind down," a 35-year-old female related to me.

"Have you had any negative consequences from marijuana?" I asked an African-American inmate who was in his early forties.

"I can't remember any," he replied.

"You complained of neck pain on your medical request form. When did you start having neck pain?" I inquired.

"My neck has hurt since I broke it in the army."

"How long ago was that?"

"It was over 20 years ago," he told me and then paused. "You know I was high on pot, when I jumped out of the helicopter and fractured my neck. I guess that's a negative consequence of smoking marijuana."

On another intake questionnaire, I noticed an inmate had admitted to daily marijuana abuse. He had been jailed multiple times.

"How long have you been using pot?" I asked him.

"I've been smoking marijuana since I was nine years old," the 26-year-old inmate with long straight red hair and a goatee stated.

"Why do you still smoke when you repeatedly end up in jail?"

"I hate life if I can't smoke pot."

"Do you hate life right now?"

"Yes, I do."

"Why don't you write a note to one of the counselors or chaplains to see if they have any ideas on how you can enjoy your life better?"

"I'd rather have a joint."

Another 300-pound inmate asked me if he could weigh himself.

"Sure," I told him.

"I've lost 60 pounds since I've been in jail," he commented after getting off the scale.

"What's your secret?"

"I haven't smoked any pot in the jail. Pot has made me fat and lazy. It's good for me to get away from that habit."

Another incarcerated individual claimed it destroyed his brilliant scientific mind.

I know most of the inmates say what I want to hear, but I feel these comments were accurate descriptions of the downside of drug use.

One of my best friends in middle school was a straight A student. He started smoking pot when he got into high school. In tenth grade, he got his girlfriend pregnant, dropped out of school, and went to work in a factory. I saw him about ten years after high school. He had been through a divorce and was taking care of his daughter alone.

Drug use and dealing can also be very dangerous. One 29-year-old dealer in our area was executed by three other drug dealers who wanted his high quality marijuana and his money. He was found with his hands tied behind his back, his mouth duct-taped, and ten bullet wounds in his back.

In a *Reader's Digest* article, "But it's only pot," Heather yielded to the temptation to smoke weed with her friends.[3] Before long, her grades dropped, she lied about her activities after school, her musical performance suffered, and she went on to use cocaine and heroin. A car accident and a cocaine overdose nearly took her life. After her brushes with death, Heather agreed to go away with her mom and dad to a beach house for the summer to get away from the drugs and her friends. She came back to high school in the fall with new goals and a new direction. She finished her senior year with good grades and was able to go on to college.

In the jail environment, most inmates aren't that fortunate. Their marijuana use has led them into dealing drugs or stealing. Unfortunately for most of them their habit started at a young age. Most inmates are into cigarettes by the age of ten, and then the drugs follow a few years after that. By the time, they are 18 they are sitting in a jail cell or prison. About 40 percent of inmates are incarcerated because of illegal drugs or committing crimes while on illegal drugs.

When it comes to driving, I've noticed a few reports lately of marijuana-impaired drivers. One driver had smoked marijuana, and taken a muscle relaxer and morphine. His driving was so erratic that another motorist stopped and called 911 to report him. The witness described him passing a vehicle on a hill and weaving from one lane to the other. He also reported that the vehicle veered off the road and nearly hit a man mowing his lawn. As the impaired driver continued, he raced up a hill. He bumped into the back of a car and then swerved around to pass. He collided head-on into a vehicle driven by a recently married city attorney.

"I leaned over, and saw my lifeless husband, and there was nothing I could do for him," the attorney's wife recounted. "I was pinned in the car, and watched Shawn die. Being married to Shawn was the best time of my life. Now, that is gone. I struggle every day."[4]

The man recklessly disregarded the lives of others and was sentenced to 142 to 270 months in prison.

Another 28-year-old man with marijuana in his blood was driving 75 miles per hour in the wrong lane on a hill and, just before Christmas, killed 16-year-old Stephanie.

"Our family of four is now a family of three, sentenced to a life of sadness and pain," her mom told a judge. "Stephanie was a wonderful person who enjoyed life to its fullest. She loved people, her friends, volleyball, music, her family. She always looked out for the underdog."[5]

"What Is in this Weed?"

Marijuana users don't always know what they are getting in their drug. A retired narcotics officer told me that one dealer was pushing marijuana that had been contaminated with poison ivy. Soon after smoking the pot, the users had trouble breathing. They had to seek treatment in the emergency room.

A jail inmate told me that he had smoked some weed laced with another unknown drug while he was in college, and he ended up high for a week. He said it scared him enough that he hasn't smoked any marijuana since.

Does Marijuana Cause any Mental Illness?

While millions of Americans have used the drug since the 1960s when it became popular, marijuana definitely affects the brain. To what extent is the question? Its lipid solubility allows it to enter the brain and affect coordination, judgment, reaction time, and peripheral vision. It also plays a role in anxiety, depression, and acute psychosis. In one Swedish military study, there was a six-fold increase in the rate of schizophrenia among men who at the time of induction had used marijuana products on 50 or more occasions.[6]

"When did you get diagnosed with paranoid schizophrenia?" I asked a 26-year-old male inmate with long dark hair parted in the middle.

"When I was a senior in high school."

"How long have you smoked marijuana?"

"Since I was eight years old," he replied.

"Why did you start?"

"I did it to escape my stepfather who beat my mom and me."

"Who did you get it from?"

"My friend's older brother."

I have heard the story frequently—a bad home situation, friends who do drugs, drug use that leads to abuse, criminal activity, mental problems, and then jail or prison.

A 24-year-old female inmate, who had long dark hair and a pleasant smile, told me she started smoking marijuana at 14 years old. She said she got into it because of her friends, but she also blamed her difficult home life. With her dad in prison and her mom in bondage to alcoholism, she left home at 16. Throughout the next eight years, she struggled with depression. I asked her if she thought that marijuana had anything to do with her depression. She answered that she smoked marijuana every day and enjoyed the good feeling of being high. However, since she has been without the drug, she has been depressed.

LUNG DISEASE

Marijuana smoking leads to lung cancer and other lung diseases just like smoking cigarettes. It deposits tars and other particulate matter in the lungs. If a patient complains to me about coughing up black sputum, the next question I ask is "Are you smoking marijuana."

COCAINE

"If you experience it, you will want more of it," an inmate told me. "The trouble is I never got back to that initial high. I kept trying to. Whatever I needed to do to get money for my cocaine, I did. After being high for days, I would get busted. Then I would sleep for three days. Jail was my safe haven. I got three hot meals and a place to sleep."

The trouble with cocaine is that it is too good. Once most people try it, they can't leave it alone. The drug gives them superhuman energy. One man was on the second floor using cocaine when the police raided the home he was in. He ran out of the bedroom and into the hall. Without any concern, he sprinted down the hall and jumped right through the window. He hit the ground and rolled several times. He didn't remember anything after that. He woke up in an ambulance handcuffed to the stretcher. According to the police and paramedics, he hit the ground and had a seizure which was due to the cocaine. Because his seizure was prolonged, he was hospitalized. His muscles were so overworked from the seizure that they released toxins that shut down his kidneys. He needed dialysis until his kidneys started functioning again.

One thin cocaine addict admitted she just couldn't leave the drug alone. The intravenous drug abuse had hardened her veins. It was difficult to find any veins to draw blood from because her blood vessels were like concrete. Finally, I drew some blood from her right upper arm.

"What would you say to young people about injecting drugs?" I asked her.

"I would tell them that injecting drugs would ruin their veins. It is a bad habit, and they shouldn't do it. They should snort it or smoke it instead," she replied. Then she smiled and confessed that she was only kidding. She knew she had a bad habit and has told her nieces to stay away from drugs. She told them her lifestyle was not worth it.

A female prostitute commented, "I use heroin and cocaine just like my mom. She was always high. Her boyfriends abused me physically and sexually since I was eight years old. I hate what I have become. Because of my obsession with drugs, I steal, prostitute, and do whatever else I need to do. I follow no laws. I am the same bad mother that my mom was to me. Because of my actions and attitude, the judge just took my kids away."

Prescription Pain Relievers for Non-Medical Purposes

According to the federal Substance Abuse and Mental Health Services Administration report in 2003, prescription pain relievers lagged only behind marijuana and cocaine as the illicit drug most people abused.[7] In the emergency room, I constantly dealt with drug-seekers asking for drugs for their back pain, headaches, or shoulder pain. If they got drugs, they would use the drugs to get high or sell them to others.

"I'm in pain," a burly, 37-year-old man complained to me while he was gripping his left shoulder.

"How did that happen?"

"I fell on it."

"Let me see if I can pinpoint where you are having your pain," I warned him as I put my hand up to palpate his collar bone and upper arm.

"Don't touch it. It hurts," he screamed.

I ordered an x-ray which was negative. I suspected he was seeking drugs, because he gave false information at the registration desk, he kept asking for pain medicine, and he refused any non-narcotic pain medicine. He left the emergency room unhappy because he didn't get the drugs he wanted.

It is unfortunate that doctors have to figure out who is lying and who is legitimate. Drug seekers waste too much of a doctor's time and mental energy.

METHAMPHETAMINES

"How was your Thanksgiving?" I greeted one of my elderly patients.

"It was depressing."

"Why is that?"

"My nephews are running from the law because they have been operating a methamphetamine lab, and my daughter attempted suicide," she responded.

I was sorry she had such a terrible weekend. I almost felt guilty for enjoying my time visiting my son and his family in Colorado.

For my patient, she was surrounded by sadness, drugs, and despair. Her daughter attempted suicide, and then was murdered several months later by her drug-abusing ex-convict boyfriend.

Methamphetamine, a highly addictive stimulant, is the fastest growing drug of abuse in the United States. According to the 2003 National Survey on Drug Use and Health, 12.3 million Americans tried methamphetamines at least once. It is a trap for people just like any other addictive substance. The user quickly develops tolerance to the drug, and then they need more of it to help them through the day. People use the drug for various reasons, and it affects the mind in various ways. Users can develop psychosis which results in a loss of reality. They may see spiders crawl up the wall, feel bugs under their skin, or feel paranoid that people are watching them. If the user overdoses, they can have abnormal heart rhythms, seizures, and even death. When they withdraw from the drug, they can experience depression, fatigue, convulsions, coma, and death.

The drug also affects the teeth. Metamphetamine users get a very dry mouth, and many of them will drink pop constantly. The sugar content of the pop and the lack of regular brushing of the teeth, results in severe tooth decay.

HEROIN

"Overdose," the paramedics explained as they pulled their gurney into the emergency room with a soaking wet, fully clothed Hispanic male who was receiving CPR. "His friends found him unconscious and threw him in the bathtub to wake him up."

We spent the next 30 minutes trying to revive this man who had no pulse and no blood pressure. The heroin he overdosed on caused him to quit breathing. Then within minutes, the heart quit, and he died. We weren't able to revive him.

Usually addicts take more heroin to get a better high. Sometimes, they take too much, and the drug stops their breathing. At other times, the addict injects a more potent heroin, and it kills them.

Heroin users inject the drug into their veins. Eventually, the veins become very hard and they have to keep trying new sites. During my medical school clerkships, I treated two young ladies who were injecting heroin into their subclavian veins under their collar bones. They missed their veins and punctured their lungs. They had to spend a few days in the hospital with tubes inserted into their chest to reinflate their lungs. After several days in the hospital, they went right back to the streets to do it again. They had no desire to go through any program to get off the drugs.

In a study of 356 heroin users, the addicts said they started to use alcohol around 13 years of age, followed by criminal activity at 15, marijuana use at 15, first arrest at 17, first heroin use at 18, and continuous heroin use at 19. In another aspect of the study, the addicts were questioned about their criminal activity. During a 12-month period, they admitted to 118,134 criminal offenses and were arrested for less than 1 percent of the offenses. Although the most frequent offenses were prostitution, drug sales, and shoplifting, 27,464 of the crimes were considered serious.[8]

When young people step over the line with substances that are harmful and illegal, the natural progression is to go on to something else. When they get into the harder drugs, their habits become more expensive and they have to rob, deal, and prostitute in order to pay the price for their drugs. Many inmates have told me their drug habits exceeded $300 a day. In an article about male prostitutes for homosexual men in the Chicago area, 75 percent of the male prostitutes said they got into prostitution for drug money and were not homosexuals themselves.[9]

DATE RAPE

"I remember going to a party and drinking some beer. Then I woke up the next morning without any clothes on. I want to know if I was raped," a young lady, who was an emergency room patient, told me.

I've heard similar scenarios from several young women. Sometimes they were just intoxicated and were never raped. However, sometimes they have been drugged and raped. Today the date-rape drugs (Rohypnol, GHB, or Ketamine) have been used to take advantage of people.[10] It is not too difficult to slip some drug into a drink and then wait for the person to pass out.

GLUE SNIFFING

A tall, lanky 16-year-old white male with black curly hair was admitted to the pediatric service because he complained of paralysis that was advancing up his legs. He was unable to walk. After extensive questioning that covered a variety of possible causes, he admitted to glue sniffing. The chronic abuse that he was involved in was causing damage to his nerves and resulting in the paralysis. His symptoms eventually resolved when he stopped sniffing glue.

"The Pact"

I read a book called *The Pact* about three young African-American men from the streets of Newark who helped each other through high school, college, and graduate school. One became a pediatrician, one an emergency room doctor, and one a dentist. Rameck Hunt, who became an emergency room doctor, described what it was like for him growing up with parents on drugs.

> From the time he took that first shot of heroin, my dad was hooked. He began to shoot up whenever and wherever he could. He returned to Assumption College the following semester in January, but he got into a fight with a group of white guys, dropped out of college, and returned to Newark.
>
> He enrolled in the Army but was discharged after two years when he was arrested for committing a robbery while on furlough. There were long periods during which he managed to function and hold a decent job while still dependent on drugs. But it would take him twenty-six years to conquer the addiction that drained him of any ambition beyond life on the streets. In 1997, after many attempts at rehabilitation, he left Newark and entered two different out-of-state rehabilitation programs back-to-back and began to turn his life around. He returned to Newark but to a different life. He now works at a drug rehabilitation center as a counselor.
>
> When I was fourteen, Dad noticed that my life seemed headed in a similar direction to his, and he tried to intervene. I wasn't using drugs, but I was hanging out with guys who, like me, were lost and acting like little thugs, trying to define our manhood by wild, foolish behavior. My father was not yet clean, but he tried to reach me. He told me he wanted my life to be better than his. He said drugs and jail were not the life he had planned for himself. He had just gotten sucked in and couldn't find his

way out. He told me he was living a lie and was tired of watching his friends die around him.

"Don't let the same thing happen to you," he pleaded.

His words touched me, but I was hardheaded. It would take a short stint in juvenile jail at age sixteen for me to finally realize that I was following my friends to a place of self-destruction.

I'm not sure when I began to suspect that my mother was abusing drugs. I just pieced together the signs on my own. I was 11 when my mother had a second child, my little sister, Mecca, whose father sometimes lived with us. But like most of the men in my mother's life, he didn't seem to be good for her. He, too, ended up behind bars. The stress of now having two little mouths to feed must have been too much for my mother. Mom was without work for a while, and we went on welfare. The bills went unpaid more often. We spent days at a time in apartments with no lights, air conditioning, or heat when the utility company turned off our electricity. I learned how to twist my little sister's hair in ponytails, and I made sure she had something to eat, even if I had to call relatives for help.

Many nights I cried myself to sleep. I tried to strike a deal with God.

"God, please, just get one of my parents off drugs," I prayed.

I figured asking Him to save them both would be too much. I swore I would never use drugs.

My mother's drug habit messed up everything. But the thing that hurt me most was that it robbed her of something I always thought came naturally: a mother's instinct. The kind of instinct that makes a mother dash into the path of a speeding car or rush into a burning building to rescue her endangered child. The kind of instinct that makes a child feel protected. When my mother's drug abuse got out of control, I no longer felt protected.

I was about 13 when my mother told me that she used drugs. She said she needed them to help her deal with her pain. She had many unfulfilled dreams. In high school, she had wanted to become a court stenographer. It seemed like such an important job, and it intrigued her. But she had gotten pregnant and never pursued it. After graduating from high school in 1974, she'd studied business administration intermittently at Essex County College for about a year and a half, but she never finished. Later, she also told me that when she was a child, a relative had molested her.

My emotions toward her swung from pity to anger and back again.

At times, my mother accused me of loving my father more than I loved her. That wasn't true. I did, however, feel less anger toward him. It is true that my mother struggled in part because my father didn't always do his share to support me financially. Yet I blamed her for leaving me without a shield. Perhaps I was angrier at her because I loved her so much, and I wondered whether she loved me back. I couldn't help suspecting that she loved the drugs more.

I never questioned my father's love. If I asked him for help, he never turned me away if he had it to give. If I happened to find him on his way to buy drugs and said, "Dad, I really need five dollars," he'd give it to me. He may have been itching and scratching because he needed a fix so badly, and may have had only $10 in his pocket. But he would pull it out and give me half. He might lie and say he had to keep the other half for food, and he might leave me and go steal some meat from a grocery store to sell and make up the half he gave me. But through a child's eyes, I saw a father sacrificing his needs for his son's.[11]

Chapter Eight

PRAYER OF AN
UNWED MOTHER

Celia, a 13-day-old baby, was lying quietly on the stretcher, unconscious, with her right arm jerking. Her body was warm, and her dark hair was dampened on her pale skin. She only had her diaper on, and an intravenous line was placed in her arm. The nurse was administering the medicine into the tubing.

A fever and seizures in a newborn was an ominous sign. The seizures stopped shortly after the drug entered her veins. As I did a physical exam on her, I didn't see any definite source of infection. I did notice some small blisters on the right side of her forehead.

"What's wrong with my baby?" Celia's mother asked me.

"She has an infection. We will be doing some tests to determine where the infection is."

"What kind of infection?"

"We have to make sure she doesn't have a serious bacterial infection of her brain, lungs, or urine. It may be a viral infection that could be serious as well. I will know more after I review the tests on her urine, blood, and spinal fluid," I explained. "She will also need a chest x-ray to look for pneumonia and a CT scan to make sure there aren't any masses or bleeds in her brain."

"Do you have to do everything that you are doing?"

"Yes, I do. I also need to do a spinal tap which is a procedure to take fluid from around the spinal cord. Then I will give her antibiotics and send her down to the pediatric intensive care unit in Grand Rapids," I told her. She was quiet.

"Do you have any questions?" I asked her knowing that I had given her too much information in a time when she was overwhelmed with emotion over her sick child.

She shook her head no, while the tears started to trickle down her cheeks. A nurse handed her a tissue and took her to a private waiting room for families of critical patients. She was all alone.

Celia's CT scan of her brain was normal. Her spinal fluid also appeared normal, but it would take several days for the culture results to return. The antibiotics were given through the intravenous line, and the child and mother were sent away by ambulance to the pediatric intensive care unit at a major center 45 minutes away.

Within a few hours, I received a phone call from the doctor I transferred the baby to.

"The neonate that you sent us most likely has herpes encephalitis (a serious infection of the brain). The blisters on the forehead were definitely herpes. We started the baby on acyclovir. The baby picked up this virus most likely during pregnancy, but it's possible the transmission occurred during delivery, or shortly after birth. As you know, the outlook for this child is poor as far as a normal neurologic outcome," the specialist explained to me confirming my worst fears.

Over the subsequent years, I saw the child several times in the emergency room. The child was severely mentally retarded and bed bound. She would require total care the rest of her life.

The mom did acquire a lawyer who promptly sent me a letter. I had to sit down with the hospital attorney and risk manager, but no lawsuit was filed. The hospital staff and I did all that we could do. The damage had already been done by the time the baby arrived in the emergency room. The baby acquired the infection from the mom, who was probably infected in the last part of her pregnancy. She didn't even know she had the infection.

Herpes Encephalitis

Herpes, when it is spread to a baby while in the womb or in the neonatal stage, severely damages the child or kills the child. Herpes infection of the brain occurs in about 1000 newborns every year. Presently, one out of four pregnant women has genital herpes. Only about 20 percent of people have the classic symptoms of genital herpes which include painful clustered bumps, blisters, or ulcers on top of red, swollen skin. The patient may complain of an itching sensation or a burning pain. Any pregnant woman with any herpes symptoms or lesions at the time of birth should have a Caesarean section to prevent the spread of the infection to the baby. The danger of herpes encephalitis is increased when a pregnant woman, who is herpes free, has sexual relations with a herpes infected partner in the last third of her pregnancy. The woman becomes infected and her body has not had a chance to build up antibodies to the virus. She has a higher chance (one in three) of passing the virus to the baby while the baby is in the womb.[1]

REALITY VERSUS THE MEDIA

The people I see aren't always enjoying unlimited happiness because of their sexual freedom. They may be suffering from venereal disease, depressed because of an abortion, or struggling as a single mom with several out of wedlock children.

On television and in the movies, the couples avoid most major problems. The media doesn't always cover the whole story. For obvious reasons, they don't show an entire life with all the choices and the resulting positive and negative consequences. The consumer wants a few hours of fantasy, not a lifetime of reality. However, what we watch does affect how we act, and what teenagers watch does influence how they act. According to an article in *Pediatrics* magazine, the amount of sex viewed on television correlated with teenage sexual experimentation and earlier sexual activity.[2] Our culture views sex as a recreational activity. In reality, when teenagers are surveyed, most wish they had waited to initiate sexual activity.

Why does God restrict sex? Why do we have boundaries? First of all, sex is a good thing. God created it for pleasure and to propagate the human race. When sex is misused, people are hurt emotionally, physically, and spiritually.

SEXUALLY-TRANSMITTED INFECTIONS

"Hey doc, how do I know if my woman has herpes?" a county inmate asked me.

"If she has painful blisters that test positive for herpes or if she gets a herpes blood test that is positive," I advised him.

"I can't tell by looking for lesions?"

"Only about 20 percent of women with genital herpes have lesions."

"Then I can't tell if it's safe to have sex?"

"The safest sex is one man with one woman for a lifetime."

As a physician, I don't have simple answers for people who live promiscuously in a diseased world. Since the world began, the safest sex is to abstain until marriage, and then be faithful in marriage to a faithful partner. To some it may sound archaic and unreasonable, but it works as God designed it to work.

In the emergency room, I examined a 20-year-old man that had hundreds of genital herpes lesions.

"Doc, give me a pill and get rid of these things."

"I can give you pills that will help the lesions go away, but they will most likely come back again. The pills don't kill the herpes virus. They help control it."

"Really," he replied with a blank stare. "You can't cure me?"

"We don't have a cure at this time. Didn't they teach you about herpes in health class?"

"I don't remember anything about herpes. Maybe I skipped that day or fell asleep."

There are about 45 million people that have the genital herpes virus. In fact, one out of five people over age 12 have it.[3]

Another problematic viral infection is the human papilloma virus (HPV) which causes genital warts and 99 percent of cervical cancers. Currently 20 million Americans are infected. It is a virus that sometimes goes away, yet if it doesn't go away it can lead to cervical cancer which claims almost 4000 lives a year. It can be spread skin to skin without intercourse, and is often spread around condoms. Nearly three out of four Americans between the ages of 15 and 49 have been infected with genital HPV in their lifetime.[4] One inmate in the jail asked me how he became infected with a virus that gave him genital warts. I told him the virus is very common, and most sexually active young people get it.

The following story is from Doug Herman, a national abstinence speaker.

I had just concluded my conversations with about a dozen junior-high students in a Nebraska school auditorium when the side exit door opened slightly. Peeking in to see if any other students were there, an eighth-grade girl with long, curly blonde hair opened the door fully and walked over to me. Her face was slightly swollen from crying; little puffy pillows framed her blue eyes.

"I just wanted to thank you for your message," she said. "Thank you for telling all my friends the truth."

"What about my presentation touched you so deeply?" I asked.

"Well, I've been sexually active. And…about six months ago I went to the doctor and discovered I had HPV." She was wringing her hands so I grabbed them in mine as she continued. "Well, a couple of months back we discovered that I have the beginnings of cervical cancer. I've already had a colposcopy and a biopsy."

"Oh, honey. I'm so sorry. I wish we could have talked before," I said.

"Me too," she replied. Then a courageous smile spread across her face.

"It's not that I'm going to die. I just have to be careful and work with the doctors….But you did get here before for my friends. And I just wanted to thank you for that."[5]

It is unfortunate that many young girls will have to undergo repeated pelvic exams and pap smears as well as procedures to detect and treat diseases associated with sexual activity. This young lady will most likely be visiting the doctor every three to six months for years. The venereal warts are treatable with medicine, laser, cryotherapy, or surgical excision. They can return however.

Another sexually transmitted disease is HIV/AIDS. It used to be a gay man's disease, but now because of intravenous drug use and women having sex with bisexual men the number of women with HIV/AIDS is consistently increasing. Presently, over one million Americans have HIV. The present antiviral drugs help keep the virus from progressing to AIDS, but the cost of the drugs ($1000 per month) and the side effects are a problem. Now we have a costly chronic disease that is continuing to spread.

Hepatitis B (1.25 million chronically infected) and Hepatitis C (3.9 million infected) are also spread sexually and by intravenous drug use. These viruses can lead to cirrhosis and then to liver cancer.

Other infections such as gonorrhea, which infects 700,000 yearly, chlamydia, which infects 2.8 million yearly, and syphilis which infects over 32,000 cases yearly can be treated with antibiotics. The treatment is usually curative, but the women may be left infertile. On a surgery rotation I did during internship, a young lady had such a widespread gonococcal infection in her pelvis that her fallopian tubes had to be removed, which ended her chance of conceiving naturally.

Our school systems have supported the condom message, but with the increasing amount of venereal disease, obviously, the "safe sex" thought is flawed. In the 1970s, when I was in high school the chance of getting a sexually-transmitted disease was one out of 32. Now, by age 24 one out of three sexually active people will have a STD.[6] The Centers for Disease Control in Atlanta, Georgia has recommended abstinence or a lifelong monogamous relationship as the only means of safe sex. It may sound impossible to the majority of teens, but in the early 1900s 97.5 percent of women demanded a trip to the altar before a trip to bed.[7]

RELATIONAL AND EMOTIONAL PAIN

The amount of emotional turmoil is not easily measured, but it is overwhelming. Lakita Garth, a national abstinence speaker, commented "They don't make a condom big enough to cover the human heart." Panic attacks, migraine headaches, depression, fibromyalgia, anxiety, anorexia, bulimia, obesity can all be symptoms of deeper emotional pain related to premarital sex, abortion, or abuse.

Women have a greater need for relationship. When women have sex without commitment, many feel violated. Those broken hearts lead to physical and mental manifestations that doctors see frequently.

How do girls know if a guy loves them? Withhold sex until the guy walks down the wedding aisle and commits his love for a lifetime. Girls need to hold out for real commitment and love. That is what young ladies deserve.

Of course, young men have a responsibility to treat the young lady with respect. Sex is a strong temptation, and once a man gives in to having sex, then he will probably keep giving in to it. How many girls will he violate in the meantime? Then when he does marry, will he have enough self-control to remain faithful to one woman throughout a lifelong marriage? Young men ought to hold out for real commitment and love also.

Heather Jamison wrote a book *Reclaiming Intimacy*[8] which details the consequences of premarital sex. After going through four years of Christian marriage without the intimacy that she desired, she decided to divorce. Before the final papers were signed, she realized that neither she, nor her husband had asked forgiveness of God or each other for engaging in premarital sex. Their anger only escalated as their marriage continued. She came to the point of true repentance to God and to her husband. Her marriage didn't dissolve. She and her husband worked through their problems and continued their journey together. It was a difficult time for them, but they sought God and now they serve with their three children as missionaries in Kenya. The following song sung by Steve Green was especially meaningful to her.

> I repent making no excuses
> I repent, no one else to blame
> I return to fall in love with Jesus
> I bow down my knees... and I repent...[9]

In Heather Jamison's epilogue, she mentioned Derek Redmond, who fell in an Olympic race because of a muscle injury. He got up and continued with a painful limp. His dad came onto the track to help him. As he finished, the crowd broke into thunderous applause.

We all fail in something. We all hurt. We all suffer. Hopefully, we can all finish strong.

Another speaker and author for purity is Dannah Gresh. She teaches seminars and retreats to young ladies and women about purity. Her book *And the Bride Wore White—Seven Secrets to Sexual Purity* details her life story and what she learned from it. My daughter was reading it for her Sunday school class. I picked it up and started reading it. I ended up buying my own copy to read. The author cited a University of Chicago study that stated people who reported being most physically pleased (by sex) and emotionally satisfied were married couples.[10] She also cited a study by Robert and Amy Levin. They took an in-depth look at the sex lives of 100,000 women and the survey was published in *Redbook* magazine. The women that were labeled "highly religious" were more likely to experience "a higher degree of sexual enjoyment and greater frequency in love making experiences per month."[11] Sometimes, as Christians, we're fooled into thinking that we are missing out on all the fun, but when we do seek God and obey His guidelines we are much better off. We enjoy life more. It is true that "no good thing will he uphold from them that walk uprightly" (Psalm 84:11 KJV).

Elisabeth Elliot wrote about her love and relationship with Jim Elliot in *Passion and Purity*. Her husband was a missionary who was killed by the Auca Indians in Ecuador in the 1950s. She commented why so many in our culture may not be finding the happiness in life that God desires for us. "There is a dullness, monotony, sheer boredom in all of life when virginity and purity are no longer protected and prized. By trying to grab fulfillment everywhere, we find it nowhere."[12]

PREGNANCY

As many young women have learned, premarital sex can also lead to babies. Nearly 900,000 teens get pregnant every year in America. The teenager must make a choice to birth, adopt, or abort. According to a 1995 survey, 51 percent of teens that become pregnant give birth; 35 percent seek abortions; 14 percent miscarry. Less than 1 percent choose to place their children for adoption.[13]

The choice a young lady makes will affect her physically as well as emotionally the rest of her life. Most of the time, the father is not willing to take on the family life responsibility. I talked to a high school counselor from New Jersey who said he gives young girls the statistics that 1 percent of guys in New Jersey marry when they are under 20 years old. It makes the girls consider the fact that their man is probably not going to marry them if they get pregnant. The young lady is usually left alone with the child.

In Doug Herman's book *Time for a Pure Revolution* by Tyndale House Publishers, he comments that 20-30 percent of teens marry their baby's father, but most are unmarried five years after the birth of their child, and less than half are married within ten years of having their child. Most of the time, these teen moms stay single a long time. Furthermore, these teenage mothers raise children that are more likely to be juvenile delinquents. Subsequently, the cost to society for adolescent childbearing and its negative social consequences is annually about $29 billion.[14]

I listened to the story of a young mother who turned her life over to God. She was going through some difficult days as outlined in this prayer that I wrote about her struggles.

PRAYER OF AN UNWED MOTHER

Dear Lord, I spent last night crying because I didn't have the money to cover my rent, but you worked things out today. Thank you. Forgive me for not having faith. You have always provided in times of my need. Even when I asked you to leave my life completely, you didn't. You were actively working. You had to teach my rebellious spirit. You know, Lord, I didn't know how real your love and care could be. I only responded to the love and attention that I could feel and touch. I had rejected the wisdom in your Word and the wisdom of my parents. I thought I knew the way to enjoy life, but I found out I was wrong. Sure, it was pleasant for a season until I reaped the seeds I had sown. I remember,

Lord, the bitter tears I tasted when I was offered the money for an abortion. "No, I can't do that," I cried. I remember the rejection, the shame, the abandonment. I felt alone in the delivery room. I had no one to comfort me and hold my hand. The intern told a joke and the medical student laughed. They were having such a good time. I wasn't. I was afraid. Everything was painful. I made it through. Thank you for watching over me.

Thank you for the love of my parents. I know I lost their trust, but I didn't lose their love. Thank you for loving me enough to chastise me. I felt your peace, when I finally gave my life back to you. You were waiting all the time. Now, Lord, you know I have a few needs. I need a husband. It has been five years that I've raised my son without a father. He needs a man to teach him manly things. I also need a husband to care for me, provide for me, pray with me, love me, and cry with me. It has been hard. I feel so lonely. Yet, I am waiting on your man, Lord. He needs to be a strong man in your Word and in his prayer life. There are so few good men, and not too many men would even consider a woman with a son. However, Lord, you know who he is. Direct him in his life. Build him up in your Word. Prepare him. I will wait, because I know your way is best. Please give me the strength for work tomorrow. Provide me with an extra income for the high winter heating bills, and continue to provide a babysitter that doesn't smoke and loves you. Thank you for all you've given. In Jesus Name, Amen.

LEGAL CONSEQUENCES

The 18-year-old white male with dark curly hair appeared out of place in the jail environment.

"What can I do for you today?" I asked him when he sat down for a medical appointment in the jail.

"I need my inhaler for my asthma."

"Are you wheezing now?"

"My lungs feel tight."

"Let me listen to your lungs," I told him as I put by stethoscope on his back. He did have some mild wheezes. "I'll have the nurses give you a treatment now, and I'll make sure you get an inhaler three times a day.

"Are you missing your senior year in high school?"

"Yes."

"You appear out of your element in here. When do you get out of here?"

"I was sentenced to a year in jail for having sex with my 15-year-old girlfriend."

"Her parents didn't appreciate that?"

"I got along with them fine until they found out I was having sex with their daughter. They called the police, and I got arrested. Now, I am spending my senior year in jail."

"It is a tough way to find out about the law, isn't it?"

"Yes," he admitted.

The statutory rape law in most states is in existence to keep men from preying on young girls. The age of consent for girls in most states is 16. By enforcing this law, the state hopes to curtail the sexual coercion and abuse of women, decrease pregnancy among teens, limit the number of fatherless children, and decrease the rate of child poverty and welfare dependency. In this case, the young man was surprised by his arrest. Yet, according to law, he was having sex with a minor.

Lack of Self-Discipline

In Galatians 5:22 Paul writes about self-control. If we don't have discipline in our life, it hurts us and those around us. God set a standard of purity for us. Do we trust Him and obey, or do we listen to a culture that disobeys the rules and seems to get away with it?

Time For a Pure Revolution, by Doug Herman calls for people to recognize the myth of the sexual revolution and seek God's way of abstinence before marriage.

Imagine if you saw a sign like this for a new national campaign aimed at teenagers: "Don't drink and drive…

but if you do, or if you ride in a car with a drunk driver, be sure to buckle up!" That would be ludicrous, wouldn't it? You probably have never heard, "Smoking cigarettes causes lung cancer and shortens your life. But if you can't stop, use multiple filters to smoke safely." Binge drinking, now pandemic in colleges and universities, is not deterred by messages saying, "Cut consumption in half." No; the fact is, it's illegal to drink under the age of 21. School violence cannot be stopped by themes promoting, "Violence is your right, so fight carefully." No; instead we have metal detectors in some schools to prevent teens from carrying weapons! Why? To instruct those who are determined to fire off weapons about the safest way to do so? Certainly not. It's to keep weapons out of schools. In that case, everyone agrees that risk elimination is the best. Why then do we settle only for risk reduction when it comes to sex outside of marriage?

If you care for our nation and its teen population, you don't want them to get hurt. And that includes challenging them to stop their high risk behavior before it kills them or someone else.[15]

Chapter Nine

BE CAREFUL LITTLE EYES

AN INMATE'S STORY

Pornography was a part of my life from the time I was very young. My mother gave me a pornographic magazine to read and look at, and I became very interested in the material. My daily life was consumed by it. Subsequently, I collected hundreds of magazines and movies over the years. Pornography was my god, and I worshipped it. I was in bondage to a progression of activities that made me constantly want more and something different. When I got married, I talked my wife into watching movies with me. She didn't want to. She was annoyed by my obsession with pornography, and my requests for her to act out some of the scenes in the movies. Eventually, she left me. I continued on with my addiction.

One day I was taking care of my sister's daughter and her friend. After I got them both drunk, I showed them some of my videos. I ended up molesting them. When they came to their senses and told their parents about what I did, I was arrested. Now I am serving my time in prison. I know what I did was immoral, disgusting, and just plain sick. My decision to dwell on pornography led to the destruction of my marriage, my sister's daughter and her friend, my career, and my finances. My desire to satisfy my lust hurt two innocent trusting girls. Even

though I asked God to forgive me and give me strength,
I still battle my mind daily.

God made women beautiful, and, as men, we are attracted to
them. Is it wrong to observe their beauty? Does viewing women in
pornographic magazines or videos interfere with a normal sexual
relationship? If we stray from God's plan for our minds and eyes,
will that lead to the destruction of our marriages, our children,
our communities, and our nation?

The business of pornography has progressed from magazines
and approximately 1000 adult movie theaters in the 1960s to the
rental and private viewing of 800 million adult films annually on
VCRs and DVDs. In addition, pornography is viewed on various
television networks, the Internet, and in hotels where 50 percent
of the guests rent adult movies.[1] Like the tobacco industry, the
pornography business is going after young people. The average
age of first viewing of Internet pornography is 11 years old,[2] and
80 percent of 15-17 year olds have had multiple hard core pornography exposures.[3] The biggest users of child porn are the 15-
20-year-old age group. The industry wants to hook young people
and profit from them for a lifetime. Their annual revenues are
$57 billion. They rake in more money than all the professional
sports teams put together and more than ABC, CBS, and NBC
combined.

God put in us a natural appreciation of beauty. At what point
is there a problem? Is there fallout from an obsession with lust?
When Bill Maier from "Focus on the Family" interviewed serial
killer David Berkowitz, he asked him if pornography had something to do with his killings. David replied that pornography
wasn't directly related to the killings, but that it made him devalue
people.

One pastor asked, "Does God want us to use people or their
images as products to be consumed?" Then he reasoned that if
we do that, then we devalue them and ourselves to less than what
God intended. Do we respect them and honor them as a creation
of God? Our choice is to seek God and true love, or choose lust
and get caught up in the anger and frustration of a false love that
cannot satisfy.

Dr. James Dobson commented that serial killers, in general, are involved in pornography. In Dobson's interview with serial killer Ted Bundy, Mr. Bundy explained that his obsession with the printed page progressed to acting out what he saw and read. He said that every serial killer he knew was obsessed with pornography.[4] The statistics bear out those facts when 86 percent of rapists and 80 percent of child molesters regularly use pornography.[5]

WHAT DOES THE BIBLE SAY?

"I will set no wicked thing before mine eyes," Psalm 101:3 (KJV). David had learned his lesson. After he viewed Bathsheba bathing, committed adultery with her, had her husband killed in the frontlines of battle, and lost his son to illness, he knew the consequences of viewing what wasn't his.

In Matthew 5:28 the Bible warns, "But I tell you that anyone who looks at a woman lustfully has already committed adultery with her in his heart" (NIV).

Women also have a responsibility "to dress modestly, with decency and propriety," as it states in 1 Timothy 2:9 (NIV).

My wife and daughter will ask me occasionally what I think about what they are wearing. I appreciate their concern, and I will tell them what I think. If I think their attire is too revealing, they will change it.

What are the right things to dwell on?

Finally, brethren, whatever things are true, whatever things are honest, whatever things are just, whatever things are pure, whatever things are lovely, whatever things are of good report; if there be any virtue, and if there be any praise, think on these things (Philippians 4:8-9 KJV).

When it comes to pornography where do we want to fight our own personal battle? Do we want to guard our eyes and minds by avoiding it as much as possible, or do we throw away safeguards and set ourselves up for the possibility of addiction? When it comes to a life of serious addiction the road back to a victorious Christian life involves a program of intense study of the Word, accountability, counseling regarding past, present, and future relationships, education, and personal responsibility. Our God opens His arms up and loves us as sinners and wants to help us live a life that is free from the bondage of sin. However, we make the decisions about what we look at and think about. Many have made decisions to pursue pornography and find it is a long road back.

Tyler's Story

Wow, what a great God we have; the very fact that I am alive and sharing this testimony is evidence of His power!

Mine is a very ordinary story in a way, I am just an ordinary Christian. But to me it is a story of extraordinary life.

I grew up as an introvert in a typically modern dysfunctional family. Having a shyness with real girls, I gravitated to "girly magazines" to satisfy my curiosity in that area during my early teens. It became a habit very quickly. Soon I had a stash of magazines carefully hidden from prying eyes, and it was my substitute for the 'real thing,' the girls that my brothers bragged about. I can recall, somehow, feeling self-righteously indignant at their moral infractions, feeling that my aberrant behavior somehow wasn't as bad as theirs, though deep down I well knew it was wrong. What did frighten me was the power that my lust for these two-dimensional pictures had over me. I tried not to think about that too much though. I was at the same time grappling with trying to understand the great why of life and beginning to come into a primitive relationship with the Lord.

At the age of 19, I met Carrie, fell in love, and we married ten months later. All thoughts of and desires for pornography evaporated. I guess that's not too unusual an experience, the 'real thing' displaces the fake substitute. At least for a time!

Over the next twenty years the battles with pornography were few and far between. For the most part I was busy taking care of my wife and children, and seeking a relationship with the Lord. However, my faith was extremely legalistic, and that would eventually prove to be near fatal.

I say the battles with pornography were few and far between. Like when I would accidentally find a Playboy magazine in a circumstance of privacy, and not be able to resist the temptation to peruse it. It worried me that I could never resist the temptation, but the times were infrequent and I found it better to try to forget, and do better in the future.

About eight years ago, during a time of great personal stress for both my wife and myself, we succumbed to the temptation together, rationalizing that "a little bit of voyeurism spiced up the sex life." For Carrie there was no great moral problem because she was still not a Christian, and her interest soon waned anyway. The turmoil for me though was horrendous. On one side the utter condemnation of a vengeful and wrathful God (my legalistic church life) and on the other the exhilaration and new heights of sexual pleasure after our relations having become stale with neglect over the years. (I had not realized this neglect at the time though, or indeed the fullness of joy God intended in sexual union between a husband and wife.)

After several attempts to rid my bedroom and my mind of this material holding me in bondage, I soon became desperate. Each time I simply found the desire for this filth too much. I can remember the last year of this trial falling to such depths that on a trip to a church convention I took a detour of several hours specifically to pick up some more videos, and spent half the time at the convention praising God and the other half shaming Him and His beloved Son. The condemnation I felt both at my weakness and my hypocrisy, going to church, even preaching (in a very minor capacity), and yet falling back into sin again at night—no, I should be honest and say, diving headlong back into sin—was becoming too much. I had been taught that obedience was the key by my church, but it simply didn't work, and, oh how miserable a creature I was.

The last six months was a bitter period of my life. Every night as I tried to find sleep, the same image came clearly into my mind, the image of a gun at my temple, and the final blast, and silence. Oh how I wanted to die. Thankfully guns of any kind are rare in Australia, let alone hand guns. But thoughts of suicide as the only way out consumed my mind, when it wasn't consumed by pornography. I was even creating my own filthy images and 'stories' in my mind, so obsessed was I. I realize now how deep the scars are that we carve into our minds as pornography becomes an addiction. Soon thoughts of actually ending it all were taking clear shape.

Thankfully our little church was at the same time going through a mighty change, from Old Covenant legalism into the New Covenant of grace. I think that this was what saved me, as in the few rational moments left I was studying these issues with our Bible study group and gradually absorbing some of this new knowledge.

But my misery was deepening. I had just a few weeks earlier been through the cycle of ridding my home of the porn, and then a few days later restocking, and I was feeling incredibly shattered at my total inability to control myself. One evening I told my wife I was going back to work for a few hours. But I had a rope on the floor behind the driver's seat, and I knew just where to tie it up out in the shed at work—on a beam next to a high workbench. I know that I had not quite reached the bitter end that night, as I did not take the rope out of the car as I went in to work. But I went out to the back pad-dock, and just stood there and cried. After a bit, I looked up into the crystal clear sky and cried out, "Lord, I can't do it!" in desperation. And then it was that I heard, so gentle, so still and so small, His voice, "Yes, Tyler, but I can."

That was a revelation. It was like a divine awareness flooded through me. Of course I couldn't overcome. That was impossible, me trying to overcome, even with His help. It was all back to front. I looked up and said, "OK, Lord, You do it." The most powerful thing was the realiza-tion that He really loved me, even right there in the midst of my putrid sin. He loved me, tenderly, affectionately. Those five words were full of love.

Wow, that was incredible! I had been struggling so much because I had always thought God hates me, detests me, and this locked me into the cycle of sin. Sin, self-condemnation, sin, self-condemnation…

I went home and rid myself of the disgusting mate-rial I had bought just a few weeks earlier. I had done this several times before, but always before with a feeling of regret at losing the objects of my lust. I had done it out of obedience to God, not desire for Him. This time it was out of desire and thirst for more of His divine awareness and JOY! For Him alone.

As soon as this all happened, I began to focus on Him, His glory, His holiness, His purity. What a joy! I rejoiced in my freedom—freedom from evil desire—because He had given me desire for Him. The chains are bro-ken, I fled to Him, to thoughts of my Savior, who saved my physical life that starry night, and who saved me eternally. And in Him I am now growing in grace and knowledge and strength. Praise our tender and merciful God.

May He be your Salvation and freedom too. This is my prayer for all who struggle as I once did.[5]

As Tyler struggled, so do many others. In our land, with such easy accessibility, the addiction is common. If a person acts out the material, it affects many more people. Consider Diane's story:

> My name is Diane. I've always felt that pornography was bad, that it was harmful. But I felt that it didn't affect me personally. No members of my family ever read pornography. My husband's family didn't read pornography. We live in a small, close-knit community. Pornography is not an issue there. I basically felt immune to its effects.
>
> A year ago in April, my world was shattered by the effects of pornography. My three-year-old daughter was raped and violated in every manner you can imagine by a twelve-year-old boy. When they arrested the young man, we were told that they would surely find sexual abuse in his background. And that this is the reason he did it on my daughter. After a thorough psycho-sexual evaluation, they came to one conclusion. There was a single motivating factor in what he did to my baby. He was exposed to pornography at a very vulnerable time in his life.
>
> What he saw on those pages not only gave him the ideas of what to do and how to do it, but it gave him the permission to treat females in a degrading and debasing manner. Since he was only twelve years old, he needed to look for a female who was younger than him, who wouldn't fight back. And so he raped and molested my daughter.
>
> I've heard it said that pornography is a victimless crime. I'm standing here before you a victim of pornography. My little girl is a victim of pornography. My husband is a victim of pornography. Even my four other children are victims. How do you explain to a fourteen-year-old boy that his favorite little sister has been raped and violated in such a heinous manner?

But I am also standing here before you, and from my heart I can tell you, that this young man was a victim. He came from a good family. This wasn't a boy who was in a gang. He'd never been in trouble with the law. He came from an intact family in a small community where everybody knows everybody. His parents sent him to a youth camp thinking that they were going to enrich his life with these two weeks in a summer youth camp. At that point, he was exposed to pornography.

He is a victim. His family is a victim. His mother loves him as much as I love my little girl. And his mother is as shattered as I am. Something is seriously wrong in this country when we protect the rights of a handful of men to make billions at the expense of women and children.[6]

This was testimony presented to our legislature about laws concerning pornography.

Can someone from the church get caught in this addiction? Unfortunately, church members, as well as leaders, are falling victim. One inmate I cared for at the county jail, who was very clean shaven, articulate, and nice in appearance told me he was headed off to prison for ten years. I asked him why. He said he was convicted of criminal sexual conduct. He was a leader in his church and became heavily involved in pornography. Eventually, he became involved with a younger member of his church and was arrested. In a survey of Promise Keepers, 53 percent said they viewed pornography in the previous week, and 47 percent admitted that porn is a major problem in their home.[7] The grip that Satan has on God's people is sad. We are very vulnerable. Even 37 percent of pastors say Internet porn is a current struggle according to a *Christianity Today* leadership survey. As men, it is our duty to love and care for the women in our lives. We have a decision to make every day about what we look at and think about.

For those that are caught up in the addiction of pornography, there is help. A friend of mine told me about his struggle with pornography. He told me about a Bible study that helped him. The devotional is called *Pure Freedom—Breaking the Addiction to*

Pornography by Mike Cleveland. It is available in Christian bookstores or on the web at www.christianbook.com.

Another program that I heard about from a pastor friend that helps with internet accountability is called "Covenant Eyes." The program can be accessed at www.covenanteyes.com.

Chapter Ten

THE OTHER SIDE OF
BROKEBACK MOUNTAIN

"Nobody cares about me," Tammy, a 36-year-old woman, blurted out with tears running down her face, as she sat on the emergency room stretcher.

"I care about you, Tammy," I told her truthfully as I handed her some Kleenex. She buried her face in the tissues and began to sob. Her 230 pounds and short blonde hair shook as she cleansed her heart of all her pain.

I had reviewed her chart before I came into the room. She had ingested 13 beers over the last six hours and had taken six sedatives. Although her suicidal gesture wasn't enough to do her any serious physical harm, it was enough to get her a psychiatric hospital admission. Her lesbian lover of three years had just left her, and she had been through similar painful rejections before. As her sobs started to slow down, she took some deep breaths and blew her nose.

"Tammy, I have a few questions I need to ask you," I began. "I have read your chart, and I know what has happened tonight. I want to get you some help."

While she regained her composure, I waited. She finally looked up at me and appeared ready to answer my questions.

"Have you tried to commit suicide before?"

"I have thought about it, but I never actually did anything."

"Were you ever able to talk to anybody about what kind of problems you were going through?"

"When I was in high school, the vice principal threatened to commit me to a mental hospital because I was so antisocial. I wouldn't leave the house or listen to anybody. To avoid going to the hospital, I did agree to see the school counselor and talk about my anger."

"What were you angry about?"

"My home life was very upsetting to me. My parents were both alcoholics and brought me along to the bars. They fought and argued frequently until they divorced during my sophomore year."

"Do you have a relationship with your parents now?"

"Not much of one. I felt so neglected growing up that I rarely communicate with them. Besides, they are both remarried now and have their own lives."

"How long have you been attracted to women?"

"Since I was a teenager."

"Have you been in other serious relationships?"

"This is my third serious relationship since high school. They usually end when my partner wants to move on and find someone else."

"Does your anger frequently cause problems in your relationships with others?"

"I get angry when my partner does whatever she wants, and she doesn't care about what I think or want."

"Were you ever abused sexually?" I asked. She looked down and hesitated. Then she looked at me.

"I was abused by my uncle when I was 7 years old," she quietly replied.

"Did you talk to the counselor in high school about that?"

"No. It was too personal."

"Abuse as a child affects people for years. Don't be afraid to talk to the counselor about that. They will help you deal with your emotions."

"I'll try to cooperate with the counselors and doctors."

After her stay in the emergency room, she was sent to a psychiatric hospital for further evaluation and treatment.

God loves this young lady. He didn't mean for her to suffer such hurt. He didn't design for her to grow up with alcoholic parents, or to be abused by an uncle, or to suffer rejection from various lovers, or to be so sad that she wanted to end her life.

GOD'S DESIGN

God designed for a man and woman to marry and live together for a lifetime. He also encouraged couples in the Bible to have children and raise them with love, training, discipline, and hard work. Many in our society try to follow God's model, but many do not believe in God and His ways.

Even when parents do their best to train their children in God's ways, they eventually must make their own decisions about what they believe and how they act.

One particular young man, Brian, came into the emergency room with severe dehydration. After getting some intravenous fluids, he felt much better. At 6 foot 2 inches, he was a solid 224 pounds. He could have played linebacker for a college football team. He said he was a homosexual and was afraid he had AIDS. At that time in 1988, AIDS was a death sentence. Over 30,000 died from AIDS in that year. I assured him that we would test him for the human immunodeficiency virus. We kept him in the hospital because he had some abnormal labs. As we were doing some further testing, his condition got worse again, and he became very confused and short of breath. In a matter of hours, his breathing became so labored that we had to put him on a ventilator.

His mother and father, as well as his brothers, came in to see him. As I talked with them over the next several days, they related to me that they attended church. They appeared to be a stable, caring family.

Another doctor and I explained to them what was happening medically to their son. We were honest with them about our concerns about AIDS and its grim prognosis. We prepared them for the worst. In the next few days, he had seizures, kidney failure, and then died.

After the autopsy was done and all the examinations were completed, the pathologist determined that the young man had AIDS and died of a fungus infection called Aspergillosis. His immune system was so weakened that a common fungus invaded his body and shut him down. There was nothing that could have helped him. His disease was too far advanced.

He was one young man that appeared to have a stable, loving home life, and he made his own decision to participate in a risky lifestyle.

If I feel it is appropriate, I will ask patients about their parents. It gives me an idea of what kind of home they were raised in and what kind of attitude they have toward their parents. When I was treating a lesbian inmate in the county jail, I asked her about her father. She said that her father was abusive and schizophrenic and hadn't been involved in her life since she was young.

As she grew up, she became a lesbian. While she was living with her longtime partner and their adopted son, she was also teaching school. She became involved sexually with a 14-year-old student. According to what the student told the state police, the teacher "wed" the student in a pagan ritual in the woods. To avoid a trial, she pleaded no contest to the criminal sexual conduct charge and was sentenced to time in prison.

A middle-aged man that I was seeing in the emergency room told me that he had been married five times. I asked him if he had any children. He said he had two daughters. One daughter was married, and one was a lesbian. It didn't surprise me that a child would choose a lesbian lifestyle after witnessing the failure of her father's heterosexual marriages.

I know you can't choose the family you are born into, but you do have a choice how you want to live your life. You do have a decision to make about what kind of relationship you want and what kind of sexuality you want to practice. The Bible does offer God's standard for how to live life.

ARE THERE DANGERS TO HOMOSEXUALITY?

The main difficulties I see with the homosexual lifestyle are suicide, disease, violence, and abuse. In *Patient Care* magazine the author quotes a 30 percent attempted suicide rate in homosexual boys.[1] Many are depressed because they get caught up in a lifestyle of drugs and alcohol, but some are unhappy because they haven't found what they're looking for in life. The homosexual, who may have experienced a chaotic family life, finds that his life of promiscuity, alcohol, and drugs has brought him further unhappiness and hopelessness. The answer for many of these young men appears to be suicide.

Another danger homosexuals face is disease. When I first entered medical school in the early 1980s, the number of patients with the human immunodeficiency virus or HIV was in the thousands, and, now, it is estimated to be about one million.

When the HIV virus infects the body, it weakens the immune system until the patient develops an AIDS (acquired immunodeficiency syndrome) defining disease.

In my internal medicine residency training, AIDS patients came into the hospital with rare diseases and cancers. They had blindness from cytomegalovirus, skin cancer from Kaposi's sarcoma, various pneumonias including pneumocystis carinii pneumonia, viral spinal cord paralysis, mental disorders, parasitic diarrhea and more. At that time, AIDS was a frightening disease that took the lives of young people within one to two years from the date of their diagnosis. Now HIV and AIDS are more of a chronic infection because of the medicines that keep the virus from replicating and taking over the immune system.

Homosexuals still die every day from AIDS, though most live with the virus for a long time. Of the one million with HIV infection, about one-third have AIDS, about one-third have the immunodeficiency virus without an AIDS-defining illness, and about one-third are unaware they have the virus. Of course, besides HIV, gay men are at risk for other sexually transmitted diseases such as syphilis, herpes, gonorrhea, venereal warts, and hepatitis.

The spread of disease is aided by the fact that most homosexuals have multiple partners. I do know some gay couples who seem happy and adjusted in a long-term relationship. However, most end up having many different partners. In a recent editorial "Sex in cities, having little to do with marriage"[2] by David Brooks, he quoted a survey that reported that 43 percent of gay men in a neighborhood in Chicago had over 60 sexual contacts in their lifetime. I asked Nigel, a 19-year-old male patient of mine, if he thought that statistic was true. He replied that he had sexual relations with hundreds of men and his 51-year-old partner had sex with thousands of men.

The next problem I see with the homosexual lifestyle is the violence. The violence against homosexuals by heterosexuals is highly publicized and condemned as it should be, but yet the homosexual murdering the homosexual or heterosexual is much more common. Consider the lives of John Gacy, Jeffrey Dahmer, Dean Corll, Juan Corona, and Randy Kraft, who were all homosexuals. John Gacy was the product of an abusive, ridiculing father. After two failed marriages and a stint in prison, he began preying on young, transient, homosexual men. He lured young homosexual men into handcuffs, sexually assaulted them, and killed them. He then buried their bodies in the crawl space of his house, his garage, or threw them in a nearby river. He was responsible for at least 33 deaths.[3] Jeffrey Dahmer confessed to killing 17 homosexual or bisexual men and then ate some of their body parts.[4] Dean Corll, who was called the "candy man," was responsible for the deaths of 27 young men.[5] Juan Corona was a migrant laborer who was married and the father of four daughters. In the spring of 1971, the police had uncovered 25 bodies in freshly dug graves in Sacramento Valley, California. There was obvious homosexual activity. A receipt for some meat and an eyewitness account of one of the victims getting into Corona's pickup truck were enough to convict him of murder and send him to prison. Randy Kraft drugged, strangled, and sexually mutilated as many as 67 men, although he was convicted of murdering 16.[6]

Because the homosexual lifestyle separates young people from their families, they become easy targets for serial killers. When the parents find out their son or daughter has been killed, they usually cannot provide much information to police, because they have not known their son or daughter's contacts or activities.

Another problem I see associated with homosexuality is child abuse. The homosexual movement influences young people, and in some cases abuses young people. In a magazine article, I read about the 1973 kidnapping, shackling, and rape of thirteen-year-old Martin Andrews by convicted pedophile Richard Ausley.[7] I was surprised that Martin Andrews, who was the victim, grew up to be a homosexual. I have since learned that about 30 percent of homosexuals say they were sexually exploited as children.[8] At the county jail, I asked one inmate why he abused and tortured several young men. He said he had battled those temptations all his life since he was sexually abused as a child. I realize he may just be saying that as part of his defense, but I hear the same story repeated frequently.

IS THERE HELP?

After I finished talking to some nurses informally about problems associated with the homosexual lifestyle, one nurse confided to me, in tears, that her son was homosexual. My talk of disease, violence, suicide, and abuse was frightening to her. She was concerned for him. I assured her there is help available if he had questions and was willing to look at his options. I referred her to a website "exodus.to" that answers questions about homosexuality. It also has a section of testimonials from homosexuals who weren't satisfied with their lifestyle and discovered a relationship with God that gave them the fulfillment they were looking for. The following is an example of one of those stories:

WHO AM I?
Bob Ragan

I did not become acquainted with the word "homosexual" until I was in high school. I knew, however, that it described the feelings I had experienced throughout my childhood.

Same-sex attractions and feelings had been around since I could remember. I assumed that this is how I was born and these feelings defined who I was as a person. I heard no discussions about homosexuality as a child and I chose not to discuss these feelings with anyone. This was the beginning of my sense of isolation and aloneness that would plague me for years to come.

A significant event took place when I was a sophomore in high school. During that year I was exposed to homosexual pornography. To this day I can see myself and feel the effect that those images had on me. I couldn't stop looking at those pictures. I could not take my eyes off of those images and that event seared one thought in my mind: You are a homosexual.

As I reflect on my life, I now see that every time the enemy was offering me counterfeit life, God was ever-present to show me the truth, the real. Just as I had same-sex attractions growing up, I also had an awareness of God as demonstrated through His creation around us. There was a hunger in me to know God just as there was a hunger to know men.

I knew about God, but I didn't know Him in a personal way. I remember as a 15 year old, crying out to Him for help in a point of anguish and desperation with my addiction to masturbation and pornography. He heard my cry. The same year I was introduced to pornography, a Franciscan priest took me to a Full Gospel Business Men's dinner where I was introduced to Jesus. My heart soared as His life and Spirit came into me. My heart recognized that this was what I was searching for. I asked Jesus to be my Savior, but I did not truly make Him Lord of my life at that time.

Dealing With God's Truth

For the next several years I was involved in the "Jesus Movement" of the early 70s. In college, I belonged to a Christian community house and I remember the precious fellowship, awesome times of praise and worship, and wonderful teaching. It was then that I became familiar with passages in Scripture which condemn sexual behaviors outside the context of heterosexual marriage.

In my conscience I agreed with God's truth regarding homosexual behavior. However, in order to cope with my strong feelings, I shut down my heart. By not dealing with my feelings, I placed myself in bondage to them. Knowing of no one who was walking in freedom from homosexuality, my feelings of aloneness and isolation deepened.

Because I had not made Jesus Lord of my life, willing to follow Him no matter what the cost, I walked away from Him. In 1976, I began dating a man that I knew. Having found my "Mr. Right." I was ready to settle down into a lifelong relationship. But that "lifelong" relationship lasted only six years.

Compromise

Since I couldn't have what I thought I wanted, I compromised my life. Now I was willing to become involved with men who did not want a committed relationship. I was willing to go out to the strip clubs and, in an alcoholic blur, drown my sorrows and lost dreams. I was walking through life oblivious of my inner turmoil. I viewed other men as mere objects to satisfy my sexual appetite.

As my life was consumed within the gay community in Washington, DC, I ignored the great emptiness I saw all around me. I ignored the fact that the bars were filled mainly with men under 40 years old. It was only at the strip bars and adult bookstores that I saw the "older" crowd. I overlooked the fact that any longterm relationships I did encounter were not what I considered healthy. Although some level of love existed within them, I consistently detected an emptiness as well.

Through all of this, God was still in the picture. Somehow I knew that He was waiting for me to come back to Him. By 1986 my heart had begun to yearn for Him again.

Pro-Gay Theology

I went to a gay bookstore and bought a book which stated that the Scriptures approve of homosexual behavior. I wanted to be convinced that homosexuality was acceptable and that thousands of years of interpretation and tradition was due to ignorance.

Even with this strong desire to be convinced, I remember laughing at the way the Scriptures were reinterpreted. It took no great discernment to see that justification of immoral behavior was being sought, and not God's greater purposes.

My spiritual hunger continued to grow but I became sidetracked. I began to investigate the New Age movement. I delved into astrology and into other areas. Then, as I was being drawn closer to the edge of darkness, God's mighty right arm reached down from on high and rescued me.

During October 1986 in San Francisco, I met a man who had a very similar background to mine. Although at that time we thought we were born as homosexuals, both of us desired a deep relationship with God. In 1987, I rededicated my life to the Lord. This time I wanted Jesus to truly be Lord of my life, especially over my sexuality.

Not knowing what else to do, I found a church in the yellow pages of the local phone directory. After a Sunday visit, I scheduled an appointment with one of the pastors and shared my story. I am so thankful that, although he admitted that he did not know how to counsel me, he said he loved me and wanted me to be a part of his church. God had His hand on me.

I wanted to be drawn into the heart of that church, and He placed me with the prayer warriors. Several couples surrounded me with love, even though I did not share my struggle with them because of my pride and fear of rejection. Then during a time of intense struggle in January 1988, I finally broke down and shared my story with one of the couples. How blessed I was when this couple just loved me, prayed for me, and did not reject me.

Two days later I went to a Christian bookstore and shared about my struggle with the owner. I purchased some literature he had and finally realized that I had not been born gay. A tremendous sense of peace flooded me. It was about 2:30 in the morning, so the only person I could call was my friend in San Francisco, where it was only 11:30 PM!

Two weeks later, I heard about Regeneration, a nearby ministry to men and women struggling with unwanted homosexuality, and I began attending their support group in northern Virginia, which had just begun three months earlier.

What a joy it was to find others who were like me, searching for a way to process and understand our homosexual feelings. How remarkable to find out that so many had gone beyond "white-knuckling" the struggle.

Through the teachings I received, I came to understand some of the roots of my gender insecurity. I came to see that my homosexual attractions were rooted in a legitimate need which I had eroticized. I bonded with men sexually to fill the need for affirmation of my masculinity. I had blocked the source of that affirmation during my childhood.

Who I Am in Christ

Although understanding root issues was necessary to my process, the foundational truth that made the real difference was knowing who I am in Christ. I had a hunger for the Scriptures like never before. As I pored over the book of Romans, the Holy Spirit revealed the truth that my old nature, the old man, was not only crucified, but was dead and buried. It was no longer I who lived, but Christ who lived in me (see Romans 6).

I began to see that I was a new creation (2 Corinthians 5:17). Neither my temptations nor feelings ultimately defined who I was as a person. The occurrence of a homosexual attraction or feeling did not mean, "I am a homosexual." I could experience temptation, but resist it and walk in freedom!

I also began to have a relationship with God as my "Abba," a word of intimacy similar to "Daddy" in the original biblical language. He was the only source of meeting my needs.

For many years I was confused about my identity, and centered it on my sexuality. Now, as a Christian, I can clearly see the truth: My relationship with God is the foundation of my identity. In the security of knowing my Heavenly Father, I never have to be confused again.[9]

Chapter Eleven

POSSESSION IS
99 PERCENT OF THE GAME

The bottom line is, they did have a choice," Wyoming Police Lieutenant Paul Robinson said. "And the choice is, you get a job and work, or you steal. And they chose to steal."[1]

The two young women he was referring to were charged with felony murder and unarmed robbery. They were taking purses from people in parking lots and using the money to pay bills, and buy alcohol and cigarettes. In the last incident, they stole a purse from a petite 81-year-old woman, who was loading groceries into her car. During the struggle to get the purse, the 200 pound 21-year-old assailant pushed the lady down, and she hit her head on the pavement. The young woman then ran to a car driven by an 18-year-old female accomplice. She hopped in, and the driver sped away.

The victim cried for help and paramedics were called. As the paramedics cared for her, she described the purse-snatcher and what happened. Then she lost consciousness. Later, at the hospital, she died of a bleed around her brain. The story was reported in the paper, and a search began. Hundreds of tips came in to the police, and they methodically followed up on them. One tipster gave the first names of the women involved. When detectives interviewed the young ladies at their apartment, they were cooperative, but they denied any involvement. On the next day, the detectives had undisclosed physical evidence that tied them to the crime scene. At that point, they confessed. They went to jail, were tried and convicted of murder.

"But my baby is not a murderer. She didn't beat, cut, stab, or shoot, things that murderers do," the mom of the suspect said after she apologized for her daughter's act. However, her thoughtless act was a crime, and it did cause a person's death. There is a consequence for that.

The victim's husband couldn't believe anyone would be so stupid to kill someone over so little. He lost his wife because these two young women had no respect for what belonged to someone else. His children lost a mother. His grandchildren lost a grandmother. His sister-in-law lost a sister, and his nieces and nephews lost an aunt. In the widower's mind, no amount of money that these young women gained was worth the void that was left.

WHEN IT GETS PERSONAL

When I was first married, I lived in an older neighborhood. I woke up, one Sunday morning, remembering I had left my yellow ten-speed bike outside on the back porch. I quickly got dressed and raced downstairs. I opened the door to discover that my bike was gone. My heart sank. It was still dark at 6 AM, and there was a lightly falling warm spring rain. I put my hat on and walked around the neighborhood. I was angry. Although I didn't find my bike, I did cool down a little before I went home to tell my wife.

I'll never forget the feeling that someone took my bike. I rode that bike to work, and I rode it four hundred miles to Mackinac Island. It meant something to me. I loved that bike. It probably didn't mean much to the person who stole it.

It's important in a society to have a sense of morality to leave other's possessions alone. In the emergency room, we leave patients in rooms and sometimes shut the door for privacy. Some patients take advantage of that privacy and load their purses with tape, bandages, wraps, and antibiotic ointment. It adds to the cost of medicine for society as a whole, but some people are out for all they can get. They don't really consider others.

I asked a 17-year-old inmate in the jail if he thought it was wrong to steal. At first he avoided the question and said he really wasn't the one who committed the armed robbery, but that he took the rap because he didn't want to see his friend go back to prison. He then stated he wasn't very happy about getting a minimum of 10 years in prison. He didn't expect the sentence to be that long. I redirected him to my original question about stealing. He answered that his mom was a prostitute who taught him how to steal from stores. His dad was in prison, and he had only seen him three times. I asked him what would make him happy in life, and he responded, "Happiness is in the Lord." He told me that when he was young, he sang in a church choir, and he learned a few things about right and wrong. Then he got involved in alcohol and marijuana, and started hanging out with the wrong friends. He realized he needed to seek God again in his life.

"Why did you steal?" I asked another inmate.

"Because it is free," he replied.

"Did you know it was wrong?"

"I didn't know it was wrong, but after I got caught a few times my mother and my uncle got all over me about it. I stopped stealing because of them."

There is hope for change in some budding young criminals. We all need to be taught. We can't be afraid to teach others.

THE COST

How much does shoplifting cost society? Employee theft, shoplifting, vendor fraud and administrative error cost the United States retailers over $30 billion every year. That is 1.7 percent of annual sales, which doesn't sound like much percentage wise. However, for an average family of four, it will cost them an extra $440 a year in higher prices. Almost half of the loss comes from employees that steal from their employers. Both shoplifting and employee theft have been on the rise over the last few years.[2]

When I was growing up, "Possession is 99 percent of the game" was quoted often. It wasn't who owned it that mattered. It was who had possession. Apparently that type of thinking still exists. A friend of mine told me his son was honest, but he tended to keep his friends' things. His friends didn't claim their possessions, and he would continue to use them. I told him I've noticed a similar pattern around our house. I did talk to one of my sons who returned a guitar that was in the garage.

Why did God include "thou shalt not steal" as part of the Ten Commandments?[3] Is it important to obey that rule? What if nobody did?

In Joshua 6 and 7, God's judgment against stealing was severe. The Lord said unto Joshua I have given into thine hand Jericho, and its king, and the mighty men of valor. God gave Joshua some peculiar instructions. Then Joshua relayed those commands to the Israelites. They walked around the city once for six days, and then, on the seventh day, they walked around the city seven times. Then the priests blew their trumpets, and the people shouted. The walls of Jericho fell flat. The Israelites rushed into the city and destroyed every man, woman, and animal. Only Rahab, the harlot, and her family, and all that she had were spared because she hid the messengers whom Joshua sent to spy out Jericho. The Israelites then burned the city.

When the Israelites went to conquer the city of Ai, they were soundly defeated. When Joshua asked God about it, God told him that Israel had sinned because someone had stolen property from Jericho when God commanded them not to. The next morning Joshua brought every tribe of Israel before him. The tribe of Judah was picked, and eventually Achan stood before Joshua. Achan confessed that he had sinned against the Lord God of Israel. He stole a garment, silver, and gold. He hid them beneath his tent. Achan, his family, their animals, and possessions were led to the valley of Achor where the Israelites stoned them and then burned them.

"Will a man rob God?" says Malachi 3:8. Do we rob God by withholding tithes and offerings? Who is really being robbed? We are.

"Bring all the tithes into the storehouse, that there may be food in mine house, and test me now herewith, saith the Lord of hosts, if I will not open for you the windows of heaven, and pour out for you a blessing, that there shall not be room enough to receive it. And I will rebuke the devourer for your sakes, and he shall not destroy the fruits of your ground; neither shall your vine cast its fruit before the time in the field, saith the Lord of hosts" (Malachi 3:10-11).

In the church today, perhaps 20-30 percent of church people tithe. Are we not willing to put faith in God? He says He will bless us so much that we won't be able to handle His blessings. I feel blessed even though I am not rich. I grew up in a middle class family. I felt loved by my mom and dad. I had food to eat, clothes to wear, and a home to live in. I went to church and learned God's way to live. I was blessed. I was taught to give my tithes and offerings to God. I obeyed. I continue to do that because I serve a great God, and I don't want to lose out on His blessings.

I want to share a story that touched my heart about tithing. I wrote it after one of the deacons of the church shared his story with me.

"Dave, how do you feel about tithing?" Brian asked.

"I would like to tithe. However, I have too many bills. The Lord didn't accumulate the debt. We did, and it is our responsibility to take care of them before we start tithing," Dave responded.

"I know where you are right now. Times seem hard, and the bills seem impossible to pay off. At one time, my wife and I were behind in our bills, and I wasn't making much money. We decided to put God first and tithe. We claimed Luke 6:38, "Give and it shall be given unto you…" as our verse. We set aside one-tenth to give to God and paid the bills with what we had left. It was hard. It took faith, but God blessed."

"What about our debts?"

"Do you owe a debt to God too?"

"Is tithing a debt?"

"According to the Bible it is."

"God can wait on His, though."

"I use to think that too. However, God blesses when you have faith in Him and give to God first."

"I'll think about what you said."

"Let me make a challenge."

"All right."

"I challenge you to tithe for one year. If you are behind in any of your bills, then I will pay those bills," Brian offered.

Dave was silent. He knew Brian was sincere. God had blessed him.

"All right," he responded.

That night he told his wife, Debbie, about the challenge.

"It is definitely a step of faith, the way our bills pile up," she replied.

"I know, but we have to start putting God first. Let's make a commitment to God right now," he suggested.

"I'm willing," She answered, and they bowed their heads.

"Dear God, we would like to commit the first tenth of our income to You. We know we have many bills to pay and groceries to buy, but we are trusting You to help us through. We don't want to rob You anymore. In Jesus name, Amen," Dave prayed.

The next Friday was payday, and Dave brought the check home. He put it in the middle of the kitchen table as Debbie was figuring the bills. She wrote out a check to the church for one-tenth of the gross income. Dave put it in an envelope and then into his Bible to take to church. Debbie paid the rest of the bills, and then whatever was left over went to pay for groceries.

The first week went well, but Dave wondered if they could make it through the winter with all the unex-pected financial emergencies. He prayed that God would keep the car running, and for extra overtime at work. He petitioned God for a warm winter, so the heating bills wouldn't be too high. One Friday, he brought his check home and gave it to Debbie.

"I don't know if this is going to be enough," she warned him.

"How close are we?"

"We can pay the bills, but there isn't any money left for groceries," she paused as they both thought out their options. "Should we hold up on the tithe just this week?"

"No, we have to keep giving our tithe," he surmised. "We have some canned fruit and vegetables downstairs. All we really need is meat and bread."

She handed him the checkbook, and he wrote the check out to the church. Then he handed her the checkbook back to write out the rest of the bills. Later, they prayed for the bread and meat. They had skimped on the groceries quite a bit since they started tithing, but they never had to cut them out completely.

When Dave arrived for work at the fire station on Monday morning, he sat down at the coffee table. He remembered Debbie's face when he left for work. She managed a weak smile. God had provided for them up to this point.

Mike, one of the other firemen, walked in with four grocery bags in his arms and a big smile on his face.

"What have you got there?" Dave asked.

"I got white, wheat, and rye bread. I'm selling each bag for fifty cents."

"Sold." Dave said as he stood up and took fifty cents out of his pocket. "Thanks. You don't know how much I appreciate this."

"Glad to help you out."

As Dave put the bag in his trunk, he thanked God for His provision. He couldn't wait to get home and tell Debbie.

After work, he drove in the driveway, stopped the car, grabbed the grocery bag out of the trunk, ran up the stairs and opened the door.

"Honey, I'm home," he shouted as he stood at the top of the stairs and waited for her to spot him with the bread.

"Dave, I got a surprise for you," she announced as she made her way from the basement. Her face broke into a smile when she saw him holding the grocery bag with loaves of bread sticking out of the top.

"I got all this bread for fifty cents."

"That is great."

"What is your surprise?"

"This morning Carol came over with a grocery bag. She explained that she and her husband had a pig butchered, and they wouldn't be able to eat all the meat. She wondered if we could use it. She pulled out some of the meat which included sausage, bacon, pork steaks, and pork chops. I thanked her for being so kind and thoughtful. I invited her in, and we talked for awhile. I told her about our step of faith in tithing. She was happy to be able to play a part in God's answer to prayer for us. After she left, I was anxious to see you and tell you what happened."

They gave each other a hug and said a prayer of thanks to God. Throughout the year, God supplied. Dave and Deb matured in their Christian walk. They took a step of faith and gave. God gave back. "But without faith it is impossible to please Him for he that cometh to God must believe that He is, and that He is a rewarder of them that diligently seek Him" (Hebrews 11:6).

Chapter Twelve

"You've Come a Long Way, Baby"

I'm having chest pain," Renee, a 36-year-old factory worker, expressed to me with a concerned look on her face. Her shoulder-length red hair and her freckles made her appear to be in her late twenties.

When I listened to her lungs, I heard wheezing. I surmised her chest tightness was due to the difficulty she was having getting a deep breath.

"I'll have the respiratory technician give you a breathing treatment to open up your lungs to see if that makes you feel better," I explained to her. Within minutes, she had the nebulizer mouthpiece in place, and she was breathing in the medicine. After fifteen minutes, the treatment finished, and I went back into her room to reassess her.

"The treatment made the pressure worse," she complained. Her concern and lack of improvement alarmed me. Could this young lady be having a heart attack? I had to make sure.

"I'll have the nurse draw some blood and get an electrocardiogram. The x-ray tech will also be in to take a chest x-ray," I assured her. Her only risk factor for coronary artery disease was that she smoked.

As I looked at her electrocardiogram, I was shocked. She was having a heart attack. I told the nurse to give her some aspirin, nitroglycerin, and some oxygen.

"You're chest pain is coming from your heart," I told her.

"I was afraid of that," she conceded to the diagnosis.

"We'll get you through this. Did the aspirin and nitroglycerin help the pressure?"

"Yes, but I still feel some pressure."

"I'll have the nurse repeat an electrocardiogram and give you some morphine for pain."

When I reviewed the repeat electrocardiogram and it was unchanged, I contacted the cardiologist. He advised me to go ahead with a powerful clot busting drug for heart attacks which would open up her clogged artery and save her heart muscle. I knew I had to administer the drug, but I also knew the dangers of using that type of medicine. Even though the patient had no contraindication to the potent blood thinner, I feared the consequence of bleeding from vessels around the brain that could disable or kill her. The chances were remote (4 out of 10,000), but the cases that went bad were tragic and unforgettable.

As the drug went in through the intravenous port, the nurse monitored the patient closely. I kept an eye on the cardiac monitor that recorded the patient's rhythm. She made it through the initial phase without any arrhythmias, but she did have some bleeding around her gums.

After another electrocardiogram didn't reveal any improvement, I phoned the cardiologist again to let him know the results of the medicine. Since she didn't have complete relief of her pain or resolution of her abnormal electrocardiogram, he agreed to accept the patient to his hospital for further care. He could perform a heart catheterization and dilate a plugged artery to see if that resolved her symptoms. Within fifteen minutes, the helicopter landed to transport her away.

"They'll take good care of you," I told her as I gave her a pat on the shoulder.

"I need to make it through this. I have 8- and 10-year-old boys at home yet."

After several hours, the cardiologist called me back.

"She ended up having a small artery that was clogged," he explained to me. "She did well without any further complications and will be staying in the hospital."

I was glad that she made it through her heart attack and catheterization without major complications. I could only hope that her close call helped her to give up the cigarettes.

THE COST

Sometimes when I talk to people about cigarettes, I mention the cost of an emergency room visit. It costs approximately $2000 for the visit, labs, x-rays, electrocardiograms, medications, and so on. Then it costs another $2500 for the emergency clot busting drug. It costs $2500 for the helicopter transport, and another $2000 for the heart catheterization. In addition, there would be a cost for the hospital stay, and if open heart surgery were necessary the cost of that would be over $75,000. The costs add up quickly.

When the national cost is considered, Tommy Thompson, former U.S. Health and Human Services Secretary, said we spent $155 billion, in 2004, on tobacco-related diseases.[1] When he spoke in Detroit, he mentioned that the Big Three automakers spent $10 billion in 2004 on health care expenses, which cost the consumer $1,525 per new vehicle sold. The care of tobacco-induced disease is a big part of that cost, and all of America is paying for it.

The one-pack-a-day smoker is also paying $1500 a year at present prices. Because the cigarette tax keeps going up, many are trying to cut down or quit. About 5 percent quit every year. It is an addiction, like other addictions, that is easy to start but difficult to quit.

Numerous patients face the consequences of cigarette smoking daily, and physicians advise patients about the dangers of smoking. Ultimately the decision is up to them. In order to quit smoking, the patient has to want to quit themselves. Smokers can get away without an adverse effect for many years, and then suddenly face the ugly side of the habit.

LUNG CANCER

"You've come a long way baby" used to flash on televisions as an advertisement for Virginia Slims cigarettes in 1968. Unfortunately, the direction the cigarette has taken women and men have been in the wrong direction for people's health. In the early 1900s, lung cancer was rare. As men started to smoke, the lung cancer rates climbed also. By 1949, it became the number one cancer. In one study of 605 male patients with lung cancer only eight were non-smokers.[2] As women started to smoke their lung cancer rates also increased to the point that it replaced breast cancer as the number one cancer in 1987. In 2004, 173,000 new cases of lung cancer were diagnosed, and 164,000 deaths were recorded due to lung cancer.[3] Cigarette smoking is responsible for over 90 percent of lung cancer cases. Approximately, one in ten smokers will develop lung cancer over their lifetime.

OTHER RELATED DISEASES

During my internship, nine out of ten of the patients I cared for on one particular day were smokers. It was a reminder to me of cigarettes disabling and lethal consequences. Recently, the Surgeon General, Richard H. Carmona, said that the list of illnesses and conditions related to cigarette smoking continues to grow.[4] He added cataracts, acute myeloid leukemia, abdominal aortic aneurysms, periodontitis (an inflammation of gum tissue) and cancers of the stomach, pancreas, cervix, and kidney to the list of conditions linked to smoking. "The toxins from cigarette smoke go everywhere the blood flows," Carmona said. Brendan McCormick, a spokesman for cigarette-maker Phillip Morris USA, said, "We agree with the medical and scientific conclusions that cigarette smoking causes serious diseases in smokers, and that there is no such thing as a safe cigarette."

According to Tommy Thompson, Secretary of Health and Human Services, smoking is responsible for 485,000 premature deaths a year. Males that smoke die an average of 13.2 years sooner than non-smokers, and females that smoke die an average of 14.5 years earlier than non-smokers. Smoking is also the number one cause of fire-related deaths.

If smoking is so dangerous, then why is it still legal and why do tobacco companies keep producing products? The answer is because 46 million Americans are addicted to it and paying $5-15 dollars a day to support their habit. In addition, the tobacco companies are profiting from sales of cigarettes to other countries.

They are aggressively marketing their product wherever they can. They have to find people who don't know or understand how bad cigarettes are for their health.

In America, cigarette smoking is the major risk factor for the top four causes of death. Heart disease killed 709,894 people in the year 2000. The youngest heart attack victim I witnessed was a 28-year-old that suddenly collapsed. He had immediate treatment administered to him, but he died. An autopsy revealed a massive heart attack. He was a cigarette and marijuana smoker. The next youngest I saw was a husky 35 year-old Caucasian male who complained of severe chest pressure. He had the pain for over 12 hours and it was radiating to his shoulders, elbows, and back. He had similar symptoms that lasted several minutes during the previous weeks. He was a smoker, but he was trying to cut down. His electrocardiogram and his blood tests revealed that he had a heart attack. He obtained treatment and survived.

The number two cause of death is cancer which killed 551,833 people in the year 2000. Almost ten million people are presently living with cancer. Of course, lung cancer is the leading killer in men and women. Peter Jennings on April 5, 2005 announced on "World News Tonight" that he had lung cancer. His voice was raspy. He was going to fight it. He did fight it, and sadly he lost August 7, 2005. The statistics for surviving lung cancer are getting better, but still about 85 percent of lung cancer patients die in five years. Peter Jennings smoked and then quit for several decades before taking up the habit again after September 11, 2001.

The third leading cause of death is stroke which accounted for 166,028 lives lost in the year 2000. I remember a lady complaining about the care her husband received at one of the major hospitals. She was upset because her husband had a stroke and remained disabled. She didn't feel the care was adequate. I listened patiently to her comments. I know medical facilities can be impersonal. However, in the back of my mind, I knew her husband was a chain smoker, and his nicotine habit was his body's worst enemy.

The fourth leading cause of death in the United States is Chronic Obstructive Pulmonary Disease (emphysema and chronic bronchitis). About 90 percent of people with this disease are smokers.

Fourteen million Americans are afflicted. Johnny Carson recently died from this at age 79. He lived a longer than normal life even though he smoked. In 1974, thirty years before he died, he told Dick Cavett that his smoking habit was killing him. Occasionally, he would be snuffing out a cigarette after a commercial break on the "Tonight Show." He retired in 1992. In 1999, he went through coronary artery bypass surgery, but that didn't convince him to quit. His brother Dick Carson said his brother expressed anger toward his cigarette habit. His wife, Alexis, also begged him to quit. He did try to quit many times, but he always started up again.[5]

SECONDHAND SMOKE

While I worked the emergency room on the night shift, I estimate that 90 percent of the sick children I saw had parents that smoked. Usually the children would have fevers, asthma, ear infections, pneumonias, sore throats, and so on. Whenever the parents complained about how the medical profession couldn't keep their children well, I would emphasize the importance of not smoking in the house. I had seen children night after night who smelled like cigarette smoke with parents who said they only smoked outside.

Whenever I speak to schools about smoking, the students that have parents that smoke become concerned. They want their parents to quit.

In a comic strip, a boy was sitting with his father in the living room. The father pulled out an empty pack of cigarettes and told his son he was heading out to the store to get some more. The son turned around and looked out the window as his dad left the room. While the son didn't notice his dad had left, he started reporting the weather. "It looks like you're out of luck, Dad. It's snowing so hard outside, all I can see is white! I can't even see across the street! The snow's so deep, the cars look like igloos! The city's diesel snowplow truck can't get through! Listen to that wind howl! Walking might be difficult since the sidewalk is nothin' more than a river of sleet and ice. You'd be better off if you stayed inside and skipped smoking for just one day," he suggested just as his dad came walking back into the living room smoking a cigarette with his pant legs and shoes covered with snow.

Smoking is also a risk factor for sudden infant death syndrome (SIDS). If the parents smoke, then the risk for SIDS for the child is twice that of a non-smoking household.

Each year close to 3000 lung cancer deaths are attributed to exposure to secondhand smoke.[6] Many restaurants and public facilities have banned smoking. Smokers are feeling the pinch.

BAD OUTCOMES

Over the years, I still think about the patients I cared for who had bad outcomes because of tobacco abuse. When I was a medical student, a 55-year-old bricklayer who smoked two packs of cigarettes a day for 40 years complained of left elbow pain. He had a normal electrocardiogram, a normal exercise stress test of his heart, and a normal Holter monitor which was used to detect any dangerous rhythms. Two hours after he turned in his monitor he dropped dead. The autopsy demonstrated that the arteries of his heart were in fairly good shape, but he must have had enough spasm in his arteries and enough disease from smoking to trigger a fatal rhythm that resulted in his death.

Another 37-year-old white male with 25 years of smoking appeared very healthy, but he was diagnosed with lung cancer. He had two small children that were two and four years old. He went through several months of chemotherapy that he didn't respond to. He died suddenly two months after his diagnosis.

While I was in residency training for Internal Medicine, I was called to the intensive care unit for a 57-year-old white male whose blood pressure was dropping. He was hospitalized for severe pneumonia. The intravenous fluids were being rapidly infused to increase his blood pressure, but it didn't help. As his pressure continued to drop and his neck veins became distended, I decided to insert a needle into the sac around his heart to see if he had fluid or blood around his heart that was tamponading his heart's ability to pump effectively. When I inserted the needle into the chest and into the pericardial sac, 30cc's of bloody fluid came out. His pressure came up. He was saved temporarily. The cardiologist came in and put a drain into the heart sac to continue to drain the blood. Through further investigation, we discovered that in addition to pneumonia the patient actually had lung cancer that had metastasized to the heart lining. The cancer was bleeding into the heart sac. He had widespread cancer. There was nothing more we could do, and the patient died the next day.

The smoking habit is ingrained. After we put one elderly woman on a ventilator, she was sedated heavily and resting peacefully. She no longer had to fight for each breath. I continued on seeing the other patients in the ICU. After I finished, I returned to the elderly woman. She still was quiet. Her thin frail body rested on the ICU bed, and her silvery hair rested on the pillow. The respirator pumped air into her lungs. Her sedation must have been wearing off, because she lifted her right hand up to her mouth as if she had a cigarette between her yellow-stained index and middle finger. Even in her sleep, her habit controlled her. She repeated the motion a few more times, until the nurse gave her more sedative medication.

MANY HAVE QUIT

My pathology professor in medical school explained to us why he quit smoking. He said he was doing an autopsy on a man who was his age, which was about forty. The man's lungs were very black and stiff because of smoking. My professor thought about that through the rest of the autopsy. How could he continue to put ash into his lungs when he could see the damage in that corpse? He threw his cigarettes in the trash on the way out of the autopsy room, and never picked up another cigarette again.

He did himself a big favor. Most people quit because they are convinced they need to. Of the 46 million smokers, 70 percent want to quit. Forty-six percent try to quit each year. The average smoker tries to quit seven times before they are successful. The numbers of smokers decrease every year. Eighty percent quit without the help of medicine, hypnosis, or acupuncture. When doctors ask their patients to stop smoking for health reasons only about 5 percent will quit. If a smoker quits before age 35, then the risk of smoking-related disease almost returns to the risk of a non-smoker.

With all this information available, we still have 22 percent of adults and 27 percent of teenagers who smoke. The rate is going down because of the price of cigarettes and the education given to people concerning the harmful effects of tobacco.[7] It is more difficult for smokers to find a place to smoke when restaurants, schools, businesses, and many public buildings ban smoking anywhere on the property. The general population is also becoming more negative towards smokers because there is more awareness of the effects of secondhand smoke. One 60-year-old man that I know was diagnosed with cancer in his voice box. His doctor told him that only heavy smokers get that kind of cancer. He told me he never smoked cigarettes, but he worked for years in a room that was smoke-filled. The public is more concerned about the rights of non-smokers over the rights of smokers, and it is making an impact on our society. Even bumper stickers are making a statement. One of my favorites is "Eternity—smoking or non-smoking."

There are quit-smoking programs at hospitals and wellness centers. They use counseling, education, support groups, and medicines to help people quit. This type of intervention is helpful for many people. There are five ways to increase your odds of success—talk with your doctor, seek counseling, investigate an aid to help you with the nicotine withdrawal, ask for support from family and friends, and don't give up.

THE BIBLE

What does the Bible say about smoking? It says nothing about the cigarette. However, smoking is responsible for more disease and death than any other preventable risk factor in the United States today. It is definitely harmful to the body. In 1 Corinthians 6:19 Paul writes that our bodies are the temple of God and we should not do anything that would harm our bodies. A verse on prevention is Proverbs 27:12 "A prudent man foreseeth the evil, and hideth himself, but the simple pass on and are punished" (KJV).

My Grandpa Carrel

I remember my grandpa as a thin five-foot six-inch white haired man who walked all over town. He was a good man, and he could eat a lot. I never knew my Grandpa Carrel to be a smoker because he quit years before I was born. However, one day I did find out he had smoked.

"Can you go check on Grandpa Carrel? He is having trouble breathing," my dad explained to me over the phone. My dad trusted my experience in the medical field even though I hadn't been to medical school yet. He knew I had a stethoscope and could check my grandpa's lung sounds.

"Sure," I responded.

When I first walked into his living room, I could see he was breathing faster than normal. He was deaf, so I just walked over to him and put my stethoscope on his back. I could hear the wheezing which was unusual for him. I took him to the emergency room, and an x-ray showed a large lung tumor with pneumonia. The doctors kept him in the hospital. When my dad arrived, the doctor asked him if my grandpa had ever smoked. My dad told him that my grandpa had a cigarette habit for about five years as a young adult. That surprised me. I'm glad he had the willpower to quit, and set a good example to his children and grandchildren.

The outlook was not good for my grandpa. No treatment was recommended for him because of the tumor's size. The doctors kept my grandpa comfortable, and he died in a couple of days at the age of 81.

Smoking Cessation Benefits

According to the American Cancer Society, American Heart Association, and the American Lung Association, the beneficial effects of quitting smoking begin 20 minutes after the last cigarette.

In 20 minutes, the blood pressure drops to normal, the pulse drops to normal, and the body temperature of the hands and feet increases to normal.

In eight hours, the carbon monoxide level in the blood drops to normal, and the oxygen level increases to normal.

In 24 hours, the chance of a heart attack decreases.

In 48 hours, the bronchial tubes relax which makes breathing easier, and lung capacity increases.

In two weeks to three months, the circulation improves and walking becomes easier. The lung function increases as much as 30 percent.

In one to nine months, coughing, sinus congestion, fatigue and shortness of breath decrease; cilia regenerate in the lungs, increasing the ability to handle mucus, clean lungs and reduce infection. Overall energy level increases.

In one year, the risk of heart attack decreases by 50 percent.

In five years, the lung cancer death rate for average smoker (one pack per day) decreases from 137 per 100,000 people to 72.

In ten years, the lung cancer rate drops to 12 per 100,000 people, almost the rate of a nonsmoker; and precancerous cells are replaced with healthy cells. There also is a decrease in cancers of the mouth, larynx, esophagus, bladder, kidney, and more.

It Is Your Choice

Is it a habit that you want to start?

Chapter Thirteen

WHO HATH WOE?

You're the doctor. You're not supposed to let my cousin die," the young lady cried out to me. She sat, grieving, with a dozen other relatives at 1:00 AM. "He is only 18 years old. Go back in that room and keep trying to save him."

I wished there was something I could've done. However, there was no coming back to life for this young man. He was killed when he missed a turn on a rural highway and slammed his car broadside into a tree at over 100 miles per hour. The car split in half from the driver's door to the passenger door. His lifeless body was found face down in the dirt underneath the car engine.

The paramedics found him without a pulse. They immediately inserted an endotracheal tube to breath for him and put in two large bore intravenous lines to give him fluids. While in transport to the emergency room, they continued CPR and gave him drugs to revive him. When they arrived, he was still without a pulse. I continued to give him intravenous fluids and drugs for another 30 minutes. Because of his lack of response, I was convinced that he ruptured his major blood vessels and bled out within a few minutes of hitting the tree. We had tried every conceivable avenue to save his life. Initially, when he arrived we knew the chance of his survival was close to zero, but we worked exhaustively against all odds. Our efforts failed to bring back his life, and we had to cease what we were doing. At 12:56 AM, I declared him dead.

According to the state trooper, there was open alcohol in the vehicle, and he was previously convicted several times for driving while intoxicated. This time his failure to make the turn on a rural highway cost him his life. Eventually, the family came to grips with the reality of their loved one's death, and they made their way down to the trauma room to view the corpse. The state troopers showed them the pictures of the demolished car, and they began to understand the finality of this young man's choice.

I talked with the family again and answered their questions. After I advised them about the required autopsy for motor vehicle deaths, they were more subdued. They were no longer angry, just sad, quiet, and tired. I left them in the family room to spend some more time together. As I began seeing other patients for various illnesses and injuries, I saw the family members slowly file out of the emergency room with their arms around each other.

Although the emergency room staff and I don't feel the intensity of the family's pain and loss, we are oppressed by the loss of life and the sadness it causes.

STATISTICS

The chaos that alcohol has caused in America is well documented. Over 100,000 people die each year because of alcohol related injuries or diseases. I advise my teenage drivers that one out of every two drivers on the road after midnight are drunk. I've seen drunk drivers come into the emergency room barely able to walk and escorted by their arresting officers. Their alcohol levels are three to four times the legal limit.

Fourteen million people suffer from alcohol abuse or alcoholism. Forty thousand infants are born with some degree of alcohol related effects.[1] Our jails and prisons contain 40 percent of inmates that have committed their crimes while under the influence of alcohol. These crimes include rape, murder, robbery, domestic abuse, drunk driving, assault and battery, and so on. The National Highway Safety Administration reports 1.5 million arrests per year for driving under the influence of alcohol. In 2002, 2.2 percent of drivers said they had driven while alcohol impaired during that year. Alcohol use is also the leading risk factor for unintentional injuries (motor vehicle accidents and drownings), suicides, and homicides. It also plays a major role in work injuries, divorces, mental disorders, and health related problems such as cirrhosis and heart disease. A recent study explained how the brains of alcoholics become smaller and lighter than the brains of non-alcoholics. Scientists believe that a number of factors including alcohol's toxic by-products, malnutrition, and cirrhosis of the liver interact to cause brain damage.[2]

In 2002, 54.9 percent of American adults admitted to one alcoholic drink in the last month. One third of adults that drink, binge drink or consume more than five drinks in a day for men and four drinks in a day for women. Binge drinkers are 14 times more likely to drink and drive than non-binge drinkers. When I told Harold, a retired man, that I was putting together a book to help people make good choices, he told me that he had made a bad choice when he took his first drink. He said he was 18 years old and working out of town. After finishing work for the week, a co-worker bought him and his friends each a six-pack of beer. They had a good time partying for several hours late into the night. When it was time to go home, he got into his car with his drinking buddies, and he started to drive. At the first intersection, he ran a red light and broadsided another car. He got out and ran, but a witness chased him down and made him return to the scene. The driver that he hit was not doing well. By the next morning, the man died. Harold went to jail and feared facing the judge who was known for his stiff sentences to drunk drivers. The judge sentenced him to one to two years in prison. He got out after one year, but still lives with the thought that his careless action cost another man his life.

For teenagers, the statistics are comparable to adults. In 2003, 44.9 percent of ninth through twelfth graders confessed to drinking alcohol in the previous month, and 28.3 percent admitted to binge drinking. Most teenage drinkers have alcohol readily available at their home, their friend's home, or at parties. Some parents sponsor parties with the thought that it is best to allow kids to drink under supervision. However, parties with alcohol can lead to other problems. One study revealed that young people that drink have an increase in the number of sexual partners and sexually transmitted diseases.[3]

Women who drink two to five drinks a day increase their breast cancer risk by 50 percent. Also oral pharyngeal cancer, esophageal cancer, prostate cancer, and liver cancer are increased by alcohol use. In 2003, 12,207 cases of chronic liver disease were alcohol related. Half of child abuse or neglect is related to alcohol or drug use, while 28 percent of suicides and two-thirds of intimate partner violence are related to alcohol.

I recall one 42-year-old man who failed to give up his drinking and developed cirrhosis of the liver. He accumulated such a large amount of fluid in his abdominal cavity that his abdomen became rigid, and he could hardly breathe. He showed up in the emergency room to have the fluid drained off. I used a five-inch needle to enter the skin. Then I attached the needle to tubing that drained the fluid into a big glass bottle. The abdominal fluid was a dark yellow color with frothy foam at the top. In fact, it looked just like a tall glass of beer. Once the fluid was drained off, he felt better and went home to drink again. He had been through alcohol rehabilitation several times, and just couldn't leave alcohol alone even though he wanted to. He returned for several weeks for the same procedure until he eventually died.

Another retired gentleman came to the emergency room several times because of a drinking binge that resulted in a fast irregular heart rhythm called atrial fibrillation. Not all atrial fibrillation is caused by alcohol, but alcohol is one of the causes. Alcohol, which is a toxin to the heart, weakens and enlarges the heart muscle. In the emergency room we converted his irregular rhythm with a shock. He was advised to abstain from alcohol and advised to follow up with his doctor for medicine to control his heart rate if needed.

In my residency, I was called to see a big husky 35-year-old man who was withdrawing from alcohol. All 250 pounds of him were shaking, and he was confused. He had pancreatitis from his heavy drinking. I ordered some medicine to help settle him down. Before the nurse could give him the medicine, he ran down the stairs and out of the building. He was outside in a hospital gown on a Michigan winter night in a sleeting rain. With the help of security, I chased him down and got him back inside.

His condition rapidly deteriorated after that, and he ended up on a ventilator in the intensive care unit. He never got better, and eventually he died leaving a wife and 13-year-old son.

An example of how alcohol affects the immune system occurred during my internship. I was caring for a 34-year-old Hispanic man that weighed 350 pounds. He worked as a landscaper and drank 24 beers a day and smoked marijuana frequently. He was in the hospital because he needed an evaluation of a mass in his chest. However, he couldn't have the mediastinoscopy to determine what the mass was because his blood pressure was too high. When I first saw him, he was complaining of a sinus headache. I gave him some medicine for the headache. Then in the evening he developed a fever and a stiff neck. When I did a spinal tap to evaluate him for meningitis, his fluid was very infected. I gave him antibiotics and put him in the intensive care unit. He became comatose and required a ventilator to help him breathe. He died two months later. His ability to fight off infection was limited because of the alcohol's effect on the immune system. Prolonged, excessive drinking shortens the life span by 10-12 years.[4]

Alcohol is a major part of emergency room work. In one study, alcohol related visits accounted for 7.9 percent of the total.[5] I have seen other totals with estimates as high as 20-25 percent. On one night in the emergency room, I saw five patients in a row that were there because of alcohol related problems. The last one was an alcoholic that was well known to our facility. He greeted me with his usual slurred "Hi, Doc" as he continued to chew on the graham crackers the nurse had given him. While stepping into the room, I had to avoid stepping on the little piles of graham crackers mixed with sputum that he had spit all over the room. To be honest, at that point I didn't want to see another drunk the rest of my life. I had listened to their profanity, their excuses, their threats, their whining, and their sad stories. I wasn't interested anymore in the problems that they had brought on themselves. I had repaired their wounds, set their broken bones, evaluated their chest pain, and pumped their stomachs when they had overdosed. I grew weary of their obnoxious behavior such as one guy who stood on a stretcher and urinated all over the trauma room because the nurse couldn't get to him fast enough with a urinal. Another uninhibited drunk punched a nurse in the face because she was scolding him.

Alcohol Withdrawal

I have seen their alcohol withdrawal symptoms frequently in the jail. One inmate, having experienced a vivid hallucination, told a visiting relative that the guards took him and 12 other inmates out to a Britney Spears concert over the weekend. Usually the inmates see imaginary spiders crawling up the wall, wild animals, or people floating around on the top of the cells. I prescribe medicine to help them get through these frightening experiences. Occasionally an alcoholic will have seizures. My first experience with a withdrawal seizure was when I was working in the hospital as an orderly. I was assigned to guard a man who had been put in four point restraints (all four extremities tied to the bed). He was 50 years old with a gray brush cut. His anger was evident. "If I ever get out of this, I am going to kill you," he said to me. I tried to talk nicely to him and settle him down. After a few hours, he had to go to the bathroom. The doctor on call gave his permission to remove the restraints. I was a little worried about his previous murder threat towards me, but his attitude had softened. As I got him to the bathroom, his shakes from alcohol withdrawal became evident. He was unsteady, and I had to help him sit down on the toilet. I put his hand on the handrail to allow him to steady himself. Then I left the bathroom and waited outside the door. When he made some abnormal gurgling sounds, I ran back into the bathroom to see what was going on. His back was arched, his head was turned to the side with foam coming out of his mouth, and his arms and legs were rhythmically contracting. He was having a grand mal seizure from alcohol withdrawal. The doctor rushed in, and within a minute, the patient stopped seizing. The nurse administered a shot to help him with his withdrawal symptoms, and we got him back to bed. After that night shift, I did not see him again, but I did read in the paper that he hung himself in jail.

Life-Changing Injuries and Incidents

I took care of a 16-year-old boy, with long blonde hair, who dove off a bridge into a river and hit his head on the bottom. He felt numbness in his arms and fingers. The water was obviously too shallow for diving. He was intoxicated. Without thinking, he got out of the water, went back up to the bridge, and jumped off again. This time, after he hit his head, he couldn't feel his arms or legs. His friends had to drag his body out of the water. He was paralyzed from the neck down. He spent months with a halo brace on his head and on a special bed frame that turned him every few hours. He would spend two hours looking at the ceiling and then two hours looking at the floor.

In the newspapers, I look for alcohol related accidents and show them to my kids. "Warrants issued in golf-cart death"[6] explained how an intoxicated golf cart driver may get a 15-year felony for passing another golf cart and causing an accident. The two golf carts touched wheels, and the one cart flipped over. The 42-year-old female passenger of the cart that flipped over died.

In another alcohol related accident, a 19-year-old left an all night beer bash and rear-ended the car of two elderly sisters carrying food to a great-nephew's graduation open house. The collision sent the women's car off the road, down an embankment, and into a river. One sister died immediately, and the other sister died later at the hospital.[7]

Attempted Suicide

"I'll kill myself the right way next time," Tom, a 44-year-old inebriated businessman assured me with slow slurred speech. With his partial balding dark hair and glasses, he appeared to belong in a boardroom somewhere as opposed to an emergency room.

"How will you do it next time?" I asked him.

"With a 12-gauge shotgun."

"Why did you want to die by car fumes this time?"

"I didn't want to shoot myself and mess up my face. I learned my lesson though. Car fumes are too slow."

"Why do you want to kill yourself?"

"I have a drinking problem, and I am no use to my wife and kids."

"Have you tried to quit?"

"I'm not going to try anymore," he answered. "I have gone to Alcoholics Anonymous, which is a good program, and it has helped many people. However, alcohol has too big a noose on me. At the AA meetings, I would tell the group how I beat my wife in an alcohol-induced rage, and how I spent the night in jail. Then the next week, I confessed to them how I was so drunk I stumbled and fell on my face. I would stand before them with my missing teeth and swollen lips that were obvious for everyone to see. Then I had stories of missed work, financial difficulties, marital problems, kids misbehaving. I told them I would conquer my alcoholism, but I didn't."

"When did you take your first drink?"

"When I was 30, my doctor told me to drink a few highballs at night to help me relax. I did that. Now, 15 years later, I am so consumed by alcohol that the only way to stop is to end my life. My longest bout of abstaining has been seven days. When I don't have it, I thirst for it. I despise those TV ads that portray the glamour and all the beautiful women, but they don't show me, or the drunken housewives, or the skid row bums, or the destroyed families."

When he finished, he looked down as he fidgeted with his hands.

"Do you go to church?"

"Yes, I do. I am a Christian. I am supposed to be doing a skit in Sunday school in a few hours."

"God still has a plan for you," I told him knowing that it would take the power of God to pull him out of the trap of alcohol.

"I know He does," he confessed. For the rest of his stay in the emergency room, he was evaluated by the mental health team for his suicide attempt, and then he was transported to an alcohol rehabilitation program.

ALCOHOL IS TOUGH ON MARRIAGES

I have known at least six nurses who divorced their husbands because of alcohol. A few of them waited until their kids were grown before they left. They endured 25 years of marriage and alcohol, and then they didn't want to hear any more lies or excuses. One nurse told me that her grown children wondered why she didn't leave him sooner. One man I talked to said he was drinking 12 beers every evening with his friends and smoking $45-60 a day of marijuana. His habits caused a separation from his church-attending wife. He said he grew up with an alcoholic father, and it was normal to drink every day. He didn't have any interest in religion. However, he loved his wife and kids. One day he went to her church and talked to the pastor. After a lengthy discussion and some soul searching, he asked Jesus Christ to come into his life and change him. With God's help, he was able to get rid of his addictions and be the kind of husband and father that God wanted him to be.

IT'S YOUR CALL

You make a choice about alcohol in your life. Where do you draw the line? Do you abstain, or drink one or two beverages at a time, or indulge until you're intoxicated? I hear people argue that most people drink responsibly and socially. Yet 30 percent are high-risk drinkers. That means that they drink more than four drinks in a day or 14 drinks in a week.[8] When you take that first drink, your chance of being a high risk drinker goes from zero to 30 percent. What part do you want to play in the unnecessary pain and suffering that alcohol causes in our society?

THE BIBLE

Look at Proverbs 23:19-23,29-33.

Hear thou, my son, and be wise, and guide thine heart in the way. Be not among winebibbers, among gluttonous eaters of flesh; for the drunkard and the glutton shall come to poverty, and drowsiness shall clothe a man with rags.
Who hath woe? Who hath sorrow? Who hath contentions? Who hath babbling? Who hath wounds without cause? Who hath redness of the eyes? They that tarry

long at the wine; they that go to seek mixed wine. Look not thou upon the wine when it is red, when it giveth color and stingeth like an adder. Thine eyes shall behold strange (things) and thine heart shall utter perverse things.

What Is the Cost?

When people think about that first drink, they want to fit in and have fun. However, you have to ask yourself: Are the pleasures worth what it may cost in the future? It may cost you a wife, a job, your kids, your home, your friends, or your life. Many drinkers start because friends or family ask them to. The alcohol may make them feel good at first. For some it even loosens them up and makes them funny. I have seen a number of happy drunks. One elderly gentleman I saw in the emergency room had a large shiner around his right eye.

"Who gave you that black eye," I asked him.

"No one gave it to me. I had to fight for it."

The progression of the occasional drink or the occasional intoxication suddenly becomes daily drinks. Then the drinks become necessary to calm the nerves. The person may sneak drinks, lie about drinking, or experience blackouts. The alcoholic then experiences legal problems, marital and family problems until they seek help, or are hospitalized or die. It is a vicious trap that is hard to recognize and get out of. Is it worth taking the risk?

I watched Tom Cruise in *A Few Good Men* get drunk at night, drive a car without difficulty, and then perform superbly in court the next morning. That is in contrast to the 40-year-old I saw in jail who said he had been locked up 44 times in our county and a half a dozen times in other counties. "I just drink and get stupid," he told me.

What About the Children?

In America, one out of five adults lived with an alcoholic while growing up. Children of alcoholics are four times more likely than other children to become alcoholics themselves. These children may have guilt because they feel they may have caused their parent's drinking, anxiety because they worry about the situation at home, embarrassment because of their drunken parent's behavior, lack of trust because of their parent's broken promises, confusion because their parent's mood may switch from love to anger without a reason, anger because of their lousy home life, and depression because their life is not happy. The children may also decide to skip school, be involved in stealing or violence, have physical symptoms such as headaches or stomachaches, abuse alcohol themselves, or consider suicide. There are educational self-help groups such as Children of Alcoholics, Al-Anon, and Alateen to help resolve problems such as anger and lack of trust which can continue into adulthood. Children of alcoholics may emotionally isolate themselves from others.[9] Of course, sometimes children choose their own course in life and do well.

THERE IS LIFE AND HOPE IN JESUS CHRIST

God provides the hope, joy, and peace for those who look for it. The church I attend has had three senior pastors who came from homes where the father battled with alcoholism. Dr. Bo Moore, our present pastor, was invited to church when he was 13 and eventually accepted Jesus Christ into his heart. He found out that there existed a God that provided the love that he needed. He didn't rely on alcohol because he discovered that God provided a better way to live.

In my hometown of Grand Rapids, Michigan, Mel Trotter Mission was founded by a former alcoholic that found new life in Christ. My parents lead a Saturday evening service there once a month. I have been there several times to talk with some of the men. They are trying to overcome their habit, but most of them have already lost their homes, jobs, and families. Tragically, when Mel Trotter was controlled by liquor, his child died from an illness because he bought alcohol instead of buying medicine for his sick child.

IS BIBLICAL MORALITY OUTDATED?

A Christian Brother's Struggle with Alcohol

I gave my heart to Jesus Christ when I was eleven years old in 1959. My godmother explained the gospel message to me. She told me she would pray for me the rest of my life.

Shortly after that, my family moved to California. My parents, without the restraints of the church or God, came out of the closet with addictive behaviors and infidelities. Liquor was readily available, although food wasn't. God became distant to me, and I self-medicated until I felt no pain. Life was a blur.

In 1967, I plunged my '57 Chevy into a Desoto at 135 miles per hour. I never saw the guy's face that I killed, but after that I would see the face I imagined for him every time I closed my eyes. I went into years of binge drinking and drugs that I remember little of. When I had my leg amputated because of gangrene, the doctors were amazed that they didn't have enough Valium to put me to sleep. I took so much Valium every day that I built up a tolerance to it. My godmother would visit me and remind me that she was praying for me. In 1990, I once and for all put the bottle and the pills down after letting them destroy my fourth marriage. I cried out to God that I needed His help desperately.

He began a good work in me, and I was asking Him to finish it. I ended up going to prison for 12 years. During that time, my godmother died.

I knew her Jesus still lived. She had always encouraged me that God would be faithful to His promises. I became faithful in the study of the Bible and grew close to God.

Now that I am out of prison, I've had opportunities to talk to young people. Occasionally, I take off my artificial leg and show them part of what alcohol cost me in my life. I ask them to seek their fulfillment in Jesus Christ without getting sidetracked by the deceptive pleasures of life which can't bring them the satisfaction they are looking for.

Chapter Fourteen

HANDS THAT SHED
INNOCENT BLOOD

Can you come down to the morgue and help me with a body?" Allen, the coroner's assistant asked me over the phone at 6 AM.

While in college, I worked night shift in a large city hospital. I transported patients, set up orthopedic equipment, performed simple procedures, and did anything I was asked to do to help the nurses, ward clerks, or doctors. Occasionally the morgue staff needed a hand. Usually I transported bodies to the morgue.

"I'll be right down," I told him, and then hurried down the stairs.

When I got to the basement, I walked down the narrow hallway to the morgue. I had been there frequently enough, but it still made me a little nervous whenever I went down there. When I opened the morgue door, I saw Allen, who was tall, thin and wearing a long blue vinyl gown, preparing the room for the autopsy.

"I need help lifting a body to the autopsy table," he informed me as he handed me a gown and gloves. "It is going to be a bloody mess."

"What happened?"

"The victim was stabbed multiple times and is laying in an inch of his own blood," he told me as I put on the gown and latex gloves. The room was dimly lit, and as I glanced around I could see various jars labeled "liver" and "kidney" that were neatly stacked on shelves.

He opened the door to the cooler and pulled out one of the trays with a body on it. The victim was an African-American male. He had a goatee and was fully clothed with multiple stab wounds in his chest. His eyes were closed, and his clothes were soaked with blood. He was in his 20s and was very muscular.

"He was found in an alley this morning. They think it was a drug deal that went bad."

"Looks like someone was a little angry," I commented.

"Definitely overkill," he surmised. He was used to dealing with the carnage left from people's anger. It had become routine for him. For me, this young man was the first murder victim I had seen. I'll never forget it. His face appeared peaceful even though his death was tragic and violent.

His dark brown shirt was bloody and had multiple knife slits. A few drops of blood splattered on his beige dress pants and his wing-tipped shoes.

"You are going to have to put your hands under his upper body, and I'll get under his waist and legs. We have to lift him up to the table," Allen instructed.

"Sure," I answered as I put my arms under his trunk and head. I could feel the cold blood soak through the gown.

"Just slowly lift him up."

We lifted him together as some of the blood dripped off my arms and onto the floor. The man weighed about 200 pounds, but with the two of us lifting it was not too heavy. We carried him over to the shiny metal autopsy table and then slowly lowered him until he rested on it. Allen positioned a curved block of wood under his neck to support his head.

"Thanks for your help."

"No problem," I replied. The experience was sobering. A young man lost his life. It was a sad. I took off the bloody gown and gloves and washed off my arms in the sink.

It was my initiation to murder. It gave me a healthy respect for the inner city and the people that resided there. Since that time, I have come in contact with other murder victims in the autopsy room. A prostitute was found dead in the city dump with a shotgun blast to her kidney. An inmate was stabbed in the neck. An elderly woman was murdered in her home. A man in his 70s was found dead in his cabin. An autopsy provided the exact cause of death. The prostitute died when the shotgun pellets ruptured the main artery supplying the kidney. The inmate was killed because the carotid artery was slit. The elderly man and woman each died of head injuries. After each case, we had unanswered questions about the murderer, the victim, their families, their friends, and the community. What led up to the murder? What kind of decisions did each individual make?

Through my work treating medical problems in the jail, I occasionally see murderers who are awaiting their trial. Sometimes I ask them questions about their life.

"What happened in your life?" I asked Christopher after I had become acquainted with him.

"My parents raised me to do the right things. They took me to church every Sunday. When I graduated from high school, I enjoyed the good times away from my parent's rules. I was dating a girl who was still in high school, and she became pregnant with my baby. I was excited about being a father, but she wanted to abort the baby.

"I was disappointed and angry when she aborted the baby and broke up with me. She started going out with another guy. When she married him, my resentment grew. One day, I got into a fight with him and released all my anger. I ended going to prison for that."

"How did you end up moving north?" I asked.

"When I got out of prison, I felt I needed a new start. I had paid my penalty. After I checked around for jobs, I located a nice job possibility up here. The company interviewed me and offered me a good salary and benefits. I took it, and everything was going well. On the job, I met a wonderful woman. Neither of us was honest with each other. I didn't tell her about my prison sentence, and she didn't relate to me her previous three marriages. We were in love, and we got married. Our life was going fine, and we had a baby boy. I loved that boy.

"My wife didn't like a few things about our relationship and that would make me angry. I thought we could work things out, but she had to ruin our life. She filed for divorce. We had a family, a nice house, and nice cars. She got the house, and then her ex-husband moved in. I felt betrayed and deceived. I had a few drinks one night, and I went to her house and killed her."

When I talked to him a few times after that, he was trying to work through his feelings. His life consisted of cement walls and bars. He had a lot of time to think. Although the future looked depressing and empty, he had been talking to his pastor and reading his Bible. He was trying to make up for lost time in his relationship with God. Tragically, his poor decisions resulted in the death of a human being and his own confinement in order to protect society.

WHAT DOES THE BIBLE SAY ABOUT MURDER?

In Exodus 20:13 God commands "thou shalt not kill." The verb means to intentionally murder another human being. Throughout the Bible, murders were committed as a result of jealousy, adultery, hatred, anger, and wrong beliefs. In James 1:19b-20 Christians are warned about anger, "…let every man be swift to hear, slow to speak, slow to wrath; For the wrath of man worketh not the righteousness of God."

In the fourth chapter of Genesis, Cain killed Abel. God asked Cain why he was angry. Cain didn't want to talk to God about it. Cain presented a bloodless offering to God of his own works. His act was disobedient to what God asked for. "Without the shedding of blood there is no remission of sin" (Hebrews 9:22; 11:4). Instead of dealing with his own sin, he took his anger out on his brother. His anger was not controlled. He was focused on himself. His brother, Abel, offered a blood sacrifice which expressed the consciousness of his sin and his faith in a substitute for his sin. God instructed Cain to do right and be accepted, or do wrong and trouble will follow. Cain chose to do wrong, and he rose up and killed Abel. He used his hands to shed innocent blood, which God hates according to Proverbs 6:17.

Sometimes people murder because of wrong ideas. Saul, later renamed Paul, in his days of persecuting the early church was involved in the murders of Christians. He thought that these

Christians were against God and the Jews. He was at the stoning of Stephen as recorded in Acts 7:58.

Today, we still have murders of Christians because of false beliefs. Religious extremists are deceived and blow themselves up with bombs and kill others because they have the false belief that they will go to heaven if they kill the unbelievers.

STATISTICS

In the United States, homicide ranks thirteenth as a cause of death. In 2001, 20,308 homicides were reported.[1] The trend in homicides demonstrate that the rates nearly doubled from the mid 1960s to the late 1970s. In 1980, the rate peaked at 10.2 per 100,000 people and remained high until 1992-2000 when the rate declined sharply. Over the last 5 years, the homicide rate has remained at levels seen in the 1960s.

Most murderers have troubled families and friends. They start down a path of alcohol, drugs, pornography, adultery, lies, deceit, and thievery. Then they end up murdering someone.

MARK

"How long have you had this swollen leg?" I inquired of Mark, a 55-year-old gentleman who was bed bound with multiple sclerosis and had just come into the emergency room from the nursing home.

"About four days," he responded.

When I examined his swollen leg, I was impressed by the redness and tension in his thigh and lower leg.

"I'll get an ultrasound to evaluate your veins," I informed him.

After a few hours of caring for the other patients, the ultrasound tech handed me the report. I went to inform Mark.

"Your leg has a big clot in it, and you'll have to stay in the hospital," I told him.

"That's fine. I'm ready for a change of scenery," he said with a positive attitude. He was relatively young for a nursing home patient, and he was conversant and pleasant.

"How long have you had multiple sclerosis?"

"Twenty years."

"What kind of symptoms did you have initially?"

"My leg gave out on me when I walked down some stairs. It kept giving out on me until that leg was so weak, I couldn't walk on it. Eventually, I was in a wheelchair. Then when I needed total care, I went to a nursing home. It took about ten years from my first problem to wheelchair dependence."

He had the progressive, more serious type of multiple sclerosis. Some patients have a single episode of some leg weakness or difficulty with vision and never have any other problems, and some have occasional symptoms due to heat or fatigue and never seem to get worse.

"Do you have any other medical illnesses?"

"No."

"Does your mom or dad have any medical problems?" I asked.

"I only know my foster parents' history."

"How long did you live with them?"

"About two years. I actually was in about ten different homes while I grew up."

I wanted to pursue that conversation, but the emergency room was full. I finished my exam and questions and got him admitted to the hospital.

A few days later, on Easter morning, I visited him in the hospital after I finished my emergency room shift. As I entered his room, the nurse was feeding him his breakfast.

"Can I finish feeding him that?" I suggested to her.

"Sure."

"Good morning, Mark," I greeted him as he finished his breakfast by swallowing the last of his egg.

"Good morning, Doctor."

"I wanted to see how you were doing."

"I'm doing fine. My leg is much better."

"I'm glad about that. It's Easter Sunday morning. You are probably missing a good service at the nursing home."

"Maybe," he responded. "Did you come to tell me a sermon?"

"I've got a good sermon on heaven."

"You can tell me that one. I don't really feel God would ever forgive me and let me into heaven."

"None of us deserve heaven, Mark. We all fall short of God's standard for heaven."

"You too?"

"Yes," I explained to him. "If I could make it to heaven on my own, then Jesus wouldn't have had to come down to earth to die for my sins."

"I didn't know that."

"The Bible explains that 'there is none righteous' in Romans 3:10. It goes on to explain that sin separates us from God. If the Bible ended at that point there would be no hope, but the story didn't end there. God proved His love toward us while we were sinners. He let His son, Jesus Christ, pay the penalty for our sins and die in our place. We have forgiveness of our sins when we believe in what Jesus did for us. We need to ask Him to save us from an eternity separated from God."

Mark listened intently. He was ready to accept God's gift of salvation that Easter Sunday morning. He bowed his head and prayed to accept Jesus Christ into his heart as his personal Savior.

After he was discharged from the hospital, I visited him in the nursing home. I read him some verses and talked with him. One day, I asked him about his life.

"Why did you live in foster care?"

"My mom was 16 when I was born. She dropped me off at the Salvation Army."

"Have you ever seen her?"

"No, I haven't."

"Why did you live in so many foster care homes?"

"I don't think too many people liked me."

"You seem likeable now."

"Thanks. I have learned a few things over the years, and I have to be nice because I need people to take care of me. I can only move my head, and I need the nurses and aides for almost everything I do."

"How did you make people mad?"

"I lied and stole all the time. If I didn't have school supplies, I stole them."

"Did you know the top two problems in adopted kids are lying and stealing?"

"I didn't know that."

"You can finish your story."

"It was because of my attitude that I didn't make it through high school. I dropped out and learned to do construction work. I worked for quite a few years doing that. When I was 29, I got married. My marriage was difficult from the start. My wife got pregnant and that seemed to make things worse. I grew frustrated and so did she. Instead of working on our marriage, we became more negative towards each other and drifted apart. Once our relationship started going bad, I didn't know how to make it whole again.

"One day on the way to work, I saw this pretty blonde-haired lady. I saw her on several different days after that on my way to work. One day I stopped at her house and told her that I was having trouble with my truck. I asked her for a pair of pliers. She went into her house and got them for me. I didn't really have any problems with my truck. I was lying, and I had something else in mind.

"When she returned, I pointed my hunting rifle at her. I asked her to go back into her house. She did. When she got in the house, she ran to her bedroom. As I got back to her bedroom, she came out from behind a door and started hitting me with an ashtray. I panicked. I thought she would do what I wanted if I had a gun pointed at her. I finally shot and killed her.

"Her work noticed that she didn't show up. They called her and didn't get an answer. They finally went to her house and found her dead. The police matched the bullet to the type of gun. They talked to the gun shops, and one store owner remembered selling a rifle to me. About seven months after the murder, the police showed up at my door. They arrested me. I was sentenced to 40 to 60 years in prison.

"While in the state penitentiary, I developed multiple sclerosis. My disease eventually paralyzed my legs and I required a wheelchair. After that they let me out of prison. At age 51 I could only eat and breathe. My wife and son wouldn't have anything to do with me."

"I visited with Mark a few times after that. One day I learned from a nurse at the nursing home that he had died. I thought about his life. He was abandoned, unruly, dishonest, uncommitted, and killed a woman.

God still cares about murderers. He can change their hearts. My friend with multiple sclerosis had a change of heart. He confessed his sin and asked for forgiveness. He asked God to save him. He suffered for his crime. His victim and her family also suffered greatly because of his senseless selfish act.

DAVID BERKOWITZ

David Berkowitz, the Son of Sam killer, also caused needless suffering. I heard his story on a Focus on the Family broadcast. Nothing can change the fact that he killed six people and injured seven in 1977. On the radio, David said he wasn't looking for any sympathy. He said he deserved death, but instead he will spend the rest of his life behind bars with regret that he injured and killed people. He was sympathetic to the families of those that he hurt and killed.

As a child David Berkowitz was adopted into a Jewish family because his birth mother couldn't care for him. While his father worked many hours in the hardware business, his mother nurtured him. When David was 14, his adopted mother developed breast cancer and died. Since David wasn't close to his dad, he spent most of his time with neighborhood friends and started drinking beer and getting into trouble. Hatred grew in his life. He said that if he would have talked to someone and asked for help maybe he could have avoided some of the problems he got into. When he graduated he did a stint in the army which didn't prove to be what he was looking for.

After the service, he became involved in Satanism and pornography which sent him down a vicious spiral to murder. He said he didn't value people. He was so hurt and rejected that he didn't care if he hurt others. When he was first in prison, he howled like an animal, had pornography posted all over his cell, and communicated through the mail with Satanists. Another inmate tried to kill him by stabbing him in the neck, but David survived. Eventually, after years in prison, another inmate encouraged him to study the Bible. While reading the Psalms one night, David broke down and asked forgiveness for his sins. God forgave him.

David has had a lot of time in prison to study the Bible and grow towards God. When given the opportunity, he tells people through radio, television, or through his website of the saving power of Jesus Christ, who turned the "Son of Sam" killer into the "Son of Hope." His hope is that his testimony may prevent others from the mistakes that he made. On his website, he states only Jesus Christ can change a serial killer and an avowed Satanist into a lover of people and a lover of God.[2]

Chapter Fifteen

Thou Shalt Not Kill (Yourself)

There is a 23-year-old white male coming in by ambulance in five minutes with a self-inflicted gunshot wound to the left chest," the physician assistant announced to me as I walked through the emergency doors for my night shift.

"Did you notify the surgeon on call?" I inquired.

"He will be in as soon as he can."

When the patient arrived, he appeared as white as the sheet that was covering him. He was unconscious.

"His blood pressure has been barely audible at 80 over 40 (120/80 is normal) with a rapid pulse of 135 (60-100 is normal). He shot himself because his girlfriend broke up with him," the paramedic informed me as I pointed the way to the trauma room.

As I pulled the sheet off his chest, I saw the dime-sized bullet wound just to the left of his sternum. When I listened for lung sounds on the left side of his chest, I couldn't hear any.

The fluids and blood were flowing into his veins from the intravenous bags being squeezed by nurses. Oxygen was being delivered to his lungs by way of an endotracheal tube. An x-ray revealed a collapsed left lung with blood filling up one third of the thoracic cavity, and a bullet was lodged next to his fifth thoracic vertebrae.

I realized that he must have missed the heart and all the major blood vessels because he was still alive and maintaining his blood pressure. As the surgeon inserted a chest tube to drain the blood and re-inflate the lung, I got on the phone to the major trauma center to give them a report of what had transpired. Soon he was on a helicopter for further treatment and subsequent care.

I saw him several years after the incident. He didn't recall the incident at all. His bullet wound healed up well. His lack of memory was probably due to the shock that he went through.

PREVALENCE

He was one of approximately 500,000 patients who are treated yearly in emergency rooms for suicide attempts.[1] Most are drug overdoses that require stomach pumping and psychiatric care. The number of actual suicides yearly is around 30,000 which have outnumbered homicides over the last few years. Among adults, it is the eleventh leading cause of death, and among adolescents, it is the third leading cause of death.[2] I wasn't aware of how common suicides were until I did a rotation on forensic pathology and spent a month in the morgue. On one Monday morning, there were three suicide victims to do autopsies on. One young man shot himself in the temple, another overdosed, and a third hung himself. It was depressing.

RISK FACTORS

The strongest risk factors for attempted suicide in adults are depression, alcohol abuse, cocaine use, and separation or divorce.

A JUDGE STRUGGLES

Professionals are not immune. A judge in our area brought this to light when he came to the emergency room with slit wrists. He had taken some sleeping pills and tried to kill himself with carbon monoxide. When that didn't work, he used a fishing knife to cut his wrists. He survived his desperate attempts. After the suicide attempt, he thought about resigning, but decided to press on with his work to show that he and others dealing with depression can lead productive lives. He detailed to the reporter how he had battled with depression and anxiety for 20 years. He had treatment from a psychiatrist and had taken an antidepressant, but his persistent sadness continued. After he burned himself accidentally, he took pain medicine and a sleeping pill in addition to his antidepressant. He felt the combined effect of all the drugs caused him to think irrationally and led to his suicide attempt. While his wrists were healing he started intensive therapy to help him work through his depression. In time he could see that his life was worth living. It took 8 weeks of counseling and medication before he was cleared to go back to work again.[3]

A Doctor Dies

At 40 years old, a medical doctor had everything going for him. He worked at a major medical center, made trips to help people in other countries, was married with three daughters, and had close friends. Despite everything good in his life, according to his friend, he had battled depression since medical school. He finally sought help and was diagnosed with severe depression. He was getting treatment, but he felt overwhelmed. Before he could get through his treatment program, he hung himself.

His dad commented, "All the nevers kind of pile up on us. He's never going to walk in this house again. He's never going to sit down to a meal with us. He's never going to walk his daughters down the aisle."[4]

I commend the judge and the doctor's family for sharing their story to help others. I'm sure it was painful for them. If people talk honestly about depression and suicide, then maybe the suicide rate will decline. In 2002, the suicides outnumbered homicides 31,655 to 17,638, respectively.[5]

Spiritual Leaders

Church leaders are not immune to problems either. Tim LaHaye wrote a book *How to Win Over Depression*. Despite his success in ministry, he struggled with depression at one point. In his book, he offered insights he gathered in his dealings with depression.[6]

I was saddened to read the newspaper story of Johnnie Carl, the conductor of the Crystal Cathedral Orchestra. He shot himself after an argument with another employee. He had grappled with depression for nearly 30 years.[7]

There are many others in ministry positions who have struggled with depression or have committed suicide. Ministers constantly deal with people and their problems. They hear complaints, make decisions, and try to maintain their own personal relationship with God. They are sometimes torn between church activities and responsibilities in their own family. Part of our responsibilities as church members is to be aware and pray for all that our pastors are going through.

DEPRESSION

Depression affects 20 million Americans. Mental health experts say major depression is the leading cause of disability in the United States. It affects nearly 10 percent of adult Americans every year, nearly twice as many women as men. Some people are helped by counseling, but medication is needed to help others. Throughout history Abraham Lincoln, Calvin Coolidge, Lyndon Johnson, Richard Nixon, Greg Louganis, Terry Bradshaw, Ted Turner, Vincent Van Gogh, Norman Rockwell, Ernest Hemingway, Judy Garland, and Sheryl Crow have all suffered from depression.[8] If it is severe, counseling and medication, as well as inpatient treatment, may be necessary. Of those with severe depression 85 percent will feel good again, but 30 percent will attempt suicide and 15 percent will kill themselves. Symptoms that warrant a visit to your doctor include persistent sadness, loss of interest in activities, decreased appetite and weight, substance abuse, disturbed sleep, feelings of worthlessness or excessive guilt, and recurrent thoughts of suicide or death.[9]

SELF-MEDICATION

I hear it often said that drinking or drugs are a way of self-medicating. In other words, a person has a mental health problem and they take alcohol or drugs to make them feel better. Of course in the mentally ill the drugs or alcohol usually make the situation worse.

In people without mental illness, the addiction itself leads to the depression. Dr. Thomas Haynes, a specialist in addiction medicine states, "Almost all addicts are depressed. So it's very difficult to diagnose depression while they're using substances." Dr. Wayne Creelman, medical director of Pine Rest Christian Mental Health Services, states regarding major depression, "Patients tell me, 'It's like I've fallen into this black hole and I can't get out.' "[10]

The bottom line is don't self-medicate. If you need help, get professional help. Don't risk your brain by taking alcohol, illegal drugs, and in some cases legal drugs.

ERNEST HEMINGWAY

While I was in college, I read *For Whom the Bell Tolls* by Ernest Hemingway. The book was about the Spanish Revolution and taught me some of the negatives of war such as wandering without shelter, cruelty, and the loss of normalcy. His writings made the suffering real to me.

As I read Hemingway's biography, I learned that he killed himself with his own shotgun after two lengthy illnesses. He was only 62.[11] I wondered why such a successful writer would end his own life. Now as I look back on it, he had a few risk factors for suicide. He was approaching an age where suicide is more common, and, in addition, had two lengthy illnesses. Elderly males are six times more likely to commit suicide. Males over 65 years old account for 19 percent of suicides. It is felt that depression and coexisting medical illness account for the high suicide rate.[12]

A FREQUENT PATIENT

I read a story about a physician who treated an elderly gentleman every week for some minor complaint. The man enjoyed interacting with the staff, and he always paid his bill. The physician finally sat down with him for two hours and did a complete history and physical. He found nothing wrong. He suggested to the man, who had lost his wife two years earlier, that he might consider befriending a widow or hire a housekeeper.

The physician said he felt guilty taking the man's money when he didn't have any medical complaint worthy of his attention. The doctor suggested the man schedule an appointment in six months. The man went out after paying his bill and hung himself later that night. The doctor felt terrible. Now he tries to screen people more thoroughly about what goes on in their minds.[13]

WICCA

Suicide can also result from demonic possession or witchcraft. A 17-year-old high school dropout in our community was a follower of Wicca, the modern name for witchcraft. He prayed to a goddess and god with the goal of gaining harmony with the cycles of nature and touching the spiritual world. It didn't help him. He saw a doctor and was put on an antidepressant. He also struggled with alcohol and drug addiction. Subsequently, he tried to kill himself several times. One attempt with a pistol that failed to fire when he pulled the trigger and another time with an overdose. After more counseling, he was still troubled. One day he argued with his sister, and he lost it. He killed her with a baseball bat and a knife.

I saw the young man in the jail a few times. He didn't say much. His trial was brief, and he was convicted of murder. Presently he is serving out his life sentence in prison. In a newspaper interview he stated, "I regret my entire life. I regret not killing myself when I had the chance."

I wonder what it would have taken to change his life before it spiraled downward. Did demonic possession or witchcraft have anything to do with his depression? The prosecuting attorney had a different thought. "He's manipulative," the attorney said. "Everybody's to blame but him. His alcoholic dad beat him. He took drugs. Pick one; that's why he said he did this. Clearly, it wasn't his fault that he butchered his family." The attorney offered another explanation: "Some people are just evil."[14]

While I was in Brazil at a mission hospital on the Amazon River a young lady came in unconscious and severely brain-damaged from a hanging. She had a large anterior abrasion on her neck where the rope had strangled her. After several days, she passed away. Apparently three young people from the Indian village had committed suicide within one month. From what I heard, the village people blamed the witchdoctor, who had recently come to the area, for putting hexes on the young people. The people felt the witchdoctor had an evil influence on the young people. Many of them were affected by his teaching and his powers. The leaders of the village, who were responsible for law enforcement, took the witchdoctor outside of the village and killed him. There were no more suicides after that.

SPORTS AND ENTERTAINMENT

Suicide has affected many in the entertainment and sports world. They have fame, money, women—and emptiness. Deion Sanders described his suicide attempt after cocaine and adultery didn't satisfy him, in his book *Power, Money, and Sex: How Success Almost Ruined My Life.* In the entertainment world, Nirvana's lead singer Kurt Cobain killed himself at age 27 after struggles with a heroin addiction,[15] and INXS (pronounced "in excess") lead singer Michael Hutchence committed suicide in a Sydney hotel room at the age of 37.[16]

PREVENTION

As a physician I try to screen patients for thoughts about suicide. Sometimes it is difficult when the patient doesn't take the questioning seriously. However, it is important to document that the patient at least denies suicidal thoughts. One patient in the emergency room had some problems with his relationships and alcohol. I thought I had better ask the middle-aged man a few questions to see if he had any thoughts of suicide.

"You got in a fight tonight?"

"If you want to call it that."

"What would you call it?"

"We were arguing, and I slipped and hit my head."

"What were you arguing about?"

"My wife was complaining that I drink too much."

"Do you?"

"Yes, I do."

"Would you say you felt hopeless because you can't quit drinking?"

"When I'm drinking, I don't feel hopeless. It is only when I'm sober that I feel hopeless."

"Have you ever thought about suicide?"

"Yes, I have been thinking about suicide," he answered me in a quieter tone of voice. "I think you ought to commit it."

I appreciated his sense of humor, and then I set up an evaluation for him with a mental health professional.

In order to help health care providers assess patients, there are a variety of programs used to estimate suicide risk. One assessment tool has been developed by the San Francisco Suicide Prevention team.[17] They ask if the person has a plan. How lethal (gun or a rope with noose) is the plan? Is the opportunity to carry out the plan available to them? Is there mental illness? Is there depression? Has there been a previous attempt? Is the person alone? Have they experienced a recent loss? Is there any substance abuse? The mnemonic is "PLAID PALS." If a person has significant risk of suicide then they need to be hospitalized. They can be taken to a mental health hospital for assessment or to an emergency room.

Can we prevent some suicides by treating people better? While I was in college there was a 44-year-old man in our church that was mentally slow. I talked to him a few times. He was likeable, but he was different. Most people didn't include him in their circle of friends. Maybe he felt shunned. I was surprised and saddened when I learned that he shot himself in the head with a handgun. After that happened I became more aware of the struggles the mentally ill go through. They are definitely at higher risk for suicide. Hopefully, in our conversations with people, we can be aware of the struggles they encounter and show genuine concern.

I listened to "A Man Called Norman" by Michael Atkins on a "Focus on the Family" broadcast. Mr. Atkins told how Norman, who was a hermit, went on a bumper car ride at the amusement park. By accident, Norman blocked some of the other cars in a corner for half the ride. When the drivers of the blocked cars finally broke free, they were mad. They individually came back at Norman and banged into his car. They hit him one after another. When Michael Atkins reflected on that experience, he realized that Norman's life was probably just like that bumper ride. People would just hit him, one after another, until he became a recluse.

Church attendance has been shown to be a deterrent to suicide. A survey in Maryland showed that people who did not attend religious services were four times more likely to commit suicide than those who attended church regularly.[18] In other studies, a belief in a higher power, a purpose in one's life, or the power of prayer were shown to be protective against suicide.[19]

Separation, divorce, or infidelity can lead to depression and suicide. When people are joined together as one, it is very painful to be ripped apart. I remember one young lady who was sobbing uncontrollably. She was on an emergency room stretcher with the back of the gurney propped up. Both her wrists were slit from a suicide attempt. Why would such a beautiful young lady want to end her life? After she settled down and had her wrist lacerations repaired, she explained her grief. She had been married for several years, and her husband had just asked two of his boyfriends to move in with them. It crushed her.

WHAT DOES THE BIBLE SAY?

Does God prohibit suicide? In Exodus 20:13 a commandment states, "Thou shalt not kill." God doesn't want us to kill ourselves. He loves us. He is the creator and author of our life. He sustains our life. Our breath is in His hands (Daniel 5:23). He has a plan for our life, and we do not belong to ourselves (1 Corinthians 6:20). Suicide cuts short what God may be doing in our lives to prepare us for future ministry. That is why Satan is anxious to discourage us and take us out of the picture. Remember, his goal is to steal, kill, and destroy. Not only does he steal the love, joy, and peace that God desires for us, but then he wants us to kill ourselves. Then when he gets us off the planet, he will continue to destroy our family, the church, and the unsaved that are watching the tragedy of our death and its consequences.

WERE THERE SUICIDES IN THE BIBLE?

In Judges 16:23-31, Samson was brought out to entertain the Philistine rulers during sacrifices to their god, Dagon. After he entertained them, they stood him by the pillars that supported the roof of the temple. The temple was crowded, and about 3000 men and women were on the roof. Samson asked God for the strength to bring down the pillars and collapse the roof to avenge the loss of his two eyes. God granted him the strength. "Let me die with the Philistines" was his final request. He died that day and killed more Philistines than he had killed in his entire life.

Ahithophel hung himself after Absalom, David's son, did not listen to his advice to go after and kill David (2 Samuel 17:23).

Zimri, who had done evil in the eyes of the Lord, committed suicide by setting the palace on fire when the Israelites surrounded him (1 Kings 16:15-20).

Saul and his armor bearer both fell on their swords before their capture (1 Samuel 31:2-5).

Judas Iscariot hung himself after he betrayed Jesus Christ (Matthew 27:3-5). After Jesus had been bound and the chief priests and elders advised that He be put to death, Judas repented and tried to give back the thirty pieces of silver. He said that he had betrayed innocent blood. The chief priests and elders said that it wasn't their problem. Judas threw the silver to the floor of the temple, and went out and hung himself.

Whatever the reason (guilt, depression, rejection, revenge, pain, poor physical health, demonic possession, stress, rebellion), suicide isn't God's plan. We are missing out on what God has for us.

What Did God Accomplish Through Those who Thought About Suicide?

In Job 7:1-6, Job states "so that my soul chooseth strangling, and death rather than my life." After Job's loss of family members, possessions, and health, he didn't feel like living. He endured his trial one day at a time with God's help. Then God blessed him with twice as much as he had before. He went on to live another 140 years, and saw four generations after him (Job 42:16).

Moses (Numbers 11:11-15) and Elijah (1 Kings 19:4) also asked for death, but God encouraged them and guided them to accomplish more.

The Philipian jailer, in Acts 16:27, wanted to kill himself, but Paul and Silas stopped him and explained to him how he could be a Christian. He believed in God that night.

Jesus Christ was also tempted by Satan to throw Himself down off the temple. Jesus resisted the temptation and went on to die for the sins of the world (Matthew 4:5-6).

There is so much to live for. Even though many of us have those times when we wonder if the pain and suffering are worth it. It is. Live on.

Chapter Sixteen

A BROKEN HEART

Describe your chest pain to me," I asked Kent, a middle-aged man, who had been to the emergency room three times in the last two weeks. Although he appeared comfortable, well groomed, and intelligent, he was distressed.

"It is a heavy sensation that makes it hard for me to take a deep breath," he explained to me.

"What makes your pressure worse?"

"I notice it most when I am not doing anything. If I am up moving around or active, I don't think about it."

"I've looked over the tests that were done on the previous visits. You have had electrocardiograms, blood tests, and a stress test which were all normal. You don't have any risk factors of smoking, sedentary lifestyle, high cholesterol, obesity, or relatives with heart disease before age 55. You exercise by riding your mountain bike for at least 30 minutes every day and that doesn't reproduce your symptoms. Your heart doesn't seem to be the problem," I assured him.

"I wanted to make sure. I didn't think it was my heart, but yet the pressure persisted."

"Do you have problems with heartburn after greasy meals or spicy foods?"

"I have occasional heartburn, but this pressure is different."

He seemed to be having an anxiety type of chest pressure.

"What is the biggest stress in your life right now?"

He hesitated. His eyes looked away as he dealt with his emotions.

"I have been separated from my wife for four months now. This week, we went out to dinner for our 25th wedding anniversary. She told me that she wasn't ready to get back together and may never be ready," he confided. I could sense his hopelessness, his grief, and his loss. His chest pressure was coming from a broken heart.

"Do you think your chest pressure is related to this emotional turmoil that you are going through?"

"Yes, I think it probably is."

"It's hard to go through marital problems. Have you been to a family counselor, or a minister?"

"I have been talking to my pastor. He has been helpful."

"That's good. I'm afraid I can't do anything more for you in the emergency room."

"That's okay. I feel better. I am ready to go home."

"I hope things work out for you. If you ever feel you need to get checked out again, don't hesitate to come back."

"Thanks."

"I will have the nurse give you a crisis number. If you ever feel overwhelmed and can't contact your other support, then call that number. You also need to follow up with your doctor. He can monitor your progress, and prescribe something for you if you need it," I explained to him.

The Consequences of Divorce

Marriages today are falling apart too frequently. Lives are left in disarray. Most of the time, I see the fallout when people come in with stress-related illness, suicide attempts, alcoholism, drug abuse, depression, and more. My heart goes out to these people. Of course, I don't know the circumstances of this man's separation. Was the marriage hopeless, or could the problems be worked through?

In the jail, the fallout of divorce is much more severe. One man was convicted of murdering his ex-wife the day before he was due in court for delinquent child support payments. His marriage of 22 years ended because of differences, but also because of his alcoholism. Another mother who went through a divorce and a job loss snapped psychologically and stabbed her two children to death. She also stabbed herself, but the wound was not life-threatening. Could counseling have prevented such tragedies?

I know marriage isn't always easy. It is hard work, and many problems and situations have to be worked through. Billy Graham's daughter said she wished her mom and dad would have argued a little more, then she would have had a more realistic observation of marriage. After her first big fight with her husband, she was shocked that there could be such disagreement between two people who loved each other.

A LIFELONG COMMITMENT

My in-laws and my parents both celebrated their 50th wedding anniversary in the past few years. I thanked them for their commitment to each other and for this accomplishment in their life. It is a blessing to be part of a family that takes commitment seriously. I know many people do not have that privilege. It is the responsibility of each couple to be serious about their marriage vows and give their family the privilege of faithfulness. Five percent of couples make it to the 50th anniversary milestone in their marriage. While 33 percent of all married people reach their 25th anniversary.

THE INCREASE IN DIVORCE AND DYSFUNCTION

What has happened to our society over this past century? In the 1930s 25 percent of couples ended their marriage in divorce. In the 1950s, 33 percent divorced. By the 1970s, 41 percent divorced, and in the 1980s we surpassed the 50 percent mark.[1]

Since our families are troubled, our society becomes more dysfunctional. Many young people live together, but the failure rate of cohabitation is worse than the marriage failure rate. In Europe, where marriage rates are plummeting and illegitimate births are the norm, the rate for cohabitation is over 50 percent for 25-34 year-olds. Europeans also lead the way on gay marriage as well. People rationalize that if marriage and cohabitation fail consistently, then why not try homosexuality where couples know better how to meet each other's needs. As we stray from God's design for marriage, we only get more chaos. Marriage, if it is based on commitment, love, respect, and a giving attitude, is still the best institution for couples. Married people do better financially and emotionally. They live longer and are better adjusted. Research also shows that children reared in stable two-parent families thrive.[2]

The effects of divorce are evident in statistics. Children in single-parent families are more likely to drop out of high school, become pregnant as teenagers, abuse drugs, and get into trouble with the law than those living with both parents. Fatherless homes account for 63 percent of youth suicides, 90 percent of homeless/runaway children, 85 percent of children with behavior problems, 71 percent of high school dropouts, 85 percent of youths in prison, and well over 50 percent of teen mothers.[3]

MARRIAGE ISN'T ALWAYS EASY

God meant marriage for the stability of society. I thought marriage was easy at first. I got my wake-up call when my wife and I watched the Gary Smalley video series "Love Is a Decision." She rated our marriage below what I thought it should have been. In my mind, if I treated my wife nice, was faithful, gave her flowers and candy on special occasions as well as in between, and attended church, then I should be above average. I was upset at her low rating of our marriage. My first thought was to blame her. Maybe she was discontent and unsatisfied with life in general. My second thought was that I was missing some ingredient that could increase her happiness. After extended discussions with her without coming up with any conclusive answers, I started reading books. The biggest help to me was reading Dr. James Dobson's book *What Wives Wish Their Husbands Knew About Women*. He interviewed and surveyed thousands of women about their depression and came up with the top ten causes of women's depression and what men could do about it. The top reason was lack of self-esteem. I began to understand a few things that would be upsetting to her. If I was asked how important my wife and my marriage was to me, I would answer that it was very important. Beside my relationship to God, it was a top priority for me.

Although in practicality, the time I spent at work, playing sports, visiting with my mom, dad, brothers, and friends probably didn't give her the time she needed. I had to realize that we both had different needs. Instead of growing apart in dissatisfaction, we built our marriage to a more satisfying level by communication. We had to give and take. We sought balance.

In Dr. Emerson Eggerichs' book *Love & Respect*, he explained the need to love our wives unconditionally as Paul said in Ephesians 5:33. He reminded me to reassure my wife of my love frequently, show affection to her, and be thoughtful and creative on birthdays and anniversaries. He added the importance of a loving caress and a hug. For the women, he talked about how to respect your man. Even if he gets you the wrong gift believe in his good will. Don't talk disrespectful and condescending. He emphasized the need to talk pleasantly to each other and not offend one another.

I read a magazine article that encouraged spending thirty minutes a day talking to your wife. The author said it was like putting money in the bank. It made sense to me. Sometimes after dinner, I sit and talk with my wife, or later in the evening we take a walk and share our thoughts on the day or discuss situations about the car, kids, work, the schedule, or finances.

When my wife and I got engaged, a woman told my wife that there would be times when she would feel like flushing me down the toilet. At the time, I couldn't imagine her being that mad at me. Of course, after twenty years of marriage, I've come close to being flushed a few times. The important thing to realize is that there will be rough times.

Marriage is a commitment. I know commitment scares some people, but it is the glue that holds many marriages together. Without commitment, it is easy to throw in the towel and call it quits. When couples give up on their first marriage, usually a second marriage runs into the same kind of problems. Couples are better off working through their problems in the first marriage. I've had many friends and relatives go through divorces, and I know not every marriage can be saved. However, we need to do better as a society in picking lifelong mates and staying together.

INFIDELITY

I enjoyed reading Jerry Jenkins book *Loving Your Marriage Enough to Protect It*. He wrote that the media has convinced too many people that adultery is no more serious than exceeding the speed limit. But it is a major problem for marriages. As a teenager, I observed two couples socialize together frequently. Eventually, the one husband married the other man's wife. I remember the devastation that occurred because of that. Jerry Jenkins advises hedges of protection for marriages. One hedge is not to spend time alone with a member of the opposite sex. One of the nurses at work told me that she allowed her husband to travel with another woman out of state for their National Guard duty. She was a little upset when they ended up staying in a hotel room together to save money. Within months this young nurse's marriage ended in divorce, and she was crushed.

A few other hedges were about touching or complimenting the opposite sex. What do you convey when you flirt? What is appropriate and what is not? He summarized Dr. James Dobson's comments that husbands and wives ought to meet each other's need for pleasure, romance, sex, and ego strokes. In other words, take care of your wife, and I'll take care of mine.

Another helpful hedge in marriage is reminding your spouse that you are keeping your vows. It is reassuring to hear that your spouse takes their wedding vows seriously. Years of faithfulness builds trust, but hedges are still important to protect us from our own weaknesses.

The last hedge was spending quality and quantity time with the family. Have fun together. Take vacations together. I've always believed in family time because my father spent time with our family. Jerry also mentioned spending individual time with each child. Dr. James Dobson put out a series called "Preparing for Adolescence," and he suggested taking each child away for a few days and listening to the tapes. I took his advice and spent time with each child before they entered the hectic teenage years. We spent time together doing something they wanted to do. It was something that took effort, but it was worth it. I love each one of my kids, and the trip alone with Dad helped them to know that.

Jerry Jenkins wrote the book about hedges for the purpose of protecting our marriages, and providing love and security for our wives and children.

ONE FLESH

I've heard reasons of divorce because of financial stress, infidelity, abuse, alcoholism, drugs, and mental illness. One deputy at the jail was divorced because his wife wanted out. Now she wants money for kid's school supplies and clothes. If he gives her money, his new wife complains. If he doesn't give her money, he feels like he is denying his kids what they need. He is caught in between and can't seem to make anybody happy. A male nurse at the jail, who has recently suffered through a divorce, offered his view on marriage and divorce with the statement "love is grand, and divorce is 200 grand."

I know some divorces are inevitable and unavoidable, but I believe many are preventable with the proper counseling and support. Our country depends on people who will take the marriage covenant seriously. A divorce rips people apart.

In Genesis 2:23-24 Adam said, "This is now bone of my bones, and flesh of my flesh; she shall be called Woman, because she was taken out of Man. Therefore shall a man leave his father and his mother, and shall cleave unto his wife; and they shall be one flesh" (KJV).

A SUCCESS STORY

In Heather Jamison's book *Reclaiming Intimacy*, she explained some of the difficulties she had in her marriage.

A little over a year into our marriage, Brian and I purchased a very small, one-bedroom house. Again, we thought a change of scenery might improve our perspectives. It didn't.

A month after we moved in, I moved out. Our fighting, which had occurred regularly since the wedding, had become more intense. Our words now seethed with hate. In two years of dating, we had argued only once. Brian had been angry with me only that one time, and then very briefly and very controlled. And I had been angry with him only that one time as well.

Now we targeted our disappointments at one another. I was disappointed that I had to work besides taking on the responsibilities at home and limiting my extracurricular college activities. Brian was disappointed that our marriage had created friction within his family. I was disappointed that boys on campus treated me better than my own husband did. Brian was disappointed that girls on campus treated him better than his own wife did. I was disappointed that I was lonely. We were both disappointed that we couldn't ever get along.

It wasn't the disappointment, though, that caused me to leave. It is what we did with our disappointments. We tried to crucify each other with our words—daily. After so many months of dishing it out and receiving it, I no longer cared about hope. I no longer cared about God's judgment if we divorced. I no longer cared about forgiving or seeking forgiveness.

So I filed for divorce. Although Brian said he didn't want a divorce, he signed the papers giving me no contest. He said he knew I was serious, and he wanted to cooperate in order to avoid further nastiness. Great, I thought. So the divorce is all of a sudden on my shoulders.

Something remarkable happened, though, when I filed for a divorce. Brian and I both got the wind knocked out of us. When we met in a public place to talk about the divorce papers, we didn't burn with anger. We were calm.

I had moved back in with my parents, and occasionally Brian would call me. Our conversations seemed different. They had an element of concern. As the months dragged on, and the court date to finalize our divorce loomed nearer, we saw each other from time to time and never fought.

I am not sure what made the change come about. Perhaps it was God's mercy acting on two hearts that were defeated. Love and trust had not been restored, but the hate had begun to dissipate. The thought occurred to me that I would be going ahead with a divorce simply because I wanted out.

I had made a decision to divorce amid emotional upheavals and a desire for peace. Now I was thinking clearly, and we were behaving a bit more congenially. I thought, how can I knowingly break God's commandment against divorce simply because I want out of my marriage? Although my relationship with God was tenuous at the time, and neither Brian nor I were going to church, I knew enough from recent experience that willingly breaking God's commandments would result in dire consequences. Would fear of God be enough of a foundation to hold my marriage together?

Brian had signed the papers months earlier, but all along he had said he was opposed to the divorce. I knew he would agree if I called it off. My thoughts turned to our daughter. She was only eight months old. Was I going to affect her life so drastically simply because I didn't want to care anymore for her daddy? These and other questions consumed me in the last few weeks leading up to our court date.

The separation had given me time to think, and in that time I realized I wanted to do what was right even if doing right didn't agree with my feelings. I hoped that the right emotions would come later. In living through the consequences of my sinfulness and selfishness, my fear of God had grown. I was too afraid to divorce and risk chastisement again. So I called off the divorce a few weeks before it was to become final.

After I moved back into our home the fights, although they still occurred, were less frequent. I think we realized, at last, that we needed to work at this relationship. Before our separation, the possibility of a divorce had kept me from controlling much of my anger. I had, at times, thought that if I made Brian mad enough he would leave me and then I wouldn't have the responsibility of filing. I could blame him and comfort myself with "poor me." Once divorce was no longer an option, I tried to accept things that I didn't like. The finality of a divorce shocked us both out of focusing solely on ourselves. It scared us and woke us up to things we needed to change.

We started going to a Christian marriage counselor who helped us understand what a Christian marriage should look like. We also started watching a preacher on the television each Sunday. At first it was hard, because we had gotten out of the habit of hearing someone speak of spiritual things. It was almost like a foreign language. Brian says he literally forced himself to listen because he knew it was the right thing to do; I followed suit. It seemed like all the preacher ever talked about, though, was Jesus' forgiveness and His death on the cross. That's exactly what Brian and I both needed to hear. After a few months of hearing about the love of Jesus and making efforts to be more kind, we found our anger slowly subsiding.

Then, as part of a course assignment, my college drama class put on a Christmas play. It was the winter that Brian and I celebrated our second wedding anniversary. Each group was responsible for its own material. I'm ashamed to admit that my group's skit wasn't spiritual in the least, but there was another group that was made up of Christians. They did something very simple for their skit, but it was life changing for me.

When it came time for the program, all five of them sat on the stage and took turns reciting different portions of a story written by Max Lucado. The piece, from Lucado's book *God Came Near*, was about Jesus' incarnation. Lucado's words painted a picture of Jesus I had never seen before. This Jesus was approachable, yet divine. He was holy, yet humble. I was mesmerized. I had to get that book. After reading it and other books by Max Lucado, I wanted to get back into church. I wanted to get to know this Jesus personally. Brian also began to read the books I had bought, and his heart was drawn to God. I remember one time when Brian was reading. I looked over at him and saw he had goose bumps on his arms. I asked him what was up, and he said, "This guy writes like you're standing in the very room with Jesus. It's as if I'm there…. It's amazing!"

So we decided to go back to church on Sunday mornings—but just church, mind you. We weren't comfortable enough to join a small group. So we went to church and sat in the back row. We also bought more Christian books to read during the week. And I started to pray for grace and mercy. At the time, that's all I could think of to pray for. I now know that many others, especially my mom, had been faithfully praying for us during that time and long before.

Our premature marriage had had a sickly start, and our hearts had been ready to pull the plug on it. But unbeknownst to us, God had been at work. He had been nursing our marriage as it were in an incubator. All that time, it had been in a place of healing warmed by His grace.[4]

What Can Be Done About the Divorce Rate?

I liked what I read in *Citizen* Magazine[5] about Judge James E. Sheridan in Lenawee County, Michigan. Alarmed by the 70 percent divorce rate in his county, he got together with pastors, judges, magistrates, and mayors to develop a policy to only marry couples who had gone through a pre-marital counseling program. After several years, the divorce rate in his county dropped, and the number of marriages increased. He said he hoped to literally change the culture.

Why did he decide to act? Initially, the number of drunk-driving cases alarmed him. When he read an article by Linda Waite of the University of Chicago, he learned that alcohol-related incidents increase as marriages begin to crumble. He said his court handled 700 new cases of "driving while intoxicated" every year. Many of these cases involved fatalities. Then he considered all the other cases in his court—assault and battery, malicious destruction of property, and disorderly conduct. He also considered some of the weddings he had performed. He realized he had used the power and responsibility given by the people to marry couples who were not ready to be married. Then later he saw them in court as defendants for driving while intoxicated.

When he developed the pre-marital counseling policy and explained it to the other civil-marriage authorities, he got 100 percent support. The policy was instituted in 1996 and is having a positive effect.

Of course his policy is not going to solve the problem of divorce in our nation. We are all responsible. How do we grow closer to each other rather than apart? I heard one preacher say that our marriage is like a triangle with God at the apex, and the husband and wife at the other corners. As the husband and wife grow closer to God, they grow closer to each other.

Chapter Seventeen

DECISION WHEEL

R andy O'Brien, a Christian comedian, said he would like to meet the guy who came up with story problems. For instance, "If Billy has 3 apples and gives 1 to Judy, then how far will the train travel?" It is hard to come up with the right answer when too little information is given.

As a young person grows up in our society, they frequently make decisions when they don't have all the information. The school hands out condoms, the homosexual group plasters posters advertising their meetings all over the hallways, and the high school counselor directs young ladies to the abortion clinic. For the majority of young people, the information they are bombarded with overwhelms any morals that are taught at home or at church.

How can we effectively teach young people how to live a victorious Christian life and avoid the traps that people fall into? I attempted to teach a boys' Sunday School class by developing a diagram that shows what the Bible says is right and wrong. I explained that certain decisions have damaging consequences that can affect them the rest of their lives, and that every person has the capacity for great good or evil.

When Charles Spurgeon was once being shown through the library of Trinity College, Cambridge, he stopped to admire a bust of Byron. The librarian said to him, "Stand here, sir, and look at it."

Spurgeon took the position indicated and, looking upon the bust, remarked, "What an intellectual countenance! What a grand genius!"

"Come, now," said the librarian, "and look at it from this side."

Spurgeon changed his position and, looking on the statue from that viewpoint, exclaimed, "What a demon! There stands a man who could defy the Deity." He asked the librarian if the sculptor had secured this effect designedly.

"Yes," he replied, "he wished to picture the two characters, the two persons—the great, the grand, the almost supergenius that he possessed; and yet the enormous mass of sin that was in his soul."[1]

I tell my class that our decisions determine what path we take, and how the course of history will be affected. We can't just break all the rules and expect to stay in the race. Ginny Owens sings about breaking the rules in the following song:

LAND OF THE GREY

There's a young mother with three children
Got a stable income and a faithful husband, too.
She's searching for her life's meaning.
So she says to her shrink. "I'm leaving home soon!"
Just decided that she couldn't take it anymore,
Didn't look back, she just snuck out the back door.
What's wrong with this picture?
We applaud this behavior
Admire how she breaks away
Oh, it's so clearly cloudy in the land of the grey.
There's a young senator, gifted politician,
So consumed by pursuing his career.
Used to care about what the people wanted,
But now he's learned how to say what they wanna hear.

A million lies and scandals bear his name,
But you'll never see him hide his face in shame—
What is wrong with this picture? We applaud this
　behavior!
He's a hero if he makes mistakes. Oh, it's so cloudy in the
　land of the grey.
What's wrong? What's right? Absolute confusion.
What's black? What's white? Everything looks hazy.
Such scenarios bring me to only one conclusion—
Maybe we've all gone crazy.
Three little kids are praying mama comes home,
And a little town feels violated and betrayed.
Meanwhile, two very unhappy people try to excuse the
　messes that they've made.
But you'll never hear it stated quite that way.
We can't handle it here in the land of the grey.[2]

A DIAGRAM FOR RIGHT AND WRONG

My diagram shows what the Bible condemns in the "Living in Darkness" part of the wheel, and what the Bible encourages in the "Living in the Light" part of the wheel. The gray area of the wheel is in between the light and dark areas and shows activities that could lead to right or wrong activities. For example, the Internet can lead to good or bad information.

In the song, "Land of the Grey," people chose wrong activities because they didn't feel there was a right or wrong. They made decisions that hurt people. According to the Bible, some actions are harmful. I made the diagram not for the purpose of condemning others, but for the purpose of directing people in the ways of God before they condemn themselves. God didn't send Jesus to condemn the world but to save the world (John 3:17).

Decision Wheel

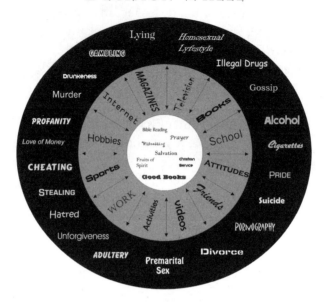

Living in Darkness

Satan wants us to live in the outer circle of darkness. He wants people to be blinded to what Jesus has to offer, and if people do find their way to God he wants to lure them back into activities that distract them from God's purpose.

The Gray Area

In the gray area, the categories listed can bring a person closer to God or turn them away from God. For instance, a book can be a good influence or a bad influence.

Knowing God by J.I. Packer, helped me understand God, but another book I read taught the New Age philosophy that every person is their own God and determines their own right and wrong.

Living in the Light

It takes a step of faith in God through Jesus Christ to live in the light.

In Hebrews 11:6, the Bible states, "But without faith it is impossible to please him."

There is evidence that Jesus Christ existed, performed miracles, and rose from the dead. Many people have sought God and found Him. At some point in every person's life, they must make a decision. They either follow man's philosophy, a false religion, or they look into the Bible and decide to obey the Bible.

If a person believes what the Bible states as truth, then that person can take more steps of faith. They can read God's Word and obey it. They can attend a church that has a Bible-preaching pastor, and develop friendships with other Christians. They can pray to God, serve others, and tell others about Jesus Christ.

DO WE NEED GOD?

I had a friend who told me that people used Christianity as a crutch. He said if people can't stand on their own two feet, then they rely on God to get them through life. I thought about his statements. I wondered if I needed God because I was weak? No, I needed God because I was crippled by my own sinful human nature. I needed God because He is the source of life (Acts 17: 25).

WHAT IS YOUR ADDICTION?

The Bible states in 1 Corinthians 6:12 that "all things are lawful unto me, but all things are not expedient; all things are lawful for me, but I will not be brought under the power of any" (KJV). When I see people addicted to drugs, cigarettes, alcohol, sex, pornography, satanism, homosexuality, gambling, and gluttony, most of them don't want to be addicted. They don't like being controlled by their addictions. Even Christians are controlled by addictions. The apostle Paul described the conflict in Romans 7:19. He said, I should do good, but I don't. I know what is wrong, but I do it anyway.

God wants us to find satisfaction in doing His work, in His way, to accomplish His purpose. He wants us to be addicted to the ministry of the saints (1 Corinthians 16:15). In James 4:7, we are instructed to submit to God, and to resist the Devil. He will flee.

We don't have to be under Satan's authority. We don't have to be controlled by Satan's traps.

The Christian Life Is not Perfect

Our decisions determine how we live on this earth. Even if we make consistently good choices, we all will experience problems and difficulties.

I've seen missionaries go through the death of a wife or a child, pastors go through sickness and disease, Christian couples lose a child in an accident, and a church lose a newly built building to a hurricane. We live in an imperfect world. God can give us peace through troubled times, but he doesn't guarantee a perfect life. Dr. Dobson's book *When God Doesn't Make Sense* goes into detail on this subject.

In contrast, poor choices can lead to an abundance of turbulence. In the first book of the Bible, we see Adam and Eve disobey God and cause sin to enter the human race. By the fourth chapter, God is telling Cain that if he does what is right he will find acceptance, but if he doesn't sin will be waiting. Cain chose to have the wrong attitude and killed his brother, Abel. Throughout life, we either live with the pain of discipline and do the right things, or we make the wrong decisions and live with the pain of regret.

Temptation

New Age philosophy teaches there is no universal right and wrong. Shirley MacLaine, an actress, stood on a cliff overlooking the beautiful blue Pacific Ocean and spread out her arms to the sky and proclaimed, "I am God." She determined her own right and wrong. No person had any right to judge her. She could do whatever she wanted within society's laws. It sounds tempting, but would it make us happy? It didn't make star football player Deion Sanders happy when he had an abundance of money, drugs, and women.

Is self-gratification what life is all about? Satan tried to tempt Jesus with wealth and power, but Jesus answered with the power of God's Word in Luke 4. "It is written, Man shall not live by bread alone, but by every word of God." "It is written, Thou shalt worship the Lord, thy God, and him only shalt thou serve." "It is written, Thou shalt not put the Lord, thy God, to the test."[3] Jesus knew the Bible, and it provided Him with the answers to Satan's temptations.

CROSSING THE LINE

When a person crosses the line into the "Living in Darkness" area, they can begin a downward spiral that makes it very difficult to get back into the "Living in the Light" area. Just this week at the county jail in Grand Rapids, Michigan, a 19-year-old hung himself. He got involved in drugs, and had to steal to support his habit. He got caught. When he faced the judge, he got prison time. He went back to his cell, waited for an opportunity, tied a sheet around his neck, and hung himself.

We've all spent some time in the "Living in Darkness" area. I've spent enough time there to realize it is not the place to be. I prefer what God has to offer. I accept the reality of my weakness, and the strength of the Lord.

God is looking for men and women who desire to be in the inner circle—a place of humility where a person bows before God and asks for the power of the Holy Spirit to live a God-controlled life.

Chapter Eighteen

NONE OF THESE DISEASES

"If thou wilt diligently hearken to the voice of the Lord thy God, and wilt do that which is right in his sight, and wilt give ear to his commandments, and keep all his statutes, I will put none of these diseases upon thee, which I have brought upon the Egyptians; for I am the Lord that healeth thee" Exodus 15:26 (KJV).

S.I. McMillen, M.D. wrote *None of these Diseases*, after he realized the inadequacy of giving patients a pill for their problems. His patients needed more. Since he couldn't spend hours with each patient explaining why God's wisdom was so important for every aspect of life, he wrote a book that outlined the spiritual, emotional, and physical health benefits of obeying God's Word.

When I was in college, I read the book and presented a report to my religion class. I explained that God's commandments were protective for the Israelites. His wisdom prevented them from the diseases which so many of the Egyptians were afflicted with. His wisdom is still applicable today.

After I presented my report to class, my professor pointed out that not all disease comes from disobedience to God. There are other purposes for illnesses aside from the consequences of wrongdoing. For example, Job lived a good life and went through catastrophe to his family, his possessions, and his health. Jesus Christ lived a perfect life without sin, and He suffered affliction, was mocked, tormented, and crucified on the cross. My professor was right, and God was right also in his commandments for living life. I want to share some of the insights from *None of these Diseases* that impacted my life.

HANDWASHING

As an example of the health benefits of God's laws, in Numbers 19:1-10 God gave Moses instructions on washing the body after dealing with sacrifices. Today, in our society, we wash our hands to prevent spread of disease. It seems like commonsense. In 1840 in Vienna and in other hospitals around the world, there was no protocol for handwashing. In fact, the doctors at that time performed autopsies in the morning and then went directly to the wards to examine patients. One out of every 6 women died on the maternity wards.[1] A young doctor named Ignaz Semmelweis observed the autopsies and the women dying. Ignaz recognized that the teachers doing the autopsies were infecting the living patients, and he instituted a handwashing policy on his ward. The mortality rate dropped to 1 out of 84. The handwashing prevented the spread of germs. It was a commandment by God, and it was a good policy that preserved the health of the people in Bible times, in Vienna, and today.

THE GIFT OF GIVING

The Bible instructs us that we ought to give to others. John D. Rockefeller Sr. didn't always follow that advice. He entered the work world with such intensity that at age 33 he made his first million. At 43, he owned the largest business in the world. At 53, he was the richest man in the world and the world's only billionaire. However, his hair was falling out, and he could only eat milk and crackers. He looked like a mummy. Those who knew him figured he had a year to live.

He only wanted to be loved, but he didn't show any consideration to others. He crushed others in his lust for bigger profits. His own workers in the oil fields of Pennsylvania hanged him in effigy. Because of his fear for those who hated him, he had bodyguards day and night. His wealth was not a source of peace or happiness, nor did it help him sleep well. In his words, he enjoyed nothing. When he realized he was approaching death and wouldn't take a dime into the next life, he began to give his millions away. Because of his generosity, penicillin was discovered, medical progress was made against hookworm, and research was begun on malaria, tuberculosis, diphtheria, and other diseases. As a result many lives were saved. When he gave toward others, his life changed. His health also changed. The self-centeredness went out of his life. He gave in love, and love and gratitude were returned to him. He practiced one of God's eternal laws found in Luke 6:38 (KJV) which reads "...give, and it shall be given unto you..." His life continued to blossom which resulted in others blossoming around him until he was laid to rest at 98 years of age.[2]

"... it is one of the basic facts of human life that the ungiven self is the unfulfilled self."[3] S.I. McMillen, M.D. further commented on this in regards to raising children:

> Far too much of our efforts and money are directed inwardly, to build up the egos of our children. We buy eight-year old Susie more expensive clothes than the family budget can afford...and foster the spirit of selfishness in her...Positive outward thinking is possible. We can buy Susie a cake mix and have her bake and frost a cake to take to an overworked or sick mother. What better investment can one make with so little money to give Susie happiness and a flying start down the road to joyful living and mental health? Some of the loveliest personalities I know are little children who sacrifice candy-money so that they may give to missions and the underprivileged. Children trained early to be considerate of others are not very likely to cause heartbreak to parents and others in the years ahead.[4]

LOVE AND HATE

I want to share some of the things I learned most from McMillen's chapters about emotions. First, a person's happiness will be determined by what they have learned about love, and how they handle anger and hate. Love is an outward reach of the mind to help and please others. We can learn about love from God, the author of love. That is why Jesus said that we need to love God with all our heart, soul, and mind. Then we will have the right attitude to love our neighbor. He said that if you love God and your neighbor, then it will not be so hard to follow all the other commandments.

> Jesus said unto him, Thou shalt love the Lord, thy God, with all thy heart, and with all thy soul, and with all thy mind. This is the first and great commandment. And the second is like it, Thou shalt love thy neighbor as thyself. On these two commandments hang all the law and the prophets.[5]

If we love someone we will not steal from them, covet what they have, kill them, lie about them, or commit adultery with them. When we mature in love, we grow up. We finish our childish things.

The prodigal son thought everything was all about him. He wanted his money, his friends, his pleasures, and he neglected his family and God. In time, he experienced the loss of everything that he thought was important. He was left with himself, and he felt empty. He got a job feeding pigs, and he ate what they ate. Because he came to the end of himself, he started to think about home and how his father's servants were better off than he was. With a humble spirit, he went home. He wasn't worthy to be a son, but at least he could be a servant. He started to think about others. He grew up. His father welcomed him back with open arms. His son came home and had an appreciative attitude.

God demonstrated His love toward us when He gave us His only son. His love was demonstrated in an action. Our love should also be demonstrated in actions—the act of obedience to His Word and the act of praying to God. We should also love Him because He first loved us. Our love towards others in our lives should be demonstrated by actions such as courtesy, kind words, helpfulness, thoughtfulness, and more. Sometimes our actions need to precede the feeling of love when we are commanded to love our enemies. The first action is forgiveness (even when we don't feel like it). How do we handle the anger and hatred that we like to harbor?

> The verbal expression of animosity toward others calls forth certain hormones from the pituitary, adrenal, thyroid, and other glands, an excess of which can cause disease in any part of the body. Many diseases can develop when we fatten our grudges by rehearsing them in the presence of others.
>
> The moment I start hating a man, I become his slave. I can't enjoy my work any more because he even controls my thoughts. My resentments produce too many stress hormones in my body and I become fatigued after only a few hours of work. The work I formerly enjoyed is now drudgery. Even vacations cease to give me pleasure. It may be a luxurious car that I drive along a lake fringed with the autumnal beauty of maple, oak, and birch. As far as my experience of pleasure is concerned, I might as well be driving a wagon in mud and rain.
>
> The man I hate hounds me wherever I go. I can't escape his tyrannical grasp on my mind. When the waiter serves me porterhouse steak with French fries, asparagus, crisp salad, and strawberry shortcake smothered with ice cream, it might as well be stale bread and water. My teeth chew the food and I swallow it, but the man I hate will not permit me to enjoy it.[6]

King Solomon must have had a similar experience, for he wrote: "Better is a meal of vegetables where there is love than a fattened calf with hatred" Proverbs 15:17 (NIV).

UPSET MIND—SICK BODY

Helen, a skinny six-year-old girl with pigtails, sat on her mom's lap. She had been losing weight and vomiting for the past six weeks. It began after she started attending school for the first time. There were hundreds of new faces, and she wasn't used to it. She did well after a week at home to adjust.

Carla, a pretty teenage girl, suffered vomiting, diarrhea, and cramps after the dentist told her she would have to get all her teeth pulled and have dentures. Brendan, a burly college student, suffered asthma attacks because he griped about the professor's assignments. Lenny's diabetes went out of control whenever he got stressed out over a test.

Does the mind (psyche) affect the body (soma)? Yes it does. How much it affects the body is hard to quantify. The term "psychosomatic" means the mind (emotional tension) produces changes in the body that can be serious. The mind sends out signals through the nervous system that affect the amount of blood flowing to an organ, the secretion of glands, and the tension of muscles. Have you ever seen a person blush because they were embarrassed? Have you broke out in a sweat, developed a dry mouth or felt your heart race because you had to speak in class? Have you ever been tense for a long period of time and developed a headache?

In the same way, our emotions affect the different illnesses that we experience. Problems such as ulcers, heartburn, headaches, nausea, diarrhea, diabetes, hives, and asthma can be caused by or affected by our feelings of hate, anger, resentment, sadness, and anxiety. Of course, the doctor is obligated to find a physical cause for such illnesses and provide a cure, but many times the emotional side is neglected. I've often thought that in order to treat the whole patient a doctor's office should include a pastoral counselor, a psychologist, a psychiatrist, a nutritionist, a dietitian, a social worker, a marriage counselor, a family therapist, a chiropractor, a physical therapist, an occupational therapist, a pharmacist, various alternative health care providers, physician's assistants, nurses, secretaries, and other support staff. There are so many aspects of the way a person lives their life that need to be considered in order to help a person be healthy. Walt Larimore, M.D. in his book *The 10 Essential of Highly Healthy People* formulates an excellent plan to work through.[7] He has patients self-evaluate themselves for their physical, emotional, relational, and spiritual health. Also Don Colbert, M.D. in his book *Deadly Emotions* discusses the psychological effect on different diseases.[8] One example he writes about is how anger and hostility play a role in high blood pressure and heart disease.

STRESS

The "Type A," "high intensity," "get out of my way," "stressed out" individual tends to have more heart disease than the mellow member of our society. The stressed person also lowers their body's immune system and is more susceptible to cancer. Their blood pressure can be increased which can lead to a greater chance of heart attack and stroke.

Our adrenal glands produce adrenaline to help us react when we need to. If a burglar breaks into my home, I need the adrenaline to give me better vision, a faster beating heart to supply my muscles with plenty of blood, and a higher blood pressure to run the necessary organs at full throttle. In contrast, if I am sitting in the middle of the day worried about burglars and all tense, then I have put my system on hyper-alert unnecessarily. We all experience stress, but how we react to the stress determines the detriment to the body.

Dr. McMillen said it is better to be a master of circumstances than a victim of circumstances. He said he lost some money which upset him. He was thinking about it when he went to bed and when he woke up at 4 AM. He didn't sleep well the next night either. He finally gave the matter over to God. He remembered that as Christians we are supposed to be thankful in all things no matter what the circumstances may be.[9] He felt relief. It was out of his hands. He said he experienced a better result by giving it to God as opposed to taking some tranquilizers to help him sleep. The Bible instructs us to give every problem over to God who is able to give us a peace that guards our hearts and minds.[10] The Bible also talks about confession for our wrongs, forgiveness of others, loving our enemies, and a variety of other issues that are important for our physical and mental well-being. Philippians 4:8 is a good prescription as a mental exercise:

> Finally, brethren, whatever things are true, whatever
> things are honest, whatever things are just, whatever

things are pure, whatever things are lovely, whatever things are of good report; if there be any virtue, and if there be any praise, think on these things (KJV).

FEAR

In the crash of 1929 J.C. Penney had a solid business, but some unwise personal commitments made him so worried he could not sleep. Then he developed shingles, a painful blistering rash, which resulted in his hospitalization. He tossed and turned all night long even though he was given sedatives. Because of the combination of circumstances, he was broken physically and mentally. Overwhelmed with the fear of death, he wrote farewell letters to his wife and son. He didn't expect to live until morning.

The next morning he heard singing coming from the chapel. After he pulled himself together, he entered the service as they were singing "God Will Take Care of You." After the song, the minister read scripture and prayed. In Mr. Penney's words: "Suddenly something happened. I can't explain it. I can only call it a miracle. I felt as if I had been instantly lifted out of the darkness of a dungeon into warm, brilliant sunlight. I felt as if I had been transported from hell to paradise. I felt the power of God as I had never felt it before. I realized then that I alone was responsible for all my troubles. I know that God, with his love, was there to help me. From that day to this, my life has been free from worry. I am seventy-one years old, and the most dramatic and glorious minutes of my life were those I spent in that chapel that morning."[11]

GUILT AND FEAR REPLACED WITH JOY

Come unto me, all ye that labour and are heavy laden,
and I will give you rest. Take my yoke upon you, and
learn of me; for I am meek and lowly in heart: and ye
shall find rest unto your souls (Matthew 11:28-29, KJV).

Before S.I. McMillen asked for God's forgiveness of his sins, he said he was weighed down with a sense of guilt and fear. After a few moments of confession, the guilt and fear were replaced with joy. Instead of trips to a psychiatrist office to get rid of the guilt complex, he made one trip to God's altar to get rid of the guilt itself. From that moment, he felt grateful to God, and he loved God.

"We love Him, because He first loved us" (1 John 4:19 KJV).

DEATH AND DISEASE

Death and disease are not from God, but are a result of Adam's sin. "Wherefore, as by one man sin entered into the world, and death by sin, and so death passed upon all men, for all have sinned" (Romans 5:12 KJV). Therefore, we can't blame God for the problems of this world, but we ought to be grateful he helps us through life.

A poet wrote "a man can see further through a tear than through a telescope." His poem was about how sorrow can be the best educator.[12] None of us wish for difficulties, but we all face them. Hopefully, we can learn something from them about compassion, humility, and the grace of God.

S.I. McMillen's daughter, Linda, developed meningitis while she was serving as a missionary with her husband and two babies in Southern Rhodesia. Dr. McMillen and his wife were saddened that their daughter, nine thousand miles away, was overcome with a potentially deadly illness. They would have been overwhelmed in their grief if it had not been for the comfort of the Holy Spirit and the Bible. The Bible instructs us not to fasten our eyes on the visible in our times of trouble, but to fasten our eyes on God's eternal purpose that is being accomplished.[13] In the next several months, their daughter recovered from the meningitis. They felt, through their tears, that they grew in their faith and trust in God.

In the sorrows of life, we should look to God. Doug Herman, when he lost his wife and child to AIDS because a man lied when he donated blood, could have become angry at God. Instead, he grew closer to God through his despair, and he was able to see further into God's purpose for his future. He felt God lead him into a ministry to talk to young people about sexual abstinence until marriage. He has taught the message to thousands of students every year. He has helped thousands through his talks, videos, and books to make biblically-wise decisions about life, sex, and relationships.[14]

ATTITUDE

Two men look out through the same bars:
One sees the mud, and one the stars.[15]

Why do we react differently to stressful situations? Can we train our minds to think differently? If we do think more positively, then will that help us be healthier? We all experience stress in life, and we all react to it. There is the external stress of the prison bars, but there can be an internal stress such as seeing the negative in every situation instead of the positive. Internally, how do we react to a car accident, a rude person, a traffic ticket, spilled milk, illness, or death. Are we glad no one was seriously hurt in the accident, or do we get angry about the inconvenience of getting the car fixed? The apostle Paul received beatings, stonings, shipwreck, hunger and thirst, yet he proclaimed that nothing could separate him from the love of Christ.[16] Others have overcome their circumstances to accomplish great things, such as Helen Keller and John Bunyan. Helen Keller overcame the bars of being blind, deaf, and dumb to bless the world with her spirit and love. John Bunyan was in prison when he wrote the bestseller *Pilgrim's Progress* which details man's struggle through life.

In order to have the proper attitude, we have to have the proper rest and balance in our life. Jesus instructed His disciples to get away and rest awhile.[17] Vacations allow us to take a break in life and get away from the everyday stress. A balanced life of worship, work, and play gives us a variety in our everyday life. If we are exposed to a repeated stress over a long period of time, it eventually breaks us down. A drop of water doesn't do much damage, but a repeated drop continuously for a long period of time can cause damage. Interrupt the drop. Take a break.

MENTAL ILLNESS

What goes wrong in people's minds that cause mental illness or brain injury? The cause varies from heredity to brain trauma, alcohol, drugs, infection, arteriosclerosis, abuse, family environment, and more. What can people do to promote mental health? The Bible teaches that we ought to work, help others, be disciplined, have fellowship with others, and, most importantly, to follow God's commandments to love Him and then love our neighbor. If a person's love is divided, the mind is unstable. For instance, we say we love God, but we also love work, alcohol, pornography, drugs, gambling, and so on. Can we love two things? We end up serving one or the other. If we develop an addiction, it will cause us to withdraw from others, live in a fantasy world, or overextend ourselves. Life becomes too complicated, and we break.

SEEK GOD

Life isn't all about me, but it is about servanthood. Serve God and serve others as is mentioned in Matthew 23:11-12: "But he that is greatest among you shall be your servant. And whosoever shall exalt himself shall be abased: and he that shall humble himself shall be exalted" (KJV).

God has the resources to take care of His people. He owns the cattle on a thousand hills. If you seek Him, He will take care of you. "Seek ye first the kingdom of God, and his righteousness, and all these things will be added unto you" (Matthew 6:33 KJV).

Chapter Nineteen

LIVING IN DARKNESS

W hy did you cut yourself tonight?" I asked Don, a thin 48-year-old who had short straight graying hair and a trimmed beard. He was propped up in a sitting position on the emergency room stretcher.

He looked at me, but he didn't answer. He seemed tired, inebriated, and embarrassed. He had superficially sliced himself with a knife across his arms and abdomen a few dozen times. His medical situation was not serious, but his mental state needed some help. He was accompanied by a woman who was standing next to his stretcher.

"Are you a friend or relative of Don's?" I asked her.

"I'm his wife," she said. "He is upset because his girlfriend dumped him."

Her frankness surprised me. I looked over at Don, who was drifting off to sleep and then started to snore. I looked back at his wife.

"How long have you been married to him?"

"One year, but we lived together for three years before we got married."

"Has he tried to commit suicide before?"

"Yes. He did cut himself a few years ago and spent some time in a mental institution."

"Why did he cut himself?"

"He was depressed because of his alcoholism."

"Do you know if he took any drugs with the alcohol that he consumed last night?"

"He didn't. He just drank a fifth of vodka after he read his girlfriend's rejection letter."

"How long have you known about his girlfriend?"

"I saw them together about one month ago. I walked up to them and called her a whore. She looked surprised. She asked me who I was. I told her that I was his wife. She scolded him for lying about his marital status. He grabbed her hand and walked away. It took her a few weeks, but she must have realized it wasn't worth keeping a dishonest married man."

"How are you doing?"

"I'm not very happy."

"I can understand that," I sympathized. "How did you find out about this suicide attempt?"

"He called me and told me he needed some help. I could tell he was drunk, and I didn't want to go to him because he has been ornery lately. However, he said he had stabbed himself and needed to go to the hospital. I told him I would be right over."

"Has he ever hurt you?"

"No, he hasn't. He is just unpleasant to be around at times."

"Does he have any medical problems?"

"He has emphysema from smoking and uses an inhaler."

"You said you have only been married one year. Were you married before?"

"I was married 27 years to an alcoholic. I finally got a divorce. Now I'm back in the same situation."

"I'm sorry to hear that. I have to take care of some other patients right now, but I will be back to talk to you later."

As the hours went by, I let him sleep off the alcohol in his system since the mental health hospital wouldn't take him until he was sober. When I went to check on him several hours later, his wife had gone to lunch, and he was sitting up eating a sandwich.

"Your wife filled me in on some of the details of your life," I informed him.

"She is my wife, but I married her for convenience. I don't love her."

"Have you been married before?"

"I have been married three times. My first wife ended up in prison for writing bad checks and for drugs. When she got out, she found a boyfriend and left. I got married a second time, but I had too many demons in my head from my first wife's betrayal. I was still bitter. I took it out on her, and we fought frequently. We didn't trust each other. I started drinking more alcohol. I became mean to her, and she finally left. However she did come back, but then I left. Eventually, we went bankrupt and divorced. Then I married Stacy. She had a house and a job. It was a convenience marriage."

"Why do you have so many problems in your life?"

"I drink too much."

"Why is that?"

"I started drinking heavily after my parents died. They were both good people, but they died too young. I was just out of high school. My dad had some health problems, and he would occasionally spend some time in the hospital. One time, my dad had kidney failure and was in the hospital for several weeks. My mom usually visited him every day. When I finally made it to the hospital after going out on a four-day drinking binge with my buddies, my dad asked me to go check on my mom. He said she hadn't been up to visit for several days. I went to their home to see what her problem was, and I found her dead. She was only 48. My dad died the next day, and he was only 49."

"That's sad."

"It was tough. Maybe it was more difficult because they lived responsible lives, and I was wasting my life on alcohol."

"When did you start drinking?"

"Not until I was 18."

"Why do you like to drink?"

"It helps me talk. It picks me up."

"Did your mom or dad ever take you to church?"

"No. If I met God, I would like to kill Him. Everything I do is wrong. I don't believe there is a heaven or a hell. When I die, I'm done. My troubles are over. I hate life. Every day is the same."

"Do you have any kids?"

"I have two daughters. They always ask for money. They spend too much. One has a job, and one doesn't work. They are 21 and 22. One is married, and one is a lesbian."

I could sense Don was deep in his own thought. Maybe he was thinking about everything he had been through in his life.

"Don, I've arranged for you to go to a hospital to treat your depression. Hopefully, they can help you work through some of your difficulties."

"I appreciate your concern, but I don't want to go to a mental hospital."

"You did attempt suicide, and you have to go," I told him. "I can't very well send you home when you came in here to get some help. I made sure you were physically out of danger. Now you need to go to a hospital where the doctors can evaluate and treat your mental condition."

The ambulance arrived and took him away. His wife went with him. Hopefully, he would find something more meaningful in his life.

I think of Don often. I hope and pray that he eventually sees God as someone that loves him. When I think about his life, I see how he has wandered through the years charting his own course. He didn't want God's help. Consequently, he made his own choices. For whatever reason, his decisions had bad outcomes. His marriages ended in divorce. His children struggled, and one after seeing the results of a dysfunctional marriage chose lesbianism. He committed adultery and lied to his girlfriend and wife. He filed for bankruptcy. He hated God. He tried to bury his problems with alcohol, and he was addicted to cigarettes that were destroying his lungs.

He still had life, and he still had an opportunity to seek God. Maybe he hadn't reached the bottom in his own mind. He hadn't come to the end of himself and his own desires. His life was circling in the realms of darkness.

DC Talk penned this song about meeting God.

Since I met you

Was at the end of my rope, had no where to go
Was at the end of my rope, I had nothing to show
Until the day that I turned to you, was at the end of my
   rope
You call me crazy, man you make my day
My state of residence was disarray
At every party and as far as anybody knew-everything was
   cool,
But the truth was bottled up inside of me
I was lonely as a man could be
And my 200 friends couldn't fill the void in my soul
It was a giant hole
Nothing made any sense
I thought there would never be an end
Then love came knocking at my door
Since I met you I've been alright
You turn all my darkness into light
And since I met you I've been okay
I've been alright
Since I met you I've been okay
You're rolling my winter into May
Since I met you I've been alright
I've been okay, been okay
You got me feeling like a million bucks
Some people write it off as Irish luck
But I know better, cause my rabbit's foot never did a bit of
   good
The truth it hit me like a sock in the eye
A revelation that I can't deny
Your love has overtaken every little part of me
You were what I needed
Now I'm carried away
Never seen the sunshine like today
You make something of my life
Sick and tired of the same ol' fluff

You took me in and you shook me up
You got me tripping on a vision of eternity
I can see it clearly[1]

The trouble with living in darkness is that a person has a hard time finding their way out without any light. Satan does blind those that do not believe (2 Corinthians 4:1-7); but Jesus Christ is the light and does give light (John 8:12). Satan will steal, kill, and destroy; but Jesus Christ offers an abundant life (John 10:10). Satan goes about seeking whom he can devour (1 Peter 5:8-14); but God loves people, can forgive them of their sin, and heal their hearts (1 John 4:9-10).

Satan offers people the pleasures of sin for a season (Hebrews 11:25), but then bondage sets in and destroys their life. People become controlled by their own habits. They are no longer free, but God can set them free (John 8:32).

Adverse Outcomes

Unfortunately, I have witnessed too many people affected by Satan's bondage that don't get out. Usually, when I see them, their life has already been snuffed out, adversely affected beyond repair, or scarred. Here are a few examples:

A 40-year-old with a three-day beard came to the hospital because he was weak. He had vomited some blood. While his history of alcohol use covered 25 years, his habit for the last several years was two-fifths of whiskey per day. He had destroyed his liver and his kidneys. He had come to the hospital for comfort only. He didn't want any treatment or procedures. He bled to death within several hours of admission.

In 1988, I saw a 24-year-old man come in with an AIDS-defining infection called pneumocystis carinii pneumonia. Even though he was treated with the appropriate antibiotics, his condition progressed to the point that he required a ventilator. He spent three months in the intensive care unit. His dad, who worked as a farmer, would come in and sit by his bedside. At that time, AIDS was killing people within a year or two. His dad didn't say much. As the days dragged on, everyone's hope faded. The young man died.

A 60-year-old man with lung cancer came into the emergency room because of trouble breathing. He had a long history of smoking. I ordered a breathing treatment for him and some pain medicine. He didn't want any resuscitation. While I was at my desk, the nurse informed me that the patient was taking his last breaths. As I went into the room, he stopped breathing and died.

Another patient I saw was a lady in her 40s. The paramedics tried to resuscitate her after she had collapsed and died of a massive blood clot. Her lesbian lover was explaining to me through tears how this lady was just getting her life back after having gastric bypass surgery and losing over one hundred pounds. She just had another surgery to remove the excessive skin which left her with fresh surgical scars across the sides of her abdomen and her lower abdomen. At home, she was recovering well from the surgery, but she developed severe shortness of breath and collapsed.

Another unsuccessful emergency room resuscitation involved a 35-year-old obese man who was found outside on the ground at his farm. He was a smoker, had high blood pressure, and high cholesterol. He died. His wife told me he never complained of chest pain or shortness of breath.

I received an emergency call for a man down in the jail. When I arrived, he was not breathing and didn't have a pulse. We began resuscitation efforts, but he died. I thought he probably died from swallowing packs of cocaine that burst in his intestines. However, the autopsy results didn't reveal any cocaine. He was only 28-years old, but he smoked marijuana and used drugs. He had a massive heart attack.

I was enjoying a quiet weekend night shift at 3 AM. when a young man came through the sliding doors with a large cut down the side of his face. Within a few seconds, another young man came through the door with a bloody hand. Both of the wounds were bleeding profusely. After I pressure bandaged the man's face, I sent him away to a plastic surgeon. The other man lost the tip of his finger. I was able to stop the bleeding, but he would need to see a hand surgeon for some skin grafting to cover the tip of his finger.

According to the police, the bars had closed and a few of the patrons, who were arguing, took their argument outside. The insults, vulgarity, and ugliness continued until the group of young men were smashing beer bottles and using the broken shards of glass as weapons against each other.

THE CHILDREN SUFFER

When adults make a bad choice, they suffer for it. Sometimes, their kids suffer also.

On two shifts in a row, I had parents bring in their dead infants from Sudden Infant Death Syndrome or SIDS. It is a tragic circumstance and a time of great emotion. Both sets of parents were smokers. We live in a society of tolerance. We allow people to smoke. Even though smoking isn't the only cause for SIDS, it is one of the risk factors. Once a child has died, there is no point in informing the parents about the risk of secondhand smoke. However, parents of children should not expose their kids to smoke. The American Academy of Pediatrics recommends no smoking during and after pregnancy and no soft bedding such as comforters and pillows. They advise placing children on their back, unless the child has a medical condition that prevents it.

A child of a cocaine addict was two years old and had a tracheostomy tube in his neck. He would come into the emergency room with trouble breathing. He wasn't a normal child physically or mentally and would suffer the rest of his life because of his mom's habit.

Mothers who use cocaine can have children with various anomalies in the brain, the gastrointestinal tract, the face, and the eyes. They commonly birth prematurely and require respiratory support which was the reason this child had a tube in his neck. Mothers that use cocaine also frequently use alcohol, cigarettes, and other drugs which further complicate their child's problems.

Can you see why "Living in Darkness" weakens a nation. According to the Bible, Satan has ruled the earth. He has exalted himself above God, and he asks us to do that also. In Luke 4:1-15, he asked Jesus to worship him. Jesus replied, "Thou shalt worship the Lord, thy God, and him only shalt thou worship." As Don said in the opening story, "If I meet God, I will kill him." In reality, Don can't kill God. He thinks he can, because he has exalted himself above God, just like Satan wants him to.

In America we are a nation of tolerance. We accept people for who they are. However, that doesn't mean that all of our activities are good for us, or good for the nation in general. As human beings, we have all lived in darkness. All of us sin and fall short of God. All of us are separated from God. We are lost. The good news is that we don't have to stay lost.

God can rescue people from the deepest pit. I have outlined in various chapters how people have found deliverance from the grips of Satan. David Berkowitz was best known as the "Son of Sam" killer in New York City, but now credits Jesus Christ for transforming his life. Others were spared from divorce, homosexuality, gambling, adultery, drugs, pornography, gluttony, and alcoholism. People do find God through Jesus Christ.

Others can be lost in intellectual darkness. I have been fascinated by the testimonies of those that have been successful in their lives and careers. They honestly investigated Jesus Christ and made a decision to accept Him as their personal Savior. I was impressed with the testimony of Lee Strobel, who holds a Master of Studies in Law degree from Yale Law School, as well as a journalism degree from the University of Missouri. He detailed his personal journey from atheism to faith in his books *The Case for Christ* and *The Case for Faith*.

I enjoyed reading *Daktar* which is the story of Viggo Olsen, M.D. and the missionary work in Bangladesh. Viggo and his wife, Joan, were agnostics as they headed to New York to begin his medical career. Joan's parents had some type of religious experience after she had gone off to college. Every visit to their house involved religious discussion until Viggo promised them he would study the Christian religion and the Bible. He wanted to prove the Bible wrong, that Christianity was not true, and that Jesus was not the Son of God.

When they got to New York, they spent time researching Christianity, the Bible, and Jesus. They also went to church whenever he wasn't working and looked for scientific errors in the

Bible and the preaching. To their surprise, the errors were not on every page as they were taught in college. A man at church gave them a book *Modern Science and the Christian Faith*. One day out of boredom, Viggo picked up the book. His boredom turned to interest and then to fascination. He read that we cannot have the law of gravity and the law of thermodynamics without a lawgiver. We cannot have a designed universe without a designer.

They spent countless hours thinking, debating, reasoning, researching, and rediscussing. They thought of the analogy of 100 Scrabble games being tossed on the floor. What would be the chances of a story or a poem being spelled out? It would be practically impossible. They believed there had to be an intelligent power. They became convinced that a personal creator God existed.

Then they debated whether God revealed Himself through Scripture. They found the Bible to be historically accurate, scientifically accurate, and prophetically accurate. They read a book called *Testimony of the Evangelist* by Simon Greenleaf, who was a highly acclaimed legal expert. His opinion, after studying the Gospels, was that these books were written by real men about real events. He felt they were not made up. He said there were too many minute details that were interconnected that detection of falsehood would be inevitable. When they researched the scientific accuracy of the Scriptures, they were surprised to learn that the Bible commented that the world was round and that it hung on nothing. That thought was in contradiction to the scientific thought of that time. When they looked into the prophetic accuracy, they were impressed that the Bible predicted that Israel would again become a nation and that prophecy was fulfilled in 1948. They were also impressed that 33 prophecies were fulfilled on the day Jesus Christ was crucified.

The last thing Olsen wanted to prove was that Jesus was not the Son of God. When he studied books and the Gospels, he saw how Jesus was virgin born, performed miracles, raised the dead, then died and was resurrected. He met with His disciples again after death, and then His disciples became fervent preachers until most of them were put to death. They must have experienced God to do what they did. Viggo and Joan discovered that Jesus

Christ wasn't preaching good works as a way to heaven. It was by admitting sin and accepting what Jesus had done on the cross that salvation was obtained.

After all their investigation, they knew Jesus Christ was the Son of God, He did die for their sins, and He did rise from the dead. They accepted Him into their hearts, and began a lifelong walk with Him that led them to mission work on the other side of the world.

Just like Dr. and Mrs. Olsen, we all spend some of our life "in darkness." In Romans 3:10, it states that "there is none righteous," and it states in Jeremiah 17:9, "the heart is deceitful above all things, and desperately wicked." In Isaiah 53:6 it tells how "we have all gone astray."

The apostle Paul described himself as the chiefest of sinners. As a Pharisee, Saul (later renamed Paul) felt he was protecting the Jewish religion by killing the followers of Jesus Christ. Then on the road to Damascus, a light from heaven blinded him. He fell to the ground. Jesus asked him why he was persecuting Him by hurting His people. Saul surrendered his life to Jesus and was willing to do whatever Jesus Christ wanted him to do. God touched his soul. Through the power of Jesus Christ, Saul was changed. It wasn't an easy road after that for him. He suffered shipwreck, beatings, a stoning, imprisonment, but he persisted for a purpose. He had a vision of eternity, and he could see it clearly when the light struck him and brought him out of his darkness.

Chapter Twenty

THE GRAY ZONE

A ct of passion or premeditated murder?" was the local newspaper headline.

Did he act in a jealous rage, or did he have it all planned? In a rare jail cell interview, the murderer confessed that he went by his ex-wife's house at 4 AM. When he recognized his ex-wife's former husband's car, he was so jealous and angry that he went up to the house and killed his ex-wife who was getting into her car to go to work. He then went into the house and attacked her former husband, but was unsuccessful in his attempt to kill him. He said his rage was an act of passion similar to the scenario played out in the movie "Secret Window" which starred Johnny Depp.

"That's not the kind of movie I needed to be seeing. It ended up having a very negative impact on me," he said.

They had met at work, and, after several months of dating, were married. Within a year, they had a son, lived in a $200,000 house, and appeared successful. He felt their marriage had gone well, but after several years they separated. She filed for divorce because of his violence. On a child visitation exchange, he became angry and beat her up in the front yard. He was enraged that her former husband was living in his house. He felt betrayed. Over the next several months, his anger and resentment continued as he spent 30 days in jail for his assault. After his release, he became depressed because he lost his job and was living with his mom. Then after watching *Secret Window* and drinking some alcohol, he drove from Indiana to Michigan and murdered her.

When I had a chance to see him in the jail for a medical problem, I had a few questions for him. I went down to the maximum security area. Before I could talk to him, the deputy said he would ask the inmate if he wanted to see the doctor. The verbal exchange that followed was unfriendly. Profanity was exchanged angrily and escalated to the point that the deputy ended the conversation abruptly. The officer walked back to where I was standing in the hallway and told me the inmate didn't want to see the doctor.

The next week, I was able to see him. I wondered why he was such an angry man. What kind of family did he come from? What kind of abuses did he suffer?

As I took care of his medical problem, I had some time to get to know him a little better. After a few minutes, I felt comfortable asking him about his family.

"Did you have any brothers or sisters?"

"I have an older brother and sister."

"How are they doing?"

"They both have families and good jobs. They have both done well in their life."

"Do you have parents?"

"My mom is still alive, but my dad died. They were good parents to me growing up. They taught me all the right things and took me to a Baptist church."

"When you left home did you continue going to church?"

"After high school I joined the army, and I didn't attend church."

"Have you thought about talking to any of the chaplains available here?"

"The pastor from my church in Indiana has visited me and is helping me. I am restoring my relationship with God."

"That's good," I encouraged him. "I will see you again in one week in the medical unit."

"Thanks, doc."

He went on to plead guilty and avoided a costly trial. He didn't want to put the victim's family through any more grief than he had already caused. He realized the seriousness of his act and accepted the consequences of life in prison without parole.

He told me he found great comfort in Psalm 51: "Have mercy upon me, O God…blot out my transgressions…cleanse me from my sin."[1]

Did the movie make him commit murder? No, I don't believe it did. He made the choice. He was thinking about himself and not about others. Did the movie influence his thinking? Yes, it did. He said it had a negative impact on him.

In the movie, "Secret Window," Johnny Depp killed two people and didn't get caught. In real life, one woman is dead, one man goes to prison, one boy misses his mom and dad, and two families are devastated.

VIDEO GAMES

In another murder case, three defendants aged 24, 18, and 16 were accused of running down people on sidewalks and then beating a man to death in the same manner that is depicted on the video game "Grand Theft Auto." After having a good time staying up all night playing video games and drinking alcohol, these young adults spotted a few people they could run over. They made a few unsuccessful attempts, but then they spotted a man on a bicycle that they were able to run over. The young thugs then proceeded to beat the man up. They took the money out of his wallet and went out to breakfast. After they ate, they returned to the man and stomped him into a coma. A few days later, the man died. The police tracked down the three suspects and arrested them. They were jailed, went through a trial, and were convicted of murder. Presently, they are serving their time in prison.

The video game didn't cause them to commit murder. These three young people made that choice. They chose to spend hours playing a violent video game that influenced their behavior and resulted in horrific inhumanity to another human being. The video game "Grand Theft Auto: San Andreas" was the top-selling game in 2004 with 5.1 million copies sold.[2] The game is described in this manner: intense violence or language; may include sexual themes. Players become gangsters, getting their kicks by stealing cars. They can relieve the tension of killing other players' characters by hiring prostitutes. The sex is off screen, but conveyed by ecstatic moaning, the car's rocking, and the vibration of the game pad. When I asked my middle school Sunday school class about the game, most of them had seen the game because their friends would play it.

The Internet

Internet users spend an average of 3 hours per day online, almost double the 1.7 hours watching television.[3] According to a recent study, "adult" websites are getting the most attention.[4] There are over 300,000 pornographic web sites. The National Center for Missing and Exploited Children found that one in five children ages 10-17, who regularly use the Internet, have received a sexual solicitation while online.[5] Gambling and pornography are number one and two in business sales online.

Music, Attitude, Activities

A 17-year-old man known as "Walking Evil" butchered his mom and two sisters one day in our city. His friends described him as enamored with heavy rock music, gothic black clothes, and drugs. In an interview from his prison cell, he claimed partial responsibility, while an unhappy childhood and the anti-depressant Prozac contributed to his crime. He smoked marijuana at age 12, and then progressed on to LSD, heroin, cocaine, alcohol, and peyote, a hallucinogen derived from cactus and used by American Indians in religious ceremonies. He was a follower of Wicca, which is a neo-pagan religion.

Following repeated fights with his family, he ran away from home and tried to commit suicide. He spent time at a mental hospital and was put on Prozac, but he said it didn't help. On the day of the murders, he argued with his 15-year-old sister and then killed her. Later he killed his mom, and then his 6-year-old sister. The dad, who has a history of alcoholism, was away on his trucking job.

The murders and the brutality were shocking. How does a young man do that? I don't pretend to understand everything that took place, but the drugs, the alcohol, the false religion led him to emptiness, hatred, and selfishness. He failed at suicide and went on to succeed at killing his own family.

FRIENDS

"You are the average of your five closest friends," I read one day on a billboard outside of a car repair shop. What are your friends like? What do they stand for?

One young man in the jail, named Kevin, appeared to be high school age. His innocent appearance made him stand out among the other inmates. On his intake survey, he was arrested for marijuana possession.

"How did you get into smoking marijuana?" I asked him.

"My friends got me into drugs. My mom and dad told me I was headed for trouble with those guys. They were right. My friends got me into smoking marijuana, and I got busted for possession."

At this time in Michigan, marijuana possession is a misdemeanor punishable by up to one year in jail and/or a $2000 fine. Most people caught with marijuana do not get put in jail, but some do depending on the circumstances.[6]

Another young lady hooked up with a drug addicted thief. The pair, described by their lawyers as "Bonnie and Clyde," stole guns from Arkansas and made their way to Michigan to sell them. They went to the home of an elderly man that the girl knew. Their intent was robbery, but the young man ended up shooting him. After they pleaded guilty, the young man was sentenced to 27 to 52 years in prison, and the young lady was sentenced to 12 ½ years to 25 years behind bars. At the sentencing, the judge told the young lady, "You showed very bad judgment being associated with this young man in the first place."

Robin Williams first came to fame with his role in the television series *Mork and Mindy*. Robin's best friend was John Belushi. They would drink and do cocaine together. Eventually, John overdosed on drugs and died. Robin was devastated, and he gave up the drugs. In the closing scene of the made-for-television movie about Robin's life, a friend offered him a line of cocaine.

"Do you want some?" the friend asked.

"Yes," he responded, and then he walked away.

I really liked that ending, because there are many things that we like that are not good for us. "There is a way which seemeth right unto a man, but the end thereof are the ways of death" (Proverbs 14:12 KJV).

MUSIC

I asked my daughter to print out the lyrics of the top ten rap songs that I saw listed in the paper.

"The lyrics are sexually graphic," she warned.

"I'm not surprised," I told her nonchalantly. As I looked through the words, I was shocked. The explicitly depicted sex was more graphic than I had imagined. I brought the words to work and showed it to some of the rap-listening nurses. They were a little surprised. When I heard the songs on the radio, it was difficult to hear the lyrics through the music. I know most people listen to songs for the music and the beat, but the lyrics are sending the wrong message. A local radio host mentioned at a community forum about violence that early hip-hop focused on lyrics of revolution and subtle black history, but modern rap has gone violent because corporations know that violence sells. The lyrics of the rap songs I reviewed were about sex, drugs, violence, profanity, armed robbery, out of wedlock children, lack of commitment, and gangs. Is it any wonder kids act out these songs in real life?

What are the lyrics of rock music or heavy metal music? It doesn't hurt to look up the words on the Internet. Troy Kunkle gained notoriety for quoting the lyrics of the group Metallica after he gunned down a 31-year-old man and robbed him of $13. He got the death sentence and was recently executed.

What does country music promote? Some songs are about family and good memories of friends. However, some of the songs are about the depressing circumstances of life and our human shortcomings. There is some truth to the joke—What do you get when you play a country music song backwards? You get your house back, your pickup truck back, your wife back, your dog back, and your job back. What kind of feelings and memories do the songs you listen to generate?

There is a wide variety of music that is uplifting. I enjoy listening to many different songs and I appreciate the creativity that goes into them. The songs I enjoy the most and the ones that I feel

best about listening to are songs that do the most for me spiritually and emotionally. One song that helps me worship the creator
God, and humbles me is Chris Tomlin's song, "Indescribable."

From the highest of heights to the depths of the sea,
Creation's revealing Your majesty.
From the colors of fall to the fragrance of spring,
Every creature unique in the song that it sings. All
   exclaiming...

(Chorus)

Indescribable, Uncontainable,
You placed the stars in the sky and You know them by
   name.
You are amazing God.
All powerful, Untameable,
Awestruck we fall to our knees and we humbly proclaim,
You are amazing God.

Who has told every lightning bolt where it should go,
Or seen heavenly storehouses laden with snow?
Who imagined the sun and gives source to its light,
Yet conceals it to give us the coolness of night?
None can fathom...
Indescribable, Uncontainable,
You placed the stars in the sky and You know them by
   name.
You are amazing God.
Incomparable, Unchangeable,
You see the depths of my heart and You love me the
   same.
You are amazing God.[7]

TELEVISION AND MOVIES

What do you remember seeing on television? Do you remember anything that helped you in life? I do remember a "Love Boat"

episode in which a married middle-aged man fell in love with a young lady in her 20s. The wife of the middle-aged man seemed almost relieved that this young lady was going to take care of her husband. She handed the young lady the creams that she needed to apply for his psoriasis, the pills he needed to take for his high blood pressure and diabetes, and the special diet he needed for his wheat gluten intolerance. The young lady didn't want the man after she found out about all the baggage that came with him. The television show etched in my mind a negative message about adultery and divorce.

What are children seeing on television now? The average person between the ages of two and eighteen sees 14,000 sexual references, innuendoes, and jokes each year on television. Fewer than 175 of those deal with the real issues of pregnancy, birth control, abstinence, or sexually transmitted diseases. On the most popular evening shows that most teenagers watch, the conversation deals with sex 29 to 59 percent of the time. On soap operas sex is 24 times more common between unmarried partners than between spouses.[8]

The gray zone of life is where we spend our time and make our decisions. It can lead us to light or darkness. I asked one of my sons how the movies he watched influenced his life. He said he watches films for entertainment. He likes to figure out the movie intellectually. He didn't really think it affected his life and decisions. Maybe that is true for him and the type of movies that he watches. However, I know movies and music have a subtle influence. There is a philosophy that is taught in movies and music.

In 2004, the best films at the box office were *The Passion of the Christ*, *Spiderman II*, and *Shrek II*. None of those movies won any awards. Hollywood awarded the movies that portrayed their message and beliefs. The top movie promoted euthanasia. In 2005, the top movie for Oscar nominations was *Brokeback Mountain* which promoted homosexuality.

A few years ago a movie *Basic Instinct* glamorized smoking. The screenwriter for that movie, Joe Eszterhas, was diagnosed with throat cancer after a lifetime of smoking. In a *New York Times* article, he admitted his movie promoted smoking, and he urged Hollywood to stop glamorizing the cigarette.[9] In the movie *A Few Good Men*, Tom Cruise drives a car while drunk without consequences, and the next morning he is brilliant as a lawyer in court. How often does that happen in real life? In reality, the drunk driver may get arrested, lose his license, and go to jail or prison. If he gets through the evening, he probably won't be brilliant the next morning. *In While You Were Sleeping*, Sandra Bullock with her sweet smile and her cute sense of humor couldn't bring herself to tell the truth and clear up a misunderstanding. It was all in fun, but honest communication is necessary in marriage, in the workplace, and in parent-child relationships.

The gray zone highlights the areas that can be used for good or bad. The media is a major portion of what is educating our society today. American children spend more time watching television than they spend on any other activity except sleeping.[10] Is that the reason we've grown into a society that has a difficult time with real life and relationships? Is that why there is a haze when we consider what is right and wrong? Is that why we are raising children that reflect the values of the media more than it reflects the values of its Christian parents? Is that why 88 percent of kids raised in Christian homes don't continue to follow the Lord after they graduate from high school?[11]

When sociologists conducted a survey of 104 of Hollywood's elite, the writers and producers answered:

93 percent seldom or never go to worship services
97 percent believe in a woman's right to abort
5 percent strongly agree that homosexuality is wrong
16 percent agree that adultery is wrong
99 percent believe that television should be "more critical" of Judeo-Christian values[12]

It is easy to see why we have lost ground morally in America. The Bible, the Ten Commandments, the sanctity of human life, God's definition of the family have all come under attack. It is easy to see why. Is it a good thing for this country? Thom S. Rainer wrote a book *The Bridger Generation.* He broke down each generation and the percentage of Bible-believers.

Builders (born 1927-1945): 65 percent Bible-based believers
Boomers (born 1946-1964): 35 percent Bible-based believers
Busters (born 1965-1983): 16 percent Bible-based believers
Bridgers (or Millennials, born 1984 or later): 4 percent Bible-based believers

We are losing the battle in America. The gray zone is taking us to the "Living in the Darkness" section more than to the "Living in the Light" section. Hosea 4:6 states that people are destroyed for lack of knowledge. Paul instructs us to love what is pure; hate what is evil; cling to what is good.[13] God has a good life for us. We need to live it and share that knowledge with others.

Chapter Twenty-One

LIVING IN THE LIGHT

Can you lead the Bible study this week?"

"Yes, I can," I responded, but in my mind I did have some hesitation. This Bible study wasn't just any gathering of believers. These were Christian brothers behind bars at Jackson State Prison. They were maximum security inmates.

When I had visited the penitentiary for the first time the week before, the walk through the yard was the most intimidating. My eyes met cold empty stares from men with graying beards and hair pulled back into pony tails. An occasional sinister smile revealed one or two yellow-stained teeth surrounded by gaps of darkness. As we walked by, three muscular men that were weight-lifting stopped and stared at our group. One sleeveless man was leaning against an open door frame with his muscular tattooed arms crossed over his chest. The atmosphere was evil. There was an element of danger. I didn't feel welcome.

Once inside the chapel, the atmosphere was more cordial. The men were smiling and shaking one another's hands. A few were laughing. The study leader kept greeting everyone, and the warmth was returned to him. He made his way to the front of the chapel and picked up his guitar. The men quieted down and began to take their seats. As he strummed out a melody, the inmates all joined in. Their voices blended in as they worshipped God with the opening praise song. The next song was livelier, and the song gained momentum until it peaked with the lyrics "set the prisoner free." After a few more songs, the study leader put down his guitar and picked up his Bible. He talked to the fifty men gathered in the auditorium for about thirty minutes about the repentant thief on the cross. They listened intently. Then he brought the meeting to a close, offered an invitation to trust in Jesus as the thief on the cross had, and ended in prayer. I was impressed by the spirit, the humility, and the teachable hearts that were present. I talked to a few of the inmates after the service, and then we went home. It was a great experience.

Now the leader wanted me to do the Bible study. I felt inadequate. How could I relate to these guys and say anything that would touch their hearts? I couldn't think of any Bible passage or topic. I couldn't relate to their life of crime since I was raised in a Christian home and had given my life to God. Anything I could say about my life, although imperfect, didn't seem appropriate. I battled with God about what to say. I gave up in frustration. There was nothing acceptable. I put it in God's hands.

As I struggled through the week with different thoughts that came into my mind, one idea seemed to persist. Help them see Jesus for who He is. Jesus could feel their pain and relate to them.

They could relate to Jesus. He was mocked for His assumed illegitimacy, beaten, scourged, misunderstood, hated, tested, tried, punished, rejected, lied about, and crucified. He knew about their lives, their hurts, their mistrust, their shame, their loneliness, their tears, their grief, and their heartaches. Jesus could offer them hope, eternity, heaven, joy, peace, forgiveness, happiness, contentment, wisdom, and faith in God. He was no ordinary man. He was God. He affected history more than any other man. He was still affecting history because He was still working in lives.

When I went in for the Bible study, the lesson was all about Jesus. I explained how I couldn't understand everything they had been through in their life, but Jesus could because He had walked in their shoes. He created the world, He lived in the world, and He suffered in many ways similar to how they had suffered. I encouraged them to focus on the life of Jesus and His teachings.

JESUS

As I think about this chapter on "Living in the Light," Jesus again comes to my mind.

He is the only one who ever lived perfectly. His sinless life was the only sacrifice acceptable for my sins and the sins of the world. I've had people say to me that they're going to heaven because of the good things they've done. However, their sin separates them from God. I ask them why Jesus came to earth, lived a life without sin, and died for their sins if they could earn their way to heaven without Him.

SALVATION

In the "Decision Wheel" diagram, salvation is one of the items listed in the "Living in the Light" section. Everyone has to make a decision whether they accept the Bible's message of salvation or not.

When I was growing up, my parents took me to church every week. I am thankful for that. At the time I had other things I would rather be doing. However, it was at church that I learned about God, heaven, and hell. I wanted to go to heaven and avoid hell, but I didn't understand what salvation was all about. At church, when I was ten, one of the leaders told a Bible story. After the story he asked if anybody wanted to know more about getting saved. I wanted to know exactly what the Bible had to say about salvation. I asked one of the men to show me. My parents had explained it to me before, and I had heard it in church many times before. Nevertheless, I didn't know it in my heart. The leader showed me four things from the Bible. First of all, he said that all men have sinned. He said it is part of our nature to disobey God. He showed me Romans 3:10 which reads "there is none righteous." He asked me if I had sinned. I hadn't robbed any banks or killed anyone, but I remembered going into a neighbor's yard to retrieve a plastic ball and finding a tennis ball. As I picked up my plastic ball, I also picked up the tennis ball. Then I looked up at the neighbor's house and saw a lady in the window. I felt guilty for wanting to take that ball out of her yard. I told the leader that I realized I was a sinner.

He told me the second thing I needed to know was that because of my sin I deserved to be separated from God for eternity. He showed me a verse in Romans 6:23 that said "the wages of sin is death." In other words, when a person works at a job they get wages for the hours they work. In the spiritual realm, the wages of all my sin is spiritual death or separation from God. If the Bible ended with that message, then we would all be without hope. Some of us are better than others, but none of us deserves to be with God.

Next, he told me that the good news is that Jesus paid the penalty for my sins. He showed me Romans 5:8 which explained that God proved His love toward me as a sinner by sending Jesus Christ to die for me. Only someone without sin could die for my sin.

Lastly, he explained that salvation is available when we ask for it (Romans 10:13). He said it is a gift from God, and it is not my gift until I receive it. I was ready to receive it.

I bowed my head in prayer and acknowledged my sin and my need for a Savior. I asked Him to save me.

I've not regretted that decision. It is the simple message of the gospel of Jesus Christ. Some have heard that message and responded the first time. Most others have heard it hundreds of times before they responded with a sincere commitment.

Study the Bible, Meditate on it, and Memorize it

When I was a young Christian, I wasn't interested in scripture memorization and Bible study. However, as I grew up, I slowly began to see the benefits. I realized God had so much to offer.

In Bill Gillham's book *What God Wishes Christians Knew About Christianity*,[1] he explained how he bought a computer and was learning how to use it. He said several computer-savvy young adults in his workplace told him about some of the unique features of the computer that he needed to learn. He agreed and he was implementing their advice when he realized how the Christian life is also about learning. If we knew everything God had to offer, we would be in His instruction manual, the Bible, much more often. In summary, he advised "Don't stop at the gift of salvation. Go for more."

THE BIBLE

The only book God has ever written is meant to show us the way to heaven and help us live life to the fullest on earth. It is a book of history, law, praise, wisdom, instruction, health, and prophecy. I love the Bible now, but I didn't always love the book. I had a difficult time understanding what it was all about. I wondered why I should read the Bible when I didn't comprehend it. A pastor told a story that helped me understand why.

A farmer and his son were out in the potato field on a hot dusty summer day. The father in the blue jean coveralls told his blonde-haired, ten-year-old son to go get some water with his potato basket.

"This basket won't hold water," the son protested as he showed his dad the wicker basket.

"Do it anyway," his dad instructed.

The son obeyed his dad and went down to the stream that flowed at the edge of the fields by the woods. He enjoyed the cool shade of the trees. He bent down on one knee and put the basket into the water. When he filled it, he brought it back to his dad while the water was leaking out. He muttered under his breath that the exercise was futile.

"The water all leaked out, Dad."

"I see. Please do it again."

The young boy didn't argue. He turned around and headed back to the stream. Once again he got down on a knee in the cool shade and dipped his basket into the clear water. When the basket was full, he brought it back to his dad with the water leaking out again.

"There is no water left," he said as he showed his dad the basket.

"Fill the basket one more time."

The son headed back to the stream and filled the basket the third time. As he headed back to his dad, the water leaked out again.

"The water is all gone."

"Do you notice anything different about the basket, son?"

His boy looked down at the basket. It still looked like the same basket to him.

"I don't notice anything different about the basket, Dad."

"Do you think it is cleaner than it was before?"

"Yes, it is."

"When you read the Bible, you may not always understand it. However, it still cleanses your heart."

After I heard that story, I wasn't disappointed when I didn't understand everything in the Bible because I knew it was transforming my life by renewing my mind.

The Gideons are a group of businessmen who hand out Bibles all around the world. I enjoy reading the stories in their monthly magazine about how people find God by reading those Bibles. One testimony I read was about Mike, a 24-year-old senior at the University of Minnesota, who was about to graduate with a degree in engineering. On a beautiful spring day, he began his usual walk to class. The easiest route to take was through a narrow gate which was between two large fenced-in fields. On this particular day, there was a man handing out New Testaments at the gate. Instead of walking all the way around the fenced-in area, it was easier to go through the gate and accept the Bible. Over the next week, he read the Bible, cover to cover, three times. Within a month, he was on his knees asking God for forgiveness and putting his faith in Jesus Christ for salvation and eternal life. He went on for further training to serve God as a missionary to Asia.[2] He closed his testimony by reflecting back on the day that he chose to go through the narrow gate. It reminded him of the passage in Matthew 7:13-14 where we are instructed to take the narrow path which few people take. It is the path that leads to life, whereas the broad path leads to destruction.

What does God promise those that study His Word? "This book of the law shall not depart out of thy mouth, but thou shalt meditate therein day and night, that thou mayest observe to do according to all that is written therein; for then thou shalt make thy way prosperous, and then thou shalt have good success" (Joshua 1:8 KJV). His Word gives us the wisdom to live life.

It doesn't guarantee an easy life. Many of the early followers of Christ paid with their life for their commitment. In contrast, if we ignore God's Word that is detrimental also. Hosea 4:6 states, "My people are destroyed for lack of knowledge." How do we get that knowledge? We get it from church, reading the Bible and good books, and from experience in life.

C.H. Spurgeon spoke about the subject of God: "No subject of contemplation will tend more to humble the mind, than thoughts of God…But while the subject humbles the mind, it also expands it. He, who often thinks of God, will have a larger mind than the man who simply plods around this narrow globe…The most excellent study for expanding the soul is the science of Christ, and Him crucified, and the knowledge of the Godhead in the glorious Trinity. Nothing will so enlarge the intellect, nothing so magnify the whole soul of man, as a devout, earnest, continued investigation of the great subject of the Deity."[3]

SHARING THE GOOD NEWS

Part of the experience of knowing God is sharing Him with others. As I do that, many people are interested to know what the Bible says about heaven. Others don't want anything to do with it. Some people believe "there is no God." Of course, if they have never learned about and accepted God, then God may seem non-existent in their life. That doesn't mean God doesn't exist or love them. It means He is not a personal part of their life. In order to get people to take a step of faith, it is important to spend time with them, share the plan of salvation with them, and live an authentic Christian life before them.

Dr. David Wood, the founding pastor of the church I attend, said "inspiration without education leads to frustration." In other words, we get inspired to tell others about Jesus Christ, but we become frustrated when we do not know how to do it effectively.

Presently Dr. Wood is involved in the worldwide training of people to spread the message of Jesus Christ. He believes it is important to have a plan for sharing the gospel, and to use it.[4]

While at a Bible conference recently, I was inspired by a song about having a heart for the souls of people.

My eyes are dry
My faith is old
My heart is hard
My prayers are cold
And I know how
I ought to be
Alive to you
And dead to me
Oh what can be done
For an old heart like mine
Soften it up with oil and wine
The oil is you, your spirit of love
Please wash me anew in the wine of your blood.

My eyes are dry
My faith is old
My heart is hard
My prayers are cold
And I know how
I ought to be
Alive to you
And dead to me
And what can be done
For an old heart like mine
Soften it up, cleanse me I cry
Let my heart break
Let tears once again
Flow down my face
For the souls of lost men[5]

"In the midst of a generation screaming for answers, Christians are studying," Howard Hendricks observed. It is good to study and learn, but there is a time to get out into the world and provide the answers. As Christians, we need to stand as if on the cliffs of the Pacific Ocean and shout for the world to hear "God is God." He is the Sovereign Creator of the universe. Seek Him, and you will find Him.

Chapter Twenty-Two

LIVING IN THE LIGHT II

How do you determine what you want to do in your life?" my college psychology professor asked our class.

"Take a career assessment inventory," one student responded.

"Realize your strengths and decide what field that would fit into," another student offered.

"Go to different mentors and spend some time with people and see what they do," a third student chipped in.

I liked all those answers, but I knew what influenced me most when I made that critical decision about life direction.

"Ask God what He wants you to do," I shared with the class. I didn't mean to be simplistic. I honestly felt that if a person pursued God, then God would reveal His will to that person.

I know that many people struggle to find their place in life. It isn't as easy for some as it is for others. However, when young people are considering the decision of a career at such an inexperienced time in their life, they need to seek the wisdom of God.

When I was 16, I felt the pressure of making a decision about what kind of career I would enter. Was I prepared to make that kind of decision? No. However, I knew God could help me. At that point in my life, I trusted in God more than myself. I believed Proverbs 3:5-6: "Trust in the Lord with all thine heart, and lean not unto thine own understanding. In all thy ways acknowledge him, and he shall direct thy paths" (KJV).

As I went through high school, I enjoyed math and science. After listening to the school counselor list the career options that required math and science skills, I considered the options of engineer, chemist, biochemist, doctor, teacher, professor, and others.

At that same time, a businessman at church mentioned that law and medicine were still worthwhile professions to go into. I remember going to a court case for school and visiting the lawyer's library. The lawyer explained how he had read most of the books in that particular room. I didn't particularly like to read. Maybe law wasn't for me.

Medicine did appeal to me. After reading and enjoying a few books about doctors, I felt God nudging me in that direction. When I entered into a college pre-medical program, I sensed God had answered my prayer for career direction.

It wasn't easy. On one distressing night of study, I prayed for God to give me some encouragement because I was overwhelmed with the amount of work. I had four tests on one Friday. The last test I was studying for was genetics. I kept falling asleep on my book at 2:30 in the morning. I considered joining the Marines. I felt physical training might be more suited for me than intellectual training. When my grades came back, I did well on three tests. I felt God answered my prayer for encouragement. The genetics test was a disaster, as I had feared, but the professor said that we were allowed to drop two of our worst test scores in the semester. I said "Thank You" to God.

After four years of pre-medical studies, I was rejected to all the medical schools I applied to. I asked Michigan State University about admission to their school. They told me I needed to enter one of their physiology masters programs and continue to learn. I didn't feel at peace about that. I was working in the hospital at the time, and I wanted to continue to learn firsthand about taking care of people.

At that time also, I was thinking about marriage. I hadn't found the right girl yet. My oldest brother asked me what I was looking for in a girl. I had to think about that. I wanted the girl to have a deep personal faith and be from the same denomination. I thought it would be nice if she was from the same town. Then I listed some of my interests such as medicine, sports, and music.

Hopefully, she would enjoy the same interests. My brother suggested I pray specifically for those qualities in a wife. I did.

I know others have been praying for years for a spouse, and God hasn't delivered. It is tough to wait for any answer to prayer. God's timing is not always our timing. The important thing is to keep seeking God's way and have faith in Him. If He provides the right partner, at the right time, then proceed in the right way. God will bless it.

I had been dating a few girls, who were very nice. However, I didn't feel any one of them was the right marriage partner for me. I was willing to stop dating and wait on God. After several months went by, I was still content. One night after church I needed a ride to my house, and I asked Bonny, one of the girls in our college and career Bible study if she could give me a ride home. She lived a few miles from where I lived.

As we were riding home, I asked her a few questions to get to know her better. She had been coming to our church for about two years, and I never saw her with any other family members.

"Do you have any brothers or sisters?"

"I have an older sister and two younger sisters. My mom had four girls in five and a half years."

She already knew I had three brothers and no sisters. I was the second born.

"Do they go to church?" I asked her because I'd never seen them at church.

"Yes, they go to the church I grew up in. I was invited by a friend to visit Heritage, and I started attending regularly. I was interested in taking the class on sign language to communicate with deaf people," she explained.

My grandparents were deaf, and I'd never taken any class on sign language. I communicated with my grandparents through my mom and dad when I needed to. I admired her willingness to learn a skill and communicate with the deaf people at church.

"Your last name is Staal. Does your dad own Staal Buick?"

"No, he doesn't, and neither do any of his relatives," she paused, then she turned her face toward me at a red light. "Does that disappoint you?"

"No, it doesn't. I just wondered since you have the same last name. What does your dad do for work?"

"He used to be a butcher, but because of tendonitis in his elbow he switched to a meat inspection job."

"My dad did cement work for the city of Grand Rapids, but now he does inspections," I told her. It was interesting to me that her dad and my dad had very similar work histories. I was just making conversation with Bonny, but I started to realize how much we had in common.

"Do you like sports?"

"My family was never athletic, but I enjoy sports. I like softball and swimming. One time, I organized some ladies to play softball, but we didn't have a league to play in. I called several churches until we had enough teams to start our own league."

"That shows initiative."

"It was something I wanted to do. I just had to find enough other people who felt the same way."

"Do you play a musical instrument?" I asked because I love music and have played the trombone since fifth grade.

"I've played an accordion for about 15 years."

"Really, my mom plays an accordion. Why did you choose an accordion?"

"I have relatives who have accordions and play polka music at their wedding receptions. I've always enjoyed the music and chose to play the accordion."

"How long have you worked at the hospital?"

"Two years."

"I've been there about two years too. Why did you apply for a job there?"

"I needed the benefits, plus I was interested in medical work."

Our conversation continued, and soon we arrived at my house. She probably wondered why I was so interested in her life when I hadn't shown much interest before. Maybe God was showing me something that I hadn't seen before. I had to take time to think.

After I prayed and thought about it, I called her and asked her out on a date. We went to a festival downtown and enjoyed music, food, arts and crafts. The next week we went out for Chinese food, and then we starting seeing each other regularly. I proposed to her 5 months later, and then we were married 5 months after that. She was my answer to prayer for a wife.

Within a year, God answered my prayer to get into medical school. I got an acceptance letter from Michigan State University College of Osteopathic Medicine. I was overjoyed that a dream and prayer of mine for the last nine years had become a reality.

Soon the excitement of medical school turned into the day-to-day struggle to cram an overwhelming amount of information into my brain. The verse I posted on my study desk was from James 1:5, "If any of you lack wisdom, let him ask of God, who giveth to all men liberally…" My prayers included a plea for wisdom, as well as the strength and health to study. He got us through the four years of medical school, and then a one-year internship and a three-year residency in internal medicine.

The next step was an emergency room and internal medicine job in Greenville, Michigan which was a rural community of 15,000 people. I practiced for a few years, and then took a two-month leave of absence to go on a mission trip to the Amazon River in the rainforest of Brazil. We prayed about what God wanted in our life, and He continued to guide us. When we returned to the United States, I continued to work in Greenville, and we continued to raise our family.

"May I let my eyes look straight ahead and fix my gaze straight before me. May I ponder the path of my feet so that all my ways will be established. May I not turn to the right or to the left but keep my foot from evil" (Proverbs 4:25-27).

FRIENDS

Second Corinthians 6:14 says "Be ye not unequally yoked together with unbelievers; for what fellowship hath righteousness with unrighteousness? And what communion hath light with darkness?"

Who you choose to spend your time with determines your future. In The Pact, three young African-American men from New Jersey agreed to stick together and help each other through school.

They chose good friends. They overcame their circumstances, and one became a dentist and two became medical doctors.[1]

GOOD BOOKS

There is wisdom in obtaining counsel from others. In our age, we can pick up a book that offers biblical advice on almost every subject. I want to share a few books that affected me.

A friend, Brian Williams, gave me the book *Knowing God* by J.I. Packer after we were roommates at a Navigator's conference when I was in college. I began reading that book as a devotional every day before I did my homework. I found it to be a foundational book for what the Bible says about God. For instance, why is jealousy a positive characteristic for God? He can be jealous in a positive way because He is the best thing for all people.

I went to hear Elisabeth Elliott speak about her missionary life. She had been married to Jim Elliott, who was killed by Waodani tribesmen in Ecuador. I bought her book *A Slow and Certain Light* about following God's will. She emphasized that God directs us slowly at times, and that we need to be seeking Him, reading His Word, and available. He will provide the light to help us see the way.

Philip Yancey in his book *Where Is God When It Hurts*, explained a few good reasons for pain. He told one story of a young lad who approached Dr. Brand as he tried to turn a key in a lock. The youngster asked if he could try. The doctor stepped aside and was astonished the young boy was able to turn the key. He told the boy "thank you" and then noticed the boy's hand was dripping blood. Dr. Brand asked if he could see the hand. The boy showed him, and Dr. Brand saw the flesh on the boy's finger was cut down to the bone. The boy had a type of leprosy that destroyed the nerves. The boy could not feel his hand. He had no pain and he could turn the key until it cut his finger down to the bone. Yancey's point was that pain does protect us.

While I was in high school, a few non-Christian students argued that we shouldn't send missionaries to jungle people. They reasoned that the natives were happy in their villages and that sending religion to them was confusing and unnecessary. I didn't know how to answer them at that time except to say that we all need to hear about Jesus and His payment for our sins. Years later, when I read the book *The Lords of the Earth* by Don Richardson, I discovered that the tribal people weren't happy because they were sacrificing their babies to appease the river gods. When the missionaries explained how God had already provided the sacrifice of His son, Jesus Christ, for the payment of their wrongdoing, some of the people accepted the message of Jesus Christ and no longer sacrificed their babies to appease the gods.

When we were preparing to go to the Amazon River in Brazil, I was reading devotions from Oswald Chamber's book *My Utmost for His Highest*. I was especially touched by a devotion that said God calls us away to a distant land so that He can work in the hearts of those that are staying home supporting and praying for us.

I rarely read any fiction novels, but I did enjoy reading *The Rising* by Jerry Jenkins and Tim LaHaye; *This Present Darkness* by Frank Peretti, and *The Testament* by John Grisham. I picked up John Grisham's novel because I knew it was a novel about Brazil, and I wanted to see what he had to say. I found fiction to be very interesting and enjoyable.

Reading a good book, whether fiction or non-fiction, has helped me understand the Christian life and God.

FRUITS OF THE SPIRIT

"But the fruit of the Spirit is love, joy, peace, long-suffering, gentleness, goodness, faith, meekness, self-control…" Galatians 5:22-23. While I was in high school, we learned about personality characteristics. All of the personalities—sanguine, choleric, phlegmatic, and melancholy—had good and bad qualities. The idea of the study was to encourage people to build on their strengths and minimize their weaknesses.

As Christians, part of the growing process is experiencing the ups and downs of life and learning what God can teach us. None of us reach perfection, but as God molds our lives, He removes our rough edges. If we are seeking God and learning, we develop the fruits of the Spirit. We experience His love and joy even in adverse circumstances and can pass it on to others. Horatio G. Spafford wrote the song "It Is Well with My Soul" after the ship carrying his daughters went down in the ocean. He had peace even in tragedy. If we have the right attitude, our faith builds. The last attribute mentioned is self-control. When we experience God as He desires us to, we don't have to seek our pleasure in activities that distract us from His good will for our lives.

IS THERE ANY GOOD ADDICTION?

Love God with all your heart, soul, and mind and love your neighbor as yourself. These are the two commandments that all the others are based upon. We can be addicted to God's ways, and that can bring lasting satisfaction. It is not our natural desire to head toward God, but it is the answer in life.

God's Word can turn on the lights, transform our minds, and help us accomplish His will in our life. Then the church of Jesus Christ can have the impact on the world that we were meant to have.

"They have addicted themselves to the ministry of the saints." I Corinthians 16:15b

Chapter Twenty-Three

LEGACY

What do I hand off to my children, grandchildren, and the world? Every day the torch is passed from one generation to the next. What legacy do you want to leave?

In 1875, Richard L. Dugdale publicly announced his study of the Jukes family in the annual report of the Prison Association of New York. After an inspection of thirteen of the county jails of New York, he found six blood-related relatives in one county jail. He tracked their ancestry back to Max Jukes, who was born in the early 1700s. Through his investigation, he found out Max was a hard drinking, jolly hunter and a fisherman, who didn't believe in God and didn't work steady. He noted that Max had many children, and of his 1029 descendents, 300 died prematurely, 100 were sent to prison for an average of 13 years each, 190 were prostitutes, and 100 were drunkards. They cost the state $1.2 million. Max Jukes was one man, but his philosophy and his actions affected thousands of his family members who came after him.

At the same time in history, Jonathon Edwards, who was a prominent Christian minister, had 729 descendents, which consisted of 300 preachers, 65 college professors, 13 college or university presidents, 60 authors, 3 U.S. congressmen, and one vice president of the United States.[1]

Every person leaves a legacy. Each individual makes choices that determine their future. In this book, I outlined what the Bible determines to be good and to be bad. I've also explained how to have a relationship with God through Jesus Christ. He gives us victory over sin. We don't have to be enslaved to Satan and his deceptive ways.

In every family, the children have a choice to make. They either follow what their father and mother believe, or they don't. An unloving, abusive, alcoholic father can have a son turn out to be a minister. In contrast, a loving, law-abiding father can have a son get involved in drugs, pornography, homosexuality, rape, and murder. In our culture, parents, who teach their children to respect God and everyone else, compete against the television, movies, the internet, music, literature, and their child's peers. Every person has a free will and makes decisions. My intent for this book is that the reader can have information which allows them to make informed choices.

THE GREAT EQUALIZER

What we are and what we teach by our words and actions have a profound affect on our family. When I worked in the hospital before I became a doctor, a man came into the emergency room with four gunshot wounds to his chest and abdomen. He was a big man at 6 feet, 6 inches tall and over 300 pounds. He was rushed immediately to the operating room where the surgeons worked to save his life. Despite their efforts, he died. I was called to take him down to the morgue. When I got into the operating room, the housekeeping staff was sweeping up the bloody gauzes, empty wrappers, and blood transfusion bags. Everybody stopped to help load the victim onto the stretcher. Physically, this man probably didn't fear too many people. However, four small bullets took his life. As I wheeled him out of the operating room, I realized, in the world of inner-city warfare, the gun is a great equalizer. A small man with a gun equals a big man without a gun.

When it comes to each person's spiritual life and leaving a legacy the great equalizer is God the Father, God the Son (Jesus Christ), and the Holy Spirit. Though a child is raised in abuse, neglect, drugs or alcoholism, the cycle of hurt, despair, and unhappiness can still be broken. It is difficult and not too many people find their way out, but every human being can have a future and a hope if they look to God and the Bible for their direction in life. "For I know the plans I have for you," says the Lord. "Plans for good and not for evil, to give you a future and a hope" (Jeremiah 29:11).

WHAT KIND OF DYSFUNCTIONAL FAMILY DO YOU COME FROM?

Every family has some dysfunction, but our choices determine who we become and what kind of legacy we leave. In Exodus 20:4-5, God is saying that the parent's example can lead a child into sin. If the home is critical, negative, abusive, addictive, dishonest, lazy, disrespectful, and uncommitted to one another, then the child, more than likely, will follow in the same pattern.

One of my friends who became a Christian after leaving a life of alcohol and drugs, told me his family drank alcohol every day. His dad drank a dozen beers every day, so when he grew up, he downed a dozen beers daily. After his wife left him, he began to wonder why she had such a problem with his drinking. He realized his habits cost him his family. One day as he went by a church his wife attended, he went in and talked to the pastor. The pastor showed him from the Bible how he could have a personal relationship with Jesus Christ. He made a decision that day to accept Jesus Christ into his life. With God's help, he gave up his alcohol. He also regained the family that he had lost.

Not every story ends that nicely. Many children of alcoholic, drug-addicted, abusive, or sexually immoral parents die of homicides, suicides, overdoses, illnesses, before they give their life over to God. Others give their life to God, but they live daily with the consequences of their bad choices early in life.

Consider Billy Schneider's story. He is a national speaker to young people about the dangers of drug use. He had a difficult childhood, made bad choices, finally accepted Jesus Christ into his life, and then found out he was infected with AIDS and developed non-Hodgkin's lymphoma. I recently read his book *Go Ahead, Jump![2]* As a child there were times Billy's alcoholic dad came home at night and woke Billy up. His dad made him stand on top of the refrigerator and told him to jump. When he jumped and his dad didn't catch him, he landed on the floor and bloodied his lip or nose. He then headed back to bed. As he cried himself to sleep, he wondered why his dad did that.

As he grew older, Billy got involved in smoking cigarettes, alcohol, drugs, immorality, criminal activity, and everything else imaginable. He was arrested 39 times, convicted 19 times, and spent 10 years in prison. He failed several drug rehabilitation programs. When he came to the end of himself, he sought help from a former drug addict friend, Tom Mahairas, who had become a minister. Billy knew he was beaten by the world. He prayed to Jesus, "Lord, I'm Yours. You can do what You want with me, but I'm through. The streets beat me. You fix me. I need a fix for my heart." He finally accepted Jesus Christ as his personal Savior.

He went into the church-sponsored drug rehabilitation program called Transformation Life Center for one year. When he got out, he wanted to know if he had the human immunodeficiency virus because of his former lifestyle. When his test results came back, he was HIV positive. After six months, he relapsed into his former lifestyle and went back to the Transformation Life Center for another three months. Over time, Billy's life was transformed. He went back to his wife and son. His wife, Linda also accepted Christ into her life. Billy was thrilled with her decision for salvation, and then her decision to gradually end her use of methadone. In time the consequences of her drug use hurt her, and she died of Hepatitis C and cirrhosis of the liver.

When I went to hear Billy speak, he talked honestly about the consequences of his bad choices. He told the young people that drugs don't give you a high. They give you a low. They can make you lose your job, your relationships, your family, your freedom, your self-worth, your hope, your future, your health, and your life.

THE GREATEST LEGACY

In Ecclesiastes 12:13, Solomon concluded his book with the thought that God is to be reverenced in His proper place as the creator, sustainer, and sovereign ruler of the universe and that God's commandments are to be obeyed. Whether we pick up that legacy and pass it on is our decision. Solomon described his conclusion as the "whole duty of man."

In John 3:16-21, we know God loves us each individually and provides a way for us to spend eternity with Him.

"For God so loved the world, that he gave his only begotten Son, that whosoever believeth in him should not perish, but have everlasting life. For God sent not his Son into the world to condemn the world, but that the world through him might be saved. He that believeth on him is not condemned; but he that believeth not is condemned already, because he hath not believed in the name of the only begotten Son of God. And this is the condemnation, that light is come into the world, and men loved darkness rather than light, because their deeds were evil. For everyone that doeth evil hateth the light, neither cometh to the light, lest his deeds should be reproved. But he that doeth truth cometh to the light, that his deeds may be made manifest, that they are wrought of God."

DO WE PASS ON A CURSE OR A BLESSING?

Sarah Groves sings about the decisions we make in her song "Generations."

I can taste the fruit of Eve. I'm aware of sickness, death, and disease. The results of her choices were vast. Eve was the first but she wasn't the last. If I were honest with myself, had I been standing at that tree, my mouth and my hands would be covered with fruit. Things I shouldn't know and things I shouldn't see.

Remind me of this with every decision. Generations will reap what I sow. I can pass on a curse or a blessing to those I will never know.

She taught us to fear the serpent. I'm learning to fear myself and all of the things I am capable of in my search for acceptance, wisdom, and wealth. To say the devil made me do it is a cop-out and a lie. The devil can't make me do anything when I'm calling on Jesus Christ.

To my great-great-great-granddaughter, live in peace. To my great-great-great-grandson, live in peace. To my great-great-great-granddaughter, live in peace. To my great-great-great-grandson, live in peace, live in peace. Eve was the first but she wasn't the last.[3]

ENDNOTES

Chapter One

1. www.marchofdimes.com

Chapter Two

1. "Time for a pure revolution" by Doug Herman. Published by Tyndale House Publishers, Inc. 2004.
2. www.cornerstone.edu/departments/president/mad?id=230.
3. Reader's Digest poll, 2004.
4. Reader's Digest poll, 2004.
5. Time, 2002.
6. USA Today, 2002.
7. Natrional Geographic Magazine, November 2004. "Was Darwin Wrong? By David Quammen. www/nationalgeographic.com/ ngm/0411/feature1/index.html.
8. "The Case for a Creator" Copyright 2004 by Strobel, Zondervan.
9. Quote of German atheistic philosopher Ludwig Feuerbach in: Hans Kung, "Freud and the Problem of God, enlarged edition, translated by Edward Quinn (New Haven: Yale University Press, 1990, 3.
10. Phillip E. Johnson, Darwin on Trial (Downers Grove, Ill, Ill.: Inter Varsity Press, second edition, 1993), 126- 27.
11. Linus Pauling, "No More War! (New York: Dodd, Mead & Co., 1958), 209.
12. "A Scientific Dissent from Darwinism," a two-page advertisement, The Weekly Standard (October 1, 2001).
13. Jonathan Wells, "Icons of Evolution" (Washington, d.C." Regnery, 2000).
14. Francis Crick, "Life Itself" (New York: Simon and Schuster, 1981), 88.
15. Marvin I. Lubenow, "Bones of Contention, 86-99.
16. Michael D. Lemonick, "How Man Began," Time (March 14, 1994), quoted in : Hank Hanegraaff, "The Face that Demonstrated the Farce of Evolution, 52.

17. Taken from "Case for a Creator" by Lee P. Strobel. Copyright 2004 by Lee Strobel. Used by permission of Zondervan.
18. Martin, "Kingdom of Cults."
19. "Unveiling Islam" by Ergun Caner and Emir Caner. Published by Kregel Publications 2002.

Chapter Three

1. "How Common Is Pastoral Indiscretion?" Leadership (Winter 1988): 12-13.
2. "The Hite Report on Male Sexuality (New York: Alfred A. Knopf, 1981).
3. "Moody Monthly" July/August 1987. "Loving Your Marriage Enough To Protect It." By Jerry Jenkins. Published by Moody Press, Chicago in 1989 and 1993. II Timothy 2:22.
4. "Loving Your Marriage Enough To Protect It" by Jerry Jenkins.
5. Grand Rapids Press "Scott Peterson affair detailed in testimony" by The Associated Press.
6. Grand Rapids Press November 13, 2003.
7. Grand Rapids Press May 22, 2003.
8. Adapted from the March/April 2004 *"Focus on the Family"* Physician magazine. Copyright © 2004, Focus on the Family. All rights reserved. International copyright secured. Used by permission.

Chapter Four

1. CDC/NCHS, National Vital Statistics System. Statistics shown are from 2001.
2. www.cdc.gov/nchs/fastats/insurg.htm
3. Grand Rapids Press-January 30, 2005, "Little common ground in abortion debate", by Ellen Goodman of the Washington Post Writers Group.
4. wwwrtl.org
5. www.ramahinternational.org/for-post-abortive-men.html.
6. John Hopkins Advanced Studies in Medicine Vol. 5, No. 6 June 2005. "Women Helping Women-Four Generations of Women's Health", by Renate Justin, M.D.
7. Right to Life of Michigan News. February/March 2005 Vol. 32/ No.1. www.rtl.org
8. K.A. Moore, et al., "Beginning Too Soon: Adolescent Sexual Behavior, Pregnancy, and Parenthood (Washington, D.C.:Child Trends, 1995)."

9. Dr. Janet Daling, Journal of the National Cancer Institute, vol. 86, No.21, pp.1584-1592, Nov.2, 1994) (Citizen Magazine January 2003) (Forbidden Grief by Theresa Burke).

10. www.ramahinternational.org/post-abortion-syndrome.html, "Help for the Post-Abortive Woman (now entitled A Solitary Sorrow), by Dr. Paul and Teri Reisser.

11. Right to Life of Michigan News "I have an announcement to make..." by Mary VerWys.

12. www.ramahinternational.org

13. "Facts in Brief-Induced Abortion," The Alan Guttmacher Institute, Washington D.C., January 1997.

14. "Her choice to Heal: Finding Spiritual and Emotional Peace after Abortion" by Sydna Masse. Published by Chariot Victor Books. www.ramahinternational.org. Used by permission.

Chapter Five

1. National Center for Health Statistics. National health and nutrition examination survey. http://www.cdc.gov/nchs/nhanes.htm

2. The Grand Rapids Press, September 30, 2003

3. www.diabetes.org/diabetes-statistics/heart-disease.jsp

4. www.diabetes.org/diabetes-statistics/heart-disease.jsp

5. Patient Care / April 2005.

6. Int J Obes Relat Metab Disord 2003;27(10):1167-77.

7. Courtlandt Forum January, 2005.

8. Courtlandt Forum January, 2005.

9. Medical Training Institute of America.

10. www.diabeticmctoday.com-Diabetic Microvascular Complications Today. January/February 2005-Volume 2, No. 1.

11. Focus on the Family Physician Sept/Oct 2003. www.healthsteward.com/orderbook.htm

12. www.shoptcs.com Welcome to the Joke Closet.

13. www.SettingCaptivesFree.com

Chapter Six

1. Grand Rapids Press, by April Vitello and Jennifer Bundy The Associated Press. January, 2003.

2. Ellen Goodstein, Bankrate.com

3. Unwin BK, Davis MK, De Leeuw JB. Pathologic Gambling. Am Fam Physician 2000;61:741-9.

4. Feigelman W, Wallisch LS, Lesieur HR. Problem gamblers, problem substance users and dual-problem individuals: an epidemiological study. Am J Public Health 1998;88:467-70.

5. Pathologic Gambling. American Family Physician Feb. 1, 2000.

6. Rex M. Rogers, "Seducing America: Is Gambling a Good Bet?" (Baker Book House, 1997; Kregel Publishers, 2004).

7. Robert Custer and Harry Milt, "When Luck Runs Out: Help for Compulsive Gamblers and Their Families (New York: Facts on File, 1985), 231, 145.

8. Vol. 118 / No 1 / July 2005 / Post Graduate Medicine / Gambling Disorders by Leena M. Sumitra, MD and Shannon C. Miller, MD. Potenza MN, Fiellin DA, Heninger GR, et al. Gambling: an addictive behavior with health and primary care implications. J Gen Intern Med 2002;17 (9):721-32.

9. Tony Evans, *Tony Evans Speaks Out On Gambling and the Lottery* (Chicago: Moody, 1995) pg. 71.

10. "Gambling Addiction-The Problem, the Pain, and the Path to Recovery" by John Eades. Published by Vine Books in 2003. Used by permission.

Chapter Seven

1. The DO January 2005.

2. Physicians Money Digest. November 2003. Pride Survey 2003.

3. Reader's Digest January 1997.

4. Grand Rapids Press by John Agar.

5. Grand Rapids Press by John Agar, January 22, 2005.

6. Marc A. Schuckit, "Are There Dangers to Marijuana?" in Drug Abuse and Alcoholism Newsletter, August 19, 1990. Published by Vista Hill Foundation, San Diego, California.

7. The DO January 2005.

8. The American Drug Scene: An Anthology 2nd Edition by James A. Inciardi, Karen McElrath 1998 Roxbury Publishing Co.

9. Citizen Magazine by Focus on the Family, December 2004.

10. The American Drug Scene: An Anthology 2nd Edition by James A. Inciardi, Karen McElrath 1998 Roxbury Publishing Co.

11. From THE PACT by Sampson Davis, George Jenkins and Rameck Hunt, with Liza Frazier Page, copyright © 2002 by Three Doctors LLC. Used by permission of Riverhead Books, an imprint of Penquin Group (USA) Inc.

Chapter Eight

1. www.genitalherpes.com
2. http://pediatrics.aappublications.org/cgi/content/full/114/3/e280.
3. www.vlatrex.com/about-herpes/index.htm Also Arch Intern Med/Vol 163, January 13, 2003.
4. www.TargetHPV.org
5. "Time for a Pure Revolution" by Doug Herman. Tyndale House Publishers, Inc. Wheaton, Illinois. Used by permission.
6. "Its Your (Sex) Life; Your Guide to Safe and Responsible Sex" (Henry J. Kaiser Family Foundation and MTV, 2002), 16.
7. Albert D. Klassen, Coin J. Williams, Eugene E. Levitt et al., "Trends in Premarital Sexual Behavior," in Charles F. Turner, Heather G. Miller, and Lincoln E. Moses, eds., AIDS: Sexual Behavior and Intravenous Drug Use (Washington, D.C.: National Academy Press, 1989), 553. Quoted in "None of These Diseases" by S.I. McMillen, M.D. and David E. Stern, M.D., Millenium Three Edition. Published by Fleming H. Revell a division of Baker Publishing Group, Grand Rapids, Michigan 49516.
8. Reclaiming Intimacy-Overcoming the Consequences of Premarital Relationships" by Heather Jamison. Kregel Publications, Grand Rapids, Michigan. All rights reserved. Used by permission.
9. Dave Noel, "I Repent," The Faithful, Steve Green, Jillybird Music, 1998. All rights reserved. Used by permission.
10. Robert T. Michael, John H. Gagnon, Edward O. Laumann, and Gina Kolata, "Sex in America" (Chicago: University of Chicago Press 1996), 124-5.
11. Robert J. Levin and Amy Levin. "Sexual Pleasure: The Surprising Preferences of 100,000 Women, Redbook 145 (September, 1970), 52.
12. Elisabeth Elliot "Passion and Purity" (Grand Rapids, Revell 2984), 21.
13. K.A.Moore, et al., "Beginning to Soon: Adolescent Sexual Behavior, Pregnancy, and Parenthood (Washington D.C. :Child Trends 1995)."
14. Bridget Mahar, ed., "The Family Portrait: A Compilation of Data, Research, and Public Opinion on the Family (Washington D.C.: Family Research Council, 2002)."
15. "Time for a Pure Revolution" by Doug Herman. Tyndale House Publishers Inc., Wheaton, Illinois. Used by permission.

Chapter Nine

1. "Porn in the U.S.A." Viewed on "60Minutes on November 23, 2003.
2. Pornography Statistics 2003, Family Safe Media.

3. Pornography Statistics 2003, Family Safe Media. Also "Battle Cry for a Generation, The Fight to Save America's Youth" by Ron Luce. Published by NEXGEN, Cook Communications Ministries of Colorado Springs, Colorado 2005.
4. http://www.moralityinmedia.org/index.htm?homepage.htm.
5. "Setting Captives Free. Pure Freedom – Breaking the Addiction to Pornography." Day 11 Mike Cleveland (Focus Publishing 502 Third Street NW, Bemidji, Minnesota 56601. www.settingcaptivesfree.com. Used by permission.
6. http://www.family.org/pastor/resources/sos/a0006443.html.
7. Pornography Statistics 2003, Family Safe Media.

Chapter Ten

1. "Patient Care" Magazine. January 2003 Vol.37 No. 1. "Teen Sexuality."
2. daybrooks@nytimes.com
3. www.crimelibrary.com/serial-killers/notorious/gacy/gacy-1.html by Rachael Bell.
4. www.crimelibrary.com/serial-killers/notorious/dahmer/naked1.html by Marilyn Bardsley.
5. www.crimelibrary.com/predators/corll/index_1.html by Marilyn Bardsley.
6. www.crimelibrary.com/predators/kraft/1.html by Michael Newton.
7. "People" magazine. March 10, 2003. "The Boy in the Box."
8. "Bringing up Boys." Chapter 9. Dr. James Dobson (Tyndale House Publishers).
9. www.exodus.to – "Who Am I" Bob Ragan's Story. Used by permission. www.regeneration ministries.org/newsletters_archives.asp

Chapter Eleven

1. Grand Rapids Press, June 9, 2005.
2. www.retailindustry.about.com/od/statistics_loss_prevention/1/aa021126a.htm.
3. Exodus 20:15.

Chapter Twelve

1. Grand Rapids Press. The Associated Press. April 16, 2005.
2. None of these Diseases.
3. Patient Care/February 2005.
4. The Grand Rapids Press on May 31, 2004 from the Los Angeles Times by James Gerstenzang.

5. People February 7, 2005 by Tom Gliatto and Alex Tresniowski.
6. Patient Care / February 2005.
7. Journal of the American Osteopathic Association, August 2004, Volume 104, Number 8.

Chapter Thirteen

1. www.niaaa.nih.gov.
2. Grand Rapids Press, June 16, 2005. www.rsoa.org.
3. www.cdc.gov/alcohol.
4. "The Truth About Alcohol" Michigan Resource Center. 1994 Channing L. Bete Co., Inc.
5. Archives of Internal Medicine (2004;164:531).
6. Grand Rapids Press, June 29, 2005.
7. Grand Rapids Press, May 30, 2005.
8. www.niaaa.nih.gov.
9. www.aacap.org/publications/factsfam/alcoholc.htm.

Chapter Fourteen

1. CDC/NCHS, National Vital Statistics System.
2. www.forgivenforlife.com

Chapter Fifteen

1. April 2005, Resident & Staff Physician
2. Supplement to the Journal of Family Practice – December 2003.
3. Grand Rapids Press, Aug 11, 2004.
4. Grand Rapids Press, April 22, 2002.
5. Kochanek KD, Murphy SL, Anderson RN, et al. Deaths: final data for 2002. Natl vital Stat. Rep. 2004;53:1-115.
6. www.christianbook.com
7. Grand Rapids Press, December 18, 2004.
8. Grand Rapids Press, August 11, 2004, Psychology Today.
9. Grand Rapids Press, August 11, 2004, Pine Rest Christian Mental Health Services.
10. Grand Rapids Press, April 22, 2002.
11. The American Tradition in Literature. Grosset & Dunlap, Inc. New York.
12. April 2005, Resident & Staff Physician.
13. April 2003, Cortlandt Forum.
14. Grand Rapids Press, April 24, 2005.

15. Grand Rapids Press, April 5, 2004.
16. Grand Rapids Press, July 10, 2005 by Kate O'Hare.
17. April 2003, Cortlandt Forum.
18. Comstock GW. Church attendance and health. J Chronic Dis 1972;25:665-672.
19. Prim Care Companion J Clin Psychiatry 2004;6(3).

Chapter Sixteen

1. The Reader's Digest, Treasury of Modern Quotations (New York: Reader's Digest, 1975), 83. "Loving Your Marrige Enough To Protect It," by Jerry Jenkins (Moody Press, 1973).
2. March 1, 2004 Newsweek.
3. www.divorcemagazine.com/statistics/statsUS.shtml.
4. Heather Jamison "Reclaiming Intimacy" by Kregel Publications, Grand Rapids Michigan, 2001. Used by permission.
5. Citizen Magazine April 2005 or www.family.org/cforum/citizenmag.

Chapter Seventeen

1. Strange Texts But Grand Truths, published in 1953 by Abingdon Press, New York and Nashville. "Classic Sermons on Spiritual Warfare" compiles by Warren Wiersbe, 1992 by Kregel Publications.
2. Ginny Owens "Land of the Grey." Used by permission.
3. "Classic Sermons on Spiritual Warfare" compiled by Warren W. Wiersbe. Published by Kregel Publications in 1992. The scripture text is Luke 4:1-13.

Chapter Eighteen

1. "None of these Diseases" by S.I. McMillen. Spire Books. Chap.2, pg.13.
2. "None of these Diseases" by S.I. McMillen. Spire Books. Chap.23, pg 126.
3. Harry J. Johnson, Blue Print for Health (Chicago, Blue Cross Association, Summer 1962), pg 19
4. "None of these Diseases" by S.I. McMillen. Spire Books. Chap.23, pg 128.
5. Matthew 22:37-40 KJV
6. "None of these Diseases" by S.I. McMillen. Spire Books. Chap. 11, pg 72
7. "10 Essentials of Highly Healthy People" by Walt Larimore, M.D., published by Zondervan, 2003

8. "Deadly Emotions" by Don Colbert, M.D., published by Thomas Nelson, Nashville Tennessee, 2003.

9. I Thessalonians 5:18 KJV

10. Phillipians 4:6,7

11. Philipians 4:8 KJV

11. "None of these Diseases" by S.I. McMillen. Spire Books. Chap 18, pg 96. How to Stop Worrying and Start Living by Dale Carnegie (New York, Simon and Schuster, Inc., 1948).

12. "None of these Diseases" by S.I. McMillen. Spire Books. Chap. 19, pg 103.

13. II Corinthians 4:17-18 KJV

14. "Time for a Pure Revolution" by Doug Herman. Published by Tyndale House, 2004

15. Fredrick Lanbridge, "A Cluster of Quiet Thoughts" (published by the Religious Tract Society).

16. II Corinthians 11:24-27

17. Mark 6:31 KJV

Chapter Nineteen

1. "Since I met you" by DC Talk. Words and music by Toby Mckeehan, Michael Tait, Kevin Max, and Mark Heimermann. 1998 Achtober Songs out of Music Blind Thief Publishing Fun Attic Music. All rights reserved. Used by permission.

Chapter Twenty

1. Authorized King James Version of the Holy Bible. New York, Oxford University Press 1967.

2. "Rating change for popular game could start crackdown" by Ron Harris of the Assoiciated Press. Printed July 21, 2005 in the Grand Rapids Press.

3. Reported by Rob McGann in an article titled, "Internet Edges Out Family Time More than TV time," January 5 2005, at web site: www.clickz.com/stats/sectors/demographics/article.php/3455061.

4. Rob McGann, Ibid. "Battle Cry For A Generation: by Ron Luce. Published by Nexgen (Cook Communications, Colorado Springs, Colorado).

5. National Coalition for the Protection of Children & Families

6. www.michiganprosecutor.org/define.htm

7. Indescribable by Laura Story © 2004 Worship Together.com Songs / Six Steps Music / Gleaning Publishing. All rights reserved. Used by permission

8. Nathalie Bartle, "Venus in Blue Jeans (Boston: Houghton Mifflin, 1998), 104-5. "And the Bride Wore White" by Dannah Gresh (p.129-30). Published in 1999 and 2004 by Moody Publishers of Chicago, Illinois.

9. "I have been an accomplice": Joe Exzterhas, writing in "The New York Times" (9 August 2002, op-ed page).

10. www.tvturnoff.org/images/facts&figures/factsheets/FastFigs.pdf.

11. Ron Luce, Ibid. www.battlecry.com

12. "Violence and Promiscuity Set the Stage for Television's Moral Collapse," Issue #: 248 www.frc.org/get.cfm?i=ISO2E4.

13. Romans 12:9 NIV

Chapter Twenty-One

1. "What God Wishes Christians Knew About Christianity-It Might Surprise You" by Bill Gillham. Published by Harvest House Publishers, 1998.

2. The Gideon/July 2005.

3. "Knowing God" by J.I.Packer, page 13. Twelfth American printing, November 1977, Inter Varsity Press.

4. David Wood Ministries at www.dwministries.org.

5. Author unknown. Presented by Mike Speck at Baptist International Network Conference, September 2004.

Chapter Twenty-Two

1. "The Pact" by Drs. Sampson Davis, George Jenkins, and Rameck Hunt with Lisa Frazier Page. 2002 by Riverhead Books.

Chapter Twenty-Three

1. www.leaderlinks.com/pastissues/2004/04_april/columntoler.htm

2. "Go Ahead, Jump" by Joanne Schneider. Published by Gospel Communications International, Inc. in 1997.

3. Generations—Sara Groves. All rights reserved. Used by permission.

ABOUT THE AUTHOR

Daniel Carrel, D.O., resides in Grand Rapids, Michigan with his wife of 25 years, Bonny Carrel. They have seven children and three grandchildren. Dr. Carrel has worked in the medical field for over 30 years. After four years of undergraduate study at Calvin College and after working for four years at Blodgett Hospital as a technician, he attended Michigan State University College of Osteopathic Medicine. He did a one year internship at Lansing General Hospital and a three year internal medicine residency at Blodgett-St. Mary's. He practiced emergency medicine in Greenville, Michigan for 13 years and worked in an internal medicine office for one year. He has spent time doing short-term missionary work in a hospital on the Amazon River in Brazil, and has worked 6 years at the Kent County jail. He presently is employed by Visiting Physicians Association making house calls on homebound patients. His other book is *In All His Ways—Internship* which is a fiction novel about his internship year.

Is Biblical Morality Outdated?

Order Form

Postal orders: 2471 Appleton Dr. NE
Grand Rapids, MI 49525

Phone orders: 616-364-6551
Online orders: dcarrel@juno.com
www.drcarrel.com

Please send *Is Biblical Morality Outdated?* to:

Name: _____

Address: _____

City: _____ State: _____

Zip: _____ Telephone: (_____) _____

Book Price: $14.99

Shipping: $3.00 for the first book and $1.00 for each additional book to cover shipping and handling within US, Canada, and Mexico. International orders add $6.00 for the first book and $2.00 for each additional book.

Or order from:

ACW Press
PO Box 110390
Nashville, TN 37222
(800) 931-BOOK

or contact your local bookstore